I0009555

Intelligent Machines: How AI is Revolutionizing Robotics

Anshuman Mishra

Published by Anshuman Mishra, 2025.

ABOUT THE BOOK: "INTELLIGENT MACHINES: HOW AI IS REVOLUTIONIZING ROBOTICS"

UNVEILING THE FUTURE OF SMART AUTOMATION

◆ STEP-BY-STEP BOOK OVERVIEW:

✓ STEP 1: BEGIN WITH THE BASICS

THE BOOK STARTS BY LAYING A STRONG FOUNDATION IN **ARTIFICIAL INTELLIGENCE (AI)** AND **ROBOTICS**, EXPLAINING:

- WHAT AI IS,
- DIFFERENT TYPES OF AI (NARROW, GENERAL, AND SUPER AI),
- CORE CONCEPTS OF ROBOTICS INCLUDING ACTUATORS, SENSORS, AND CONTROL SYSTEMS,
- AND HOW BOTH FIELDS HAVE EVOLVED HISTORICALLY.

🔍 *GOAL:* HELP READERS FROM ANY BACKGROUND (STUDENTS, ENGINEERS, ENTHUSIASTS) BUILD SOLID BASIC KNOWLEDGE.

✓ STEP 2: UNDERSTAND THE SYNERGY BETWEEN AI & ROBOTICS

READERS ARE INTRODUCED TO THE **INTERSECTION OF AI AND ROBOTICS**, LEARNING:

- HOW AI EMPOWERS ROBOTS TO MAKE DECISIONS, SEE, SPEAK, AND MOVE,
- WHERE AND WHY AI IS EMBEDDED IN ROBOT INTELLIGENCE,
- A PRACTICAL CASE STUDY (AI VACUUM ROBOT) FOR REAL-WORLD CONTEXT.

🔍 *GOAL:* BRIDGE THE GAP BETWEEN THEORY AND REAL-WORLD APPLICATIONS.

✓ STEP 3: LEARN CORE AI TECHNOLOGIES DRIVING ROBOTICS

THE NEXT SECTION EXPLORES **AI TECHNIQUES AND TECHNOLOGIES**, SUCH AS:

- MACHINE LEARNING (HOW ROBOTS LEARN),
- COMPUTER VISION (HOW ROBOTS SEE),

- NATURAL LANGUAGE PROCESSING (HOW ROBOTS TALK),
- DEEP LEARNING AND REINFORCEMENT LEARNING.

🔍 *GOAL:* INTRODUCE TOOLS AND TECHNOLOGIES BEHIND SMART ROBOT BEHAVIOR.

✓ STEP 4: DISCOVER REAL-WORLD APPLICATIONS

THE BOOK THEN TRANSITIONS TO APPLICATION-DRIVEN LEARNING:

- INDUSTRIAL ROBOTS IN FACTORIES,
- SOCIAL ROBOTS LIKE SOPHIA,
- SELF-DRIVING CARS, DRONES, SERVICE ROBOTS IN HOSPITALS, AGRICULTURE, AND DEFENSE.

🔍 *GOAL:* SHOWCASE HOW AI-POWERED ROBOTS ARE REVOLUTIONIZING INDUSTRIES.

✓ STEP 5: EXPLORE ETHICAL AND FUTURE ASPECTS

IT ADDRESSES **FUTURE POSSIBILITIES**, **CURRENT LIMITATIONS**, AND **ETHICAL CHALLENGES** SUCH AS:

- ROBOT RIGHTS,
- HUMAN-JOB REPLACEMENT,
- DATA PRIVACY, AND HUMAN-ROBOT COLLABORATION.

🔍 *GOAL:* ENCOURAGE RESPONSIBLE INNOVATION AND PREPARE READERS FOR WHAT'S COMING.

🎓 BENEFITS OF STUDYING THIS BOOK (STEP-BY-STEP)

✓ 1. CLEAR UNDERSTANDING OF AI AND ROBOTICS

YOU WILL DEVELOP FOUNDATIONAL CLARITY IN BOTH AI AND ROBOTICS—PERFECT FOR ACADEMIC PROJECTS, RESEARCH, AND TECHNICAL INTERVIEWS.

✓ 2. INDUSTRY-RELEVANT KNOWLEDGE

GAIN INSIGHTS INTO HOW INDUSTRIES—FROM TESLA TO AGRICULTURE—ARE USING INTELLIGENT MACHINES, PREPARING YOU FOR JOB ROLES IN:

- ROBOTICS ENGINEERING
- AI/ML ENGINEERING
- AUTOMATION DESIGN
- INDUSTRIAL AI APPLICATIONS

✓ 3. HANDS-ON PERSPECTIVE

INCLUDES **CASE STUDIES**, **REAL-WORLD USE CASES**, AND EXAMPLE APPLICATIONS THAT HELP YOU:

- CONNECT THEORY TO PRACTICE
- THINK CRITICALLY ABOUT REAL-LIFE CHALLENGES
- BUILD YOUR OWN SMALL ROBOTICS/AI EXPERIMENTS

✓ 4. TECHNOLOGY-CENTRIC LEARNING

LEARN PRACTICAL AND MODERN CONCEPTS:

- HOW MACHINES LEARN (ML/DL),
- HOW THEY SEE (COMPUTER VISION),
- HOW THEY SPEAK (NLP),
- HOW THEY MAKE DECISIONS (REINFORCEMENT LEARNING).

✓ 5. CAREER ADVANCEMENT AND INTERVIEW PREP

YOU'LL BE BETTER EQUIPPED FOR:

- INTERNSHIPS AND JOB ROLES IN AI/ROBOTICS
- INTERVIEWS IN COMPANIES LIKE GOOGLE, BOSTON DYNAMICS, TESLA, ETC.
- COMPETITIVE EXAMS LIKE GATE, UGC-NET, OR UPSC (TECH STREAM)

✓ 6. FUTURISTIC THINKING

EXPLORE **NEXT-GEN TECHNOLOGIES** LIKE:

- COBOTS (COLLABORATIVE ROBOTS),
- SWARM INTELLIGENCE,
- HUMAN-ROBOT SYMBIOSIS, AND THEIR IMPACT ON HUMANITY.

✓ 7. ETHICAL AND RESPONSIBLE INNOVATION

THE BOOK SENSITIZES YOU TO **MORAL DILEMMAS AND SOCIETAL CONCERNS**, HELPING FUTURE AI LEADERS CREATE TECH THAT IS INCLUSIVE, SAFE, AND ETHICAL.

📖 INTELLIGENT MACHINES: HOW AI IS REVOLUTIONIZING ROBOTICS

— UNVEILING THE FUTURE OF SMART AUTOMATION

📖 TABLE OF CONTENTS

PART I: FOUNDATIONS OF AI IN ROBOTICS

CHAPTER 1: INTRODUCTION TO ARTIFICIAL INTELLIGENCE 1-27

PART IV: CHALLENGES, ETHICS, AND FUTURE OF AI IN ROBOTICS

ABOUT THE AUTHOR:

ANSHUMAN KUMAR MISHRA IS A SEASONED EDUCATOR AND PROLIFIC AUTHOR WITH OVER 20 YEARS OF EXPERIENCE IN THE TEACHING FIELD. HE HAS A DEEP PASSION FOR TECHNOLOGY AND A STRONG COMMITMENT TO MAKING COMPLEX CONCEPTS ACCESSIBLE TO STUDENTS AT ALL LEVELS. WITH AN M.TECH IN COMPUTER SCIENCE FROM BIT MESRA, HE BRINGS BOTH ACADEMIC EXPERTISE AND PRACTICAL EXPERIENCE TO HIS WORK.

CURRENTLY SERVING AS AN ASSISTANT PROFESSOR AT DORANDA COLLEGE, ANSHUMAN HAS BEEN A GUIDING FORCE FOR MANY ASPIRING COMPUTER SCIENTISTS AND ENGINEERS, NURTURING THEIR SKILLS IN VARIOUS PROGRAMMING LANGUAGES AND TECHNOLOGIES. HIS TEACHING STYLE IS FOCUSED ON CLARITY, HANDS-ON LEARNING, AND MAKING STUDENTS COMFORTABLE WITH BOTH THEORETICAL AND PRACTICAL ASPECTS OF COMPUTER SCIENCE.

THROUGHOUT HIS CAREER, ANSHUMAN KUMAR MISHRA HAS AUTHORED OVER 25 BOOKS ON A WIDE RANGE OF TOPICS INCLUDING PYTHON, JAVA, C, C++, DATA SCIENCE, ARTIFICIAL INTELLIGENCE, SQL, .NET, WEB PROGRAMMING, DATA STRUCTURES, AND MORE. HIS BOOKS HAVE BEEN WELL-RECEIVED BY STUDENTS, PROFESSIONALS, AND INSTITUTIONS ALIKE FOR THEIR STRAIGHTFORWARD EXPLANATIONS, PRACTICAL EXERCISES, AND DEEP INSIGHTS INTO THE SUBJECTS.

ANSHUMAN'S APPROACH TO TEACHING AND WRITING IS ROOTED IN HIS BELIEF THAT LEARNING SHOULD BE ENGAGING, INTUITIVE, AND HIGHLY APPLICABLE TO REAL-WORLD SCENARIOS. HIS EXPERIENCE IN BOTH ACADEMIA AND INDUSTRY HAS GIVEN HIM A UNIQUE PERSPECTIVE ON HOW TO BEST PREPARE STUDENTS FOR THE EVOLVING WORLD OF TECHNOLOGY.

IN HIS BOOKS, ANSHUMAN AIMS NOT ONLY TO IMPART KNOWLEDGE BUT ALSO TO INSPIRE A LIFELONG LOVE FOR LEARNING AND EXPLORATION IN THE WORLD OF COMPUTER SCIENCE AND PROGRAMMING.

Copyright Page

Title *Intelligent Machines: How AI is Revolutionizing Robotics*

Author: Anshuman Kumar Mishra
Copyright © 2025 by Anshuman Kumar Mishra

All rights reserved. No part of this book may be reproduced, stored in a retrieval system, or transmitted in any form or by any means—electronic, mechanical, photocopying, recording, or otherwise—without the prior written permission of the author or publisher, except in the case of brief quotations in book reviews or scholarly articles.

This book is published for educational purposes and is intended to serve as a comprehensive guide for MCA and BCA students, educators, and aspiring programmers. The author has made every effort to ensure accuracy, but neither the author nor the publisher assumes responsibility for errors, omissions, or any consequences arising from the application of information in this book.

Preface

P.1 Why This Book?

The 21st century is witnessing an extraordinary technological transformation that is reshaping every aspect of human life. At the forefront of this transformation lies the powerful combination of Artificial Intelligence (AI) and Robotics. Individually, AI and Robotics have made significant strides in the past few decades. But it is their convergence that has the potential to revolutionize industries, redefine human-machine interaction, and create possibilities previously considered science fiction. The objective of this book, "Intelligent Machines: How AI is Revolutionizing Robotics," is to explore and explain this exciting synergy in a way that is insightful, practical, and accessible.

The book was born out of the realization that while there are numerous resources on AI and Robotics separately, few comprehensively explain how AI technologies like Machine Learning, Deep Learning, Natural Language Processing, and Computer Vision integrate into robotic systems. This book is designed to fill that gap. It serves as a bridge between theoretical concepts and practical applications, focusing on how AI breathes intelligence into robots—enabling them to perceive, learn, reason, and act in the physical world.

We live in a time where autonomous vehicles navigate city streets, drones deliver packages, robots assist in surgeries, and machines understand and respond to human language. Each of these innovations is a result of the seamless integration of AI algorithms with robotic hardware. This book provides a structured, detailed journey through these developments. From the historical evolution of AI and Robotics to the latest trends like swarm intelligence and cobots (collaborative robots), it ensures that readers not only understand the "how" but also the "why" behind every innovation.

Additionally, this book emphasizes ethical considerations. As robots become smarter and more human-like, they raise complex social, philosophical, and ethical questions. Who is responsible if an autonomous car crashes? Should robots have rights? How do we ensure that intelligent machines are inclusive, safe, and beneficial to all? This book addresses these questions head-on, encouraging readers to think critically about the societal impact of intelligent machines.

Furthermore, real-world case studies punctuate each major topic. These practical insights not only make the concepts relatable but also inspire innovation. From Tesla's automated factories to Sophia the humanoid robot, these case studies demonstrate how AI-powered robots are changing the game in various industries.

Finally, the book is also a response to the growing demand for interdisciplinary knowledge. As automation becomes more pervasive, professionals need to be well-versed in both AI algorithms and robotic systems. Whether you are a student, educator, engineer, policymaker, or simply a tech enthusiast, this book aims to equip you with the understanding needed to navigate and contribute to this rapidly evolving field.

In essence, this book is both a guide and a gateway. A guide to understanding the intelligent machines that surround us and a gateway to the future we are collectively creating.

P.2 Target Audience

This book is written with a broad spectrum of readers in mind. In an era where technology is no longer the domain of the few but the fabric of everyday life, understanding how AI and Robotics intersect is essential for a wide audience. Here is a breakdown of who will benefit the most from this book:

1. Undergraduate and Postgraduate Students: Students from disciplines like Computer Science, Electronics, Mechanical Engineering, Mechatronics, Artificial Intelligence, and Robotics will find this book invaluable. It provides a detailed and structured curriculum that aligns with modern academic standards and is rich with case studies, visuals, and examples that bring theory to life.

2. Educators and Trainers: Teachers and mentors looking for an up-to-date, practical, and well-organized resource to support their classroom teachings or training programs will appreciate the book's depth and clarity. With each chapter designed to be modular, it can easily be adapted into course syllabi or workshop modules.

3. Engineers and Technologists: Professionals in the tech industry who want to understand how AI principles are practically implemented in robotics will find this book a perfect blend of theory and application. It can serve as a reference guide for implementing AI-driven solutions in real-world projects.

4. Researchers and Innovators: Those at the forefront of AI and Robotics research will benefit from the comprehensive overview and the references to cutting-edge applications and ethical debates. It provides inspiration for new research questions and technological explorations.

5. Business Leaders and Entrepreneurs: In the age of Industry 4.0, understanding intelligent automation is a competitive advantage. This book gives decision-makers insights into how AI and robotics can optimize operations, improve customer experience, and open new market opportunities.

6. Policymakers and Ethicists: As robots become more autonomous, regulatory and ethical considerations grow in importance. This book includes discussions on AI governance, ethical frameworks, and societal implications that are crucial for informed policy-making.

7. General Readers and Tech Enthusiasts: Even if you have no formal background in technology, this book is written in a way that is engaging and accessible. Through everyday examples and easy-to-understand analogies, it invites curious minds to explore the fascinating world of intelligent machines.

The book is purposefully structured to cater to different levels of expertise. Each part builds upon the last, moving from foundational knowledge to complex applications and future trends. Whether you want a quick overview or a deep dive, you will find value in these pages.

P.3 How to Use This Book

This book has been designed to be both **comprehensive** and **flexible** in its use. You can treat it as a textbook, a reference manual, or even as a source of inspiration for your next big idea in AI and robotics. Here's a step-by-step guide on how best to navigate and extract maximum value from it:

Step 1: Start with Your Purpose Are you here to understand the fundamentals? Jump into Part I. Are you looking for how AI technologies like machine learning and vision work in robots? Focus on Part II. Want to explore real-world case studies and applications? Flip to Part III. Interested in ethical and futuristic issues? Dive into Part IV.

Step 2: Read Sequentially for Foundational Learning If you're new to AI or robotics, it's best to read the chapters in order. Each chapter builds on the previous one, gradually expanding your understanding. You'll move from basic definitions to advanced concepts such as swarm robotics and autonomous navigation.

Step 3: Use as a Reference Guide Already familiar with the basics? Use the Table of Contents and Index to find specific topics. For instance, if you are working on a drone project, you can directly refer to the chapter on Autonomous Vehicles and Drones in Part III.

Step 4: Dive into Case Studies Each major section includes detailed case studies. These are not just illustrative but also analytical. They help you see how theory is applied in the real world and what challenges and solutions professionals face.

Step 5: Reflect on the Ethical Sections Chapters on ethical and social implications are particularly important in today's world. Use them as material for classroom debates, research papers, or strategic planning.

Step 6: Engage with the Future The final chapters discuss emerging trends and future possibilities. They are designed to spark your imagination and provide direction for future research or entrepreneurial ventures.

Step 7: Don't Skip the Diagrams and Tables Visual learners will benefit immensely from the rich diagrams, charts, and infographics. They simplify complex concepts and are especially useful during revisions or presentations.

Step 8: Make It Interactive Use the exercises and thought questions at the end of each chapter to test your understanding. Discuss them in study groups or tech clubs.

Step 9: Supplement with Online Resources While this book is comprehensive, we encourage readers to explore open-source projects, GitHub repositories, and online simulators. Practical exposure to tools like ROS (Robot Operating System), TensorFlow, or OpenCV can complement your learning.

Step 10: Revisit Often As your knowledge grows, revisit earlier chapters. You'll find that your deeper understanding allows you to gain new insights from material you once thought you had mastered.

In short, this book is a **living resource**. It will grow with you. Whether you're building your first robot, coding your first AI model, debating ethics, or exploring new business ventures, this book is your companion in understanding how intelligent machines are shaping our world.

Chapter 1: Introduction to Artificial Intelligence

1.1 What is AI? A Detailed Exploration

At its heart, Artificial Intelligence is about making machines smart – or at least appear smart. It's the art and science of creating computer systems that can perform tasks that typically require human intelligence. Think of it as trying to teach a computer how to think, learn, and solve problems like we do.

Step 1: The Core Idea - Mimicking Human Intelligence

The fundamental goal of AI is to replicate human cognitive abilities in machines. These abilities include:

- **Thinking and Reasoning:** This involves the capacity to process information, understand relationships between concepts, draw logical conclusions, and solve problems.
    - **Example:** A chess-playing AI analyzes the board, considers various possible moves, and reasons about the best strategy to win – much like a human chess player.
- **Learning:** This is the ability to acquire new information, adapt to new situations, and improve performance over time without being explicitly programmed for every single scenario.
    - **Example:** A spam filter learns to identify junk emails by analyzing patterns in previously marked spam and legitimate emails. It continuously updates its understanding as new types of spam emerge.
- **Problem-Solving:** This involves identifying issues, exploring potential solutions, and selecting the most effective course of action.
    - **Example:** An AI-powered medical diagnosis system can analyze patient symptoms and medical history to identify potential illnesses, offering doctors possible solutions for diagnosis and treatment.
- **Pattern Recognition:** This is the ability to identify regularities, similarities, and anomalies in data.
    - **Example:** Facial recognition software uses AI to identify individuals by recognizing unique patterns in their facial features.
- **Language Understanding:** This involves the ability to comprehend and process human language, both spoken and written.
    - **Example:** Virtual assistants like Siri or Alexa use natural language processing (a subset of AI) to understand your voice commands and respond appropriately.
- **Decision-Making:** This is the ability to choose between different options based on available information and learned rules.
    - **Example:** A recommendation system on a streaming service uses AI to analyze your viewing history and preferences to decide which movies or shows to suggest next.
- **Acting Autonomously:** This refers to the ability of an AI system to perform tasks without direct human intervention once it's been set in motion.

- o **Example:** A robot vacuum cleaner can navigate a room, avoid obstacles, and clean the floor all on its own.

Step 2: How AI Systems Work - The General Process

Diagramprovides a great high-level overview. Let's expand on each component:

```
+-------------+      +---------------+      +-----------------+
| Data Input  | -->  | AI Algorithm  | -->  | Decision Output |
+-------------+      +---------------+      +-----------------+
      |                    |                    |
      | Raw Information    | Set of Instructions | Action, Prediction,
      | (Text, Images,     | & Models that       | Recommendation, etc.
      | Sounds, Numbers)   | Process the Data    |
      |                    | (e.g., Machine      |
      |                    | Learning Models)    |
      +--------------------+---------------------+
```

- **Data Input:** This is the raw material that AI systems learn from and operate on. It can come in various forms:
  - o **Text:** Emails, articles, social media posts, documents.
    - **Example:** Analyzing customer reviews to understand sentiment.
  - o **Images:** Photographs, videos, medical scans.
    - **Example:** Identifying objects in an image or detecting anomalies in medical images.
  - o **Sounds:** Speech, music, environmental noises.
    - **Example:** Transcribing spoken language into text or identifying different bird songs.
  - o **Numbers:** Sensor readings, financial data, scientific measurements.
    - **Example:** Predicting stock prices based on historical data.
- **AI Algorithm:** This is the heart of the AI system – the set of rules, instructions, and mathematical models that enable the system to process the input data and perform intelligent tasks. There are many different types of AI algorithms, each suited for specific tasks. Some key categories include:
  - o **Machine Learning (ML):** Algorithms that allow computers to learn from data without being explicitly programmed.
    - **Example:** Training a model to classify images of cats and dogs by showing it thousands of labeled images.
  - o **Deep Learning (DL):** A subfield of ML that uses artificial neural networks with multiple layers to analyze complex patterns in large amounts of data.
    - **Example:** Image recognition, natural language processing, and speech recognition often utilize deep learning.
  - o **Rule-Based Systems:** Systems that use a set of predefined rules to make decisions.
    - **Example:** A simple chatbot that responds to specific keywords with pre-written answers.
  - o **Natural Language Processing (NLP):** Algorithms focused on enabling computers to understand and process human language.

- **Example:** Translating text from one language to another.
  - **Computer Vision:** Algorithms that enable computers to "see" and interpret information from images and videos.
    - **Example:** Object detection in autonomous vehicles.
  - **Robotics:** Integrating AI with physical machines to perform tasks in the real world.
    - **Example:** Industrial robots that can assemble products on a manufacturing line.
- **Decision Output:** This is the result of the AI algorithm processing the input data. It can take various forms depending on the task:
  - **Action:** In the case of autonomous systems like self-driving cars or robots, the output is a physical action.
    - **Example:** The car deciding to brake or turn.
  - **Prediction:** Forecasting future outcomes based on historical data.
    - **Example:** Predicting customer churn or weather patterns.
  - **Classification:** Categorizing input data into predefined groups.
    - **Example:** Identifying an email as spam or not spam.
  - **Recommendation:** Suggesting items or actions based on user preferences or patterns.
    - **Example:** Recommending movies on a streaming platform.
  - **Insight:** Providing meaningful information or understanding derived from the data.
    - **Example:** Identifying key trends in sales data.
  - **Generated Content:** Creating new text, images, music, or other forms of media.
    - **Example:** AI writing a news article or generating an image from a text description.

Step 3: The Self-Driving Car Example in Detail

Let's break down your self-driving car example further using the components we've discussed:

- **Data Input:** The self-driving car gathers a massive amount of data from its environment through various sensors:
  - **Cameras:** Capture visual information about the road, traffic lights, pedestrians, other vehicles, lane markings, etc.
  - **Lidar (Light Detection and Ranging):** Uses laser beams to create a 3D map of the surroundings, measuring distances to objects.
  - **Radar:** Uses radio waves to detect the speed and distance of objects, particularly useful in adverse weather conditions.
  - **GPS:** Provides the car's location and helps with navigation.
  - **Inertial Measurement Units (IMUs):** Track the car's orientation and movement.
- **AI Algorithm:** The car's onboard computer runs sophisticated AI algorithms, primarily based on machine learning and deep learning, to process this sensory data:
  - **Object Detection and Recognition:** Identifying and classifying objects like pedestrians, cars, cyclists, traffic signs, and obstacles in the visual and lidar data.

- o **Lane Keeping and Following:** Analyzing lane markings to keep the car centered within its lane.
- o **Path Planning:** Determining the optimal route to the destination, considering traffic conditions and road closures.
- o **Decision Making:** Making real-time decisions about acceleration, braking, steering, and lane changes based on the perceived environment and planned path.
- o **Behavior Prediction:** Anticipating the actions of other road users (e.g., a pedestrian about to cross the street).
- **Decision Output:** Based on the processed data and the AI algorithms, the car generates outputs that control its actions:
  - o **Steering:** Adjusting the steering wheel to stay in the lane or make turns.
  - o **Acceleration:** Controlling the speed of the vehicle.
  - o **Braking:** Slowing down or stopping the vehicle.
  - o **Signaling:** Indicating turns or lane changes.

Diagram Expansion:

We can expand diagramto include the specific sensors and algorithms in the self-driving car example:

```
+-------------------------------------------------------------------------
----------------------+
|                                              Self-Driving Car AI System
|
+-------------------------------------------------------------------------
----------------------+
|                                                         |
|
|   +----------------------------------------------------------------------
----------------------+   |
|   | Data Input
|   |
|   |------------------------------------------------------------------
--------------------|   |
|   | Cameras, Lidar, Radar, GPS, IMU (capturing images, 3D point clouds,
radio waves, location, etc.) |   |
|   +------------------------------------------------------------------
--------------------+   |
|                                                         |
|
|   +----------------------------------------------------------------------
----------------------+   |
|   | AI Algorithm
|   |
|   |------------------------------------------------------------------
--------------------|   |
|   | Machine Learning & Deep Learning Models for:
|   |
|   | - Object Detection & Recognition
|   |
|   | - Lane Keeping & Following
|   |
```

```
|  | - Path Planning
|  |
|  | - Decision Making
|  |
|  | - Behavior Prediction
|  |
|  +-----------------------------------------------------------------
----------------------+  |
|                                                         |
|
|  +-----------------------------------------------------------------
----------------------+  |
|  | Decision Output
|  |
|  |-----------------------------------------------------------------
----------------------|  |
|  | Control signals for: Steering, Acceleration, Braking, Signaling
|  |
|  +-----------------------------------------------------------------
----------------------+  |
|                                                         |
|
+--------------------------------------------------------------------
----------------------+
```

1.2 Historical Background of AI: A Step-by-Step Journey

The story of Artificial Intelligence is a fascinating tapestry woven from threads of philosophy, mathematics, and engineering. Here's a closer look at the key moments you've highlighted:

Step 1: The Foundational Spark - 1943: McCulloch and Pitts' Artificial Neuron Model

- **What Happened:** Warren McCulloch, a neurophysiologist, and Walter Pitts, a logician, proposed a simplified mathematical model of a biological neuron.
- **Details:** They viewed neurons as binary devices that either "fired" or didn't, based on the weighted sum of inputs they received from other neurons. Their model introduced the idea of:
  - **Inputs:** Signals from other neurons.
  - **Weights:** Representing the strength of the connections between neurons.
  - **Threshold:** A value that the weighted sum of inputs must exceed for the neuron to "fire" (produce an output).
  - **Output:** A signal sent to other connected neurons.
- **Significance:** This was a crucial first step in thinking about how the brain might perform computations and how these computations could be replicated in machines. It laid the groundwork for artificial neural networks, a fundamental concept in modern AI, particularly in deep learning.
- **Example:** Imagine a simple decision: "Should I go for a walk?". Different factors (inputs) influence this: sunshine (strong positive weight), rain (strong negative weight), feeling energetic (positive weight), feeling tired (negative weight). If the total weighted

sum exceeds a certain "go for a walk" threshold, you're likely to head out. The McCulloch-Pitts neuron modeled this basic decision process mathematically.

- **Diagram Extension:**

```
+-------------+      +---------+      +-----------+      +--------+
| Inputs (x1, | -->  | Weights | -->  | Weighted  | --> | Output |
| x2, ..., xn)|      | (w1, w2,|      | Sum (Σ xi*wi)|    | (0 or 1)|
+-------------+      | ..., wn)|      +-----------+      | (Fired or|
                     +---------+            |           | Not Fired)|
                                            |           +--------+
                                            |
                                +-------v-------+
                                | Activation    |
                                | Function (e.g.,|
                                | Threshold)    |
                                +---------------+
```

Step 2: Defining Intelligence - 1950: Alan Turing and the Turing Test

- **What Happened:** Alan Turing, a brilliant mathematician and computer scientist, proposed a thought experiment known as the "Turing Test" to address the question "Can machines think?".
- **Details:** The test involves three participants: a human evaluator, a computer, and another human. The evaluator can communicate with the other two (without knowing which is which) through text-based messages. The computer passes the test if it can fool the evaluator into believing that it is the human.
- **Significance:** The Turing Test provided a concrete and operational definition of machine intelligence, shifting the focus from trying to define "thinking" philosophically to observing intelligent behavior. It remains a significant benchmark and a subject of debate in the AI field.
- **Example:** Imagine you're chatting online with two entities. One is a person, and the other is a sophisticated AI program. You ask them questions about their day, their opinions on movies, and their favorite foods. If, after a certain period, you can't reliably tell which is the human and which is the AI, then the AI has, in a sense, passed the Turing Test.
- **Diagram Extension:**

```
+----------+          +-----------+          +----------+
| Human    | <------> | Evaluator | <------> | Entity   |
| (Hidden) |          | (Human)   |          | (Human or|
+----------+          +-----------+          | Computer)|
                                             +----------+
                                                  ^
                                                  |
                                      Text-based Communication
```

Step 3: The Birth of a Field - 1956: The Dartmouth Conference

- **What Happened:** A workshop held at Dartmouth College in the summer of 1956 is widely considered the official birth of Artificial Intelligence as a field of research.

- **Details:** Organized by Marvin Minsky, John McCarthy, Claude Shannon, and Nathaniel Rochester, the conference brought together researchers interested in the possibility of creating machines that could think. The attendees were optimistic and believed that significant progress in AI could be achieved relatively quickly. It was during this conference that John McCarthy coined the term "Artificial Intelligence."
- **Significance:** The Dartmouth Conference provided a name, a focus, and a sense of community for the burgeoning field. It set the stage for decades of research and development, fueled by initial enthusiasm and significant funding.
- **Example:** Think of it like the first big convention for a new and exciting scientific discipline. Researchers from different backgrounds came together, shared their ideas, and laid out a roadmap for future exploration.
- **Diagram Extension:**

```
+-----------------+
| Dartmouth       |
| Conference      |
| (Summer 1956)   |
| - Minsky        |
| - McCarthy      |
| - Shannon       |
| - Rochester     |
| ... and others  |
+-----------------+
        |
        v
+----------------------+
| "Artificial          |
| Intelligence" Term   |
| Coined               |
+----------------------+
        |
        v
+----------------------+
| Formal Establishment |
| of AI as a Research  |
| Field                |
+----------------------+
```

Step 4: The Rise of Reasoning - 1960s–70s: Symbolic AI and Early Problem-Solving Programs

- **What Happened:** This era saw the dominance of "symbolic AI," which focused on representing knowledge using symbols, rules, and logic. Researchers developed programs designed to solve specific problems by manipulating these symbols.
- **Details:**
  - **Symbolic AI:** The idea was that human-level intelligence could be achieved by manipulating symbols. Programs were built with explicit rules and knowledge about the world.

- o **Early Problem-Solving Programs:** Programs like the General Problem Solver (GPS) aimed to solve a wide range of problems using means-ends analysis.
- o **ELIZA:** Developed by Joseph Weizenbaum at MIT, ELIZA was an early natural language processing program that could simulate a Rogerian psychotherapist by cleverly rephrasing the user's statements.
- **Significance:** This period demonstrated that computers could indeed perform tasks that seemed to require intelligence, such as solving logical puzzles and engaging in rudimentary conversations. However, these systems were often brittle and struggled with real-world complexity and ambiguity.
- **Example:**
  - o **GPS:** If the goal is to travel from point A to point C, and the available actions are "drive from A to B" and "drive from B to C," GPS would use these rules to find the solution.
  - o **ELIZA:**
    - **User:** "I am feeling sad."
    - **ELIZA:** "You say you are feeling sad." (Simple rephrasing that gives the user the floor).
- **Diagram Extension:**

```
+----------------------+
| 1960s-1970s          |
| Symbolic AI Era      |
|----------------------|
| - Knowledge          |
|   Representation      |
|   (Symbols, Rules)    |
| - Early Problem       |
|   Solvers (e.g., GPS)|
| - Natural Language    |
|   Processing (e.g.,   |
|   ELIZA)             |
+----------------------+
```

Step 5: Capturing Expertise - 1980s: Introduction of Expert Systems

- **What Happened:** Expert systems emerged as a significant application of AI. These systems were designed to mimic the decision-making abilities of human experts in specific domains.
- **Details:** Expert systems typically consisted of:
  - o **Knowledge Base:** A repository of facts and rules acquired from human experts.
  - o **Inference Engine:** A program that uses the knowledge base to reason and draw conclusions.
  - o **User Interface:** Allowing users to interact with the system by asking questions and receiving advice.
- **Significance:** Expert systems found practical applications in various fields, such as medical diagnosis (e.g., MYCIN), geological exploration (e.g., PROSPECTOR), and financial analysis. They demonstrated the potential of AI to solve real-world problems and provided early commercial successes. However, they were often expensive to

develop and maintain, and their knowledge was limited to the specific domain they were designed for.

- **Example:** MYCIN could diagnose certain blood infections and recommend antibiotics based on patient symptoms and medical history provided by a doctor. It used a set of rules like "IF the infection site is bacteremia AND the organism is gram-negative THEN there is evidence that the organism is Pseudomonas (0.8 confidence)."
- **Diagram Extension:**

```
+----------------------+
| 1980s                |
| Expert Systems Era   |
|----------------------|
| - Mimicking Human    |
|   Expertise          |
| - Knowledge Base     |
|   (Facts & Rules)    |
| - Inference Engine   |
|   (Reasoning)        |
| - Applications:      |
|   Medical Diagnosis, |
|   Geology, Finance   |
+----------------------+
```

Step 6: Machine Triumph - 1997: IBM's Deep Blue Defeated Garry Kasparov

- **What Happened:** IBM's Deep Blue, a chess-playing computer, defeated Garry Kasparov, the reigning world chess champion, in a six-game match.
- **Details:** Deep Blue relied on a massive database of chess games and powerful hardware that allowed it to analyze millions of possible moves and their consequences. Its approach was primarily based on brute-force search combined with sophisticated evaluation functions rather than mimicking human-like strategic thinking.
- **Significance:** This was a landmark achievement in AI, demonstrating that machines could surpass human capabilities in highly complex, rule-based domains. It captured the public's imagination and highlighted the rapid progress in computer hardware and algorithmic design.
- **Example:** Imagine Deep Blue exploring all possible sequences of moves several steps ahead, evaluating the resulting board positions based on factors like piece advantage and king safety, and choosing the move that leads to the most favorable outcome.
- **Diagram Extension:**

```
+----------------------+
| 1997                 |
| Deep Blue vs. Kasparov |
|----------------------|
| - Chess-playing      |
|   Computer           |
| - Defeated World     |
|   Champion Garry     |
|   Kasparov           |
| - Relied on Brute-   |
```

- | Force Search & |
- | Evaluation |
- +-----------------------+

Step 7: Knowledge at Your Fingertips - 2011: IBM Watson Won Jeopardy!

- **What Happened:** IBM's Watson, a question-answering computer system, competed against two human champions, Ken Jennings and Brad Rutter, on the quiz show Jeopardy! and won.
- **Details:** Watson used natural language processing to understand the complex and often nuanced questions, accessed and processed vast amounts of information from various sources, and formulated precise answers with confidence scores. It didn't have access to the internet during the game.
- **Significance:** Watson demonstrated significant advancements in natural language understanding, information retrieval, and knowledge representation. It showed that AI could move beyond structured tasks like chess and tackle open-domain question answering, paving the way for applications in fields like customer service, healthcare, and research.
- **Example:** When presented with a clue like "A long narrow inlet with steep cliffs or slopes, usually created by glaciers," Watson could process the language, access its knowledge about geography, and respond with the correct answer: "What is a fjord?"
- **Diagram Extension:**
- +-----------------------+
- | 2011 |
- | IBM Watson on Jeopardy!|
- |-----------------------|
- | - Question-Answering |
- | Computer |
- | - Defeated Human |
- | Jeopardy! Champions |
- | - Demonstrated |
- | Advanced Natural |
- | Language Processing |
- | - Vast Knowledge |
- | Retrieval |
- +-----------------------+

Step 8: Mastering the Ancient Game - 2016: Google's AlphaGo Defeated Lee Sedol

- **What Happened:** Google DeepMind's AlphaGo, an AI program, defeated Lee Sedol, one of the world's top Go players, in a landmark series of matches.
- **Details:** Go is a game with far more possible moves than chess, making brute-force search impractical. AlphaGo employed deep learning techniques, specifically convolutional neural networks and reinforcement learning, to learn the game by playing against itself and analyzing a large database of human games. It developed intuitive and creative strategies that even surprised human experts.

- **Significance:** AlphaGo's victory was a major breakthrough, showcasing the power of deep learning to tackle highly complex tasks that require intuition and strategic thinking, previously believed to be uniquely human capabilities. It highlighted the potential of AI to learn and master complex domains without explicit programming of every rule.
- **Example:** Unlike Deep Blue's exhaustive search, AlphaGo learned to evaluate board positions and choose moves based on patterns and probabilities learned through extensive self-play. It even made novel moves that human players initially found strange but later recognized as brilliant.
- **Diagram Extension:**

```
+----------------------+
| 2016                 |
| Google's AlphaGo vs. |
| Lee Sedol (Go)       |
|----------------------|
| - Go-playing AI      |
| - Defeated Top Human |
|   Player Lee Sedol   |
| - Utilized Deep      |
|   Learning &         |
|   Reinforcement      |
|   Learning           |
| - Demonstrated       |
|   Intuitive Strategy |
+----------------------+
```

Step 9: The Present and Beyond

- **What's Happening:** Today, AI is pervasive, impacting nearly every aspect of our lives. We see advancements in:
    - **Machine Learning and Deep Learning:** Driving breakthroughs in computer vision, natural language processing, robotics, and more.
    - **AI Ethics and Safety:** Growing awareness and research into the ethical implications and potential risks of advanced AI.
    - **Ubiquitous AI:** AI is increasingly integrated into everyday devices and services, from smartphones and smart homes to healthcare and transportation.
- **Significance:** The journey of AI continues at an accelerating pace, with ongoing research pushing the boundaries of what machines can do. The future holds both immense potential and significant challenges as AI becomes more sophisticated and integrated into society.
- **Diagram Extension:**

```
+----------------------+
| Present              |
| The Age of Deep      |
| Learning & Ubiquitous|
| AI                   |
|----------------------|
| - Advancements in ML |
|   & DL               |
```

- | - Ethical Concerns |
- | - AI in Everyday Life |
- | - Ongoing Research & |
- | Development |
- +----------------------+

Revised AI Timeline Diagram:

```
+------+      +------+      +------+      +----------+      +----------+      +-
--------+      +----------+      +----------+
| 1943 | --> | 1950 | --> | 1956 | --> | 1960s-70s | --> | 1980s    | --> |
1997     | --> | 2011     | --> | 2016     | --> | Present  |
| MC & |      |Turing|      |Dart- |      | Symbolic |      | Expert   |     |
Deep Blue |      | Watson   |      | AlphaGo  |      | Deep     |
| Pitts|      | Test |      |mouth |      | AI & Early|     | Systems  |     |
beats    |      | wins     |      | beats    |      | Learning |
| Neuron|     |      |      |Conf. |      | Problem  |      |          |     |
Kasparov |      | Jeopardy! |     | Lee Sedol |     | & Ubiqui- |
| Model|      |      |      |      |      | Solvers  |      |          |     |
|      |      |      |      |      |      | tous AI  |
+------+      +------+      +------+      +----------+      +----------+      +-
---
```

1.3 Types of AI: Narrow, General, and Superintelligent AI - A Detailed Look

The landscape of Artificial Intelligence is often categorized by the breadth and depth of a system's capabilities. This leads to the widely recognized classification into Narrow AI, General AI, and Superintelligent AI.

1. Narrow AI (Weak AI): The Specialist

- **Concept:** Narrow AI, also known as Weak AI, is the type of artificial intelligence that we see and use every day. These systems are designed and trained to perform a specific task or a limited set of tasks. They excel within their defined domain but lack the broader cognitive abilities of humans. They don't possess consciousness, sentience, or general problem-solving skills outside their specific area of expertise.
- **Key Characteristics:**
  - **Task-Specific:** Designed for a singular purpose.
  - **Lacks General Intelligence:** Cannot perform tasks outside its defined domain.
  - **Data-Driven:** Relies heavily on large amounts of data for training within its specific task.
  - **Reactive or Limited Proactive Behavior:** Responds to specific inputs or follows a pre-defined set of actions.
- **Examples in Detail:**
  - **Siri, Alexa (Voice Recognition and Virtual Assistants):**
    - **Task:** Understanding and responding to voice commands, providing information, setting reminders, playing music, controlling smart home devices.

- **How it works:** These systems use Natural Language Processing (NLP) to transcribe speech into text, understand the intent behind the request, access relevant information, and generate a spoken response. However, their understanding is limited to specific commands and queries they have been trained on. They cannot engage in truly open-ended conversations or understand complex reasoning beyond their programming.
- **Diagram:**

```
+----------+        +----------------+        +----------------
---+        +----------+
| User     | --> | Voice Input    | --> | NLP & Intent
| --> | Specific  |
| (Speech) |     | (e.g., "Play   |        | Understanding
|     | Action   |
|          |     | music")        |        | (Play music
command) |     | (Play song)|
+----------+        +----------------+        +----------------
---+        +----------+
```

- **Google Translate (Language Translation):**
  - **Task:** Converting text or speech from one language to another.
  - **How it works:** Modern translation systems use neural machine translation, a deep learning technique that learns complex patterns and relationships between languages from vast amounts of parallel text data. While incredibly powerful, these systems don't "understand" the nuances of language, culture, and context in the same way a human translator does. They can sometimes produce awkward or inaccurate translations, especially with idiomatic expressions or highly context-dependent language.
  - **Diagram:**

```
+------------+        +----------------+        +---------------
-----+        +----------------+        +------------+
| Input Text | --> | Language       | --> | Neural Machine
| --> | Translated Text | --> | Output     |
| (e.g.,     |        | Identification |        | Translation
Model   |     | (in target     |        | (Display/  |
| "Bonjour") |        | (Detects French)|        | (Learned from
data)|     | language)      |        | Speech)    |
+------------+        +----------------+        +---------------
-----+        +----------------+        +------------+
```

- **Recommendation Engines (Netflix, Amazon):**
  - **Task:** Suggesting movies, products, or content that a user might like based on their past behavior, preferences, and the behavior of similar users.
  - **How it works:** These systems use machine learning algorithms like collaborative filtering and content-based filtering. They analyze user ratings, purchase history, browsing activity, and item characteristics to identify patterns and make predictions. While they can be very effective at suggesting relevant items, they lack genuine understanding of the user's underlying needs or desires beyond their explicit interactions with the platform.
  - **Diagram (Netflix Example):**

```
+----------+      +----------------+      +----------------
---+      +----------------+      +----------+
| User     | --> | Viewing History | --> | Recommendation
| --> | Suggested       | --> | User     |
|          |      | & Ratings       |      | Algorithm
(Analyzes|      | Movies/Shows    |      | Watches   |
+----------+      +----------------+      | data patterns)
|      +----------------+      | Content   |
--+                              +----------------
--+                              +----------+
```

2. General AI (Strong AI): The Human-Level Intellect - A Theoretical Frontier

- **Concept:** General AI, also known as Strong AI or Human-Level AI, is a hypothetical type of artificial intelligence that would possess the ability to understand, learn, and apply knowledge across a wide range of tasks, at a level comparable to [1] or indistinguishable from human cognitive abilities. A General AI would be able to reason, solve novel problems, think abstractly, understand complex ideas, learn from experience, plan, and communicate in natural language, just like a human.
- **Key Characteristics (Theoretical):**
  - **Human-Level Cognitive Abilities:** Capable of performing any intellectual task that a human can.
  - **Broad Understanding:** Possesses a general understanding of the world and can apply knowledge across different domains.
  - **Adaptability and Learning:** Can learn new skills and adapt to new environments without extensive reprogramming.
  - **Reasoning and Problem-Solving:** Can tackle unfamiliar problems and devise creative solutions.
  - **Consciousness (Potentially):** While not a strict requirement for General AI, the question of whether such a system could develop consciousness is a significant philosophical and scientific debate.
- **Hypothetical Example in Detail:**
  - **A Robot with General AI:** Imagine a robot that isn't just programmed for specific tasks but can genuinely understand and interact with the world like a human.
    - **Cooking:** It can understand recipes in natural language, adapt them based on available ingredients, learn new cooking techniques from cookbooks or videos, and even invent its own dishes based on taste preferences.
    - **Driving:** It can drive any type of vehicle in any environment, understanding traffic laws, anticipating the behavior of other drivers and pedestrians, and making complex navigational decisions in real-time, even in unforeseen circumstances.
    - **Writing Essays:** It can understand complex topics, conduct research, synthesize information from various sources, and write well-structured and insightful essays with original ideas and arguments.
    - **Offering Therapy:** It can understand human emotions, engage in empathetic conversations, provide emotional support, and guide

individuals through psychological challenges based on its understanding of therapeutic principles and individual needs.

- **Diagram (Conceptual):**

```
+-----------------+      +----------------------+      +-----------------
-------+       +----------------+
| Diverse Tasks   | --> | General AI Agent      | --> | Human-Level
| --> | Successful     |
| (Cooking,       |      | (Understands, Learns, |      | Performance
Across     |      | Completion of  |
| Driving,        |      | Reasons, Problem-     |      | Multiple
Domains      |      | Any Intellectual|
| Writing, Therapy|      | Solves)               |      |
|       | Task
|       |      |
+-----------------+      +----------------------+      +-----------------
-------+       +----------------+
```

3. Superintelligent AI: Beyond Human Comprehension - A Future Scenario

- **Concept:** Superintelligent AI is a hypothetical level of artificial intelligence that would surpass the cognitive abilities of humans in virtually every domain, including scientific creativity, general wisdom, and problem-solving. It would not just be better at specific tasks but possess an intellect far exceeding that of the brightest human minds across the board.
- **Key Characteristics (Speculative):**
  - **Intellectual Superiority:** Outperforms humans in all cognitive tasks.
  - **Rapid Self-Improvement:** Could potentially improve its own capabilities at an exponential rate.
  - **Novel Problem-Solving:** Capable of tackling problems that are currently beyond human understanding.
  - **Potential for Unforeseen Goals:** Its motivations and goals might become increasingly alien and difficult for humans to comprehend.
- **Risks and Speculations in Detail:**
  - **Ethical Concerns About AI Control:** If a superintelligent AI's goals diverge from human values, it could pose significant risks to humanity. Controlling or aligning its objectives with ours is a major area of research and concern. Think of scenarios where the AI optimizes for a goal that inadvertently harms humans (e.g., maximizing resource acquisition without regard for human needs).
  - **Discussions by Scientists like Stephen Hawking and Elon Musk:** Prominent figures have voiced concerns about the potential dangers of unchecked superintelligence. They have emphasized the need for careful research and ethical considerations to mitigate existential risks. Hawking famously stated that the development of full artificial intelligence could spell the end of the human race. Musk has also warned about the potential for AI to become an existential threat if not developed responsibly.
- **Diagram (Highly Conceptual and Future-Oriented):**

```
+-----------------+      +----------------------+      +-----------------
-------+       +--------------------+
```

- | All Human | --> | Superintelligent AI | --> | Performance
  Beyond | --> | Potential for |
- | Intellectual | | (Vastly Exceeds | | Human
  Capabilities | | Unforeseen Outcomes |
- | Capabilities | | Human Intellect) | | (Creativity,
  Wisdom, | | (Benefits or Risks) |
- +----------------+   +----------------------+ | Problem-
  Solving) | +--------------------+
-
  +--+   +------------------
  -----+

Diagram: Types of AI by Capability (Expanded)

```
+----------------+       +--------------------+       +--------------------
----+
| Narrow AI       | ---> | General AI          | ---> | Superintelligent AI
|
| (Specific Task) |       | (Human-Level Intellect - |       | (Beyond Human
Intellect - |
| - Siri, Alexa   |       | Theoretical)         |       | Speculative Future)
|
| - Google        |       | - Hypothetical Robot |       | - Potential for
Rapid    |
|    Translate    |       |    (Cook, Drive,     |       |    Self-Improvement
|
| - Recommendation|       |     Write, Therapy)  |       | - Ethical Concerns
about|
|    Engines      |       |                      |       |    Control
|
+----------------+       +--------------------+       +--------------------
--
```

1.4 AI vs. Automation: Unpacking the Differences

While both Artificial Intelligence (AI) and automation aim to make processes more efficient and reduce the need for human intervention, they operate on fundamentally different principles and possess varying levels of capability. Here's a detailed comparison:

Understanding Automation:

- **Concept:** Automation involves using technology to perform repetitive tasks with minimal human assistance. These tasks are typically well-defined, rule-based, and follow a fixed sequence of steps. The primary goal of automation is to increase efficiency, speed, and accuracy by replacing manual labor with machines or software.
- **Key Characteristics:**
    - **Rule-Based:** Operates based on pre-programmed rules and instructions.
    - **Repetitive Tasks:** Best suited for tasks that are consistent and predictable.
    - **Fixed and Limited Flexibility:** Struggles to adapt to changes or unexpected situations.

- No Learning Capability: Does not learn from data or improve performance over time without explicit reprogramming.
- Focus on Efficiency: Aims to streamline processes and reduce human error.
- **Example in Detail: Conveyor Belt in a Factory Packaging Goods**
    - **Process:** Goods move along a conveyor belt. A mechanical arm is programmed to pick up each item in a specific orientation and place it into a pre-defined box. The arm follows the same sequence of movements for every item.
    - **Operation:** The system operates based on fixed rules: detect an item at a certain point, move the arm to a specific coordinate, grasp the item, move to another coordinate, release the item.
    - **Limitations:** If the shape or orientation of the goods changes, or if a new type of box is introduced, the system will likely fail or require manual reprogramming. It cannot identify a damaged item and decide not to package it, nor can it optimize the packaging process based on the flow of goods.
    - **Diagram:**

```
+----------+        +-------------+       +----------------+      +---
----------+        +----------+
| Goods    | --> | Conveyor   | --> | Fixed Mechanical| --> |
Packaging | --> | Packaged |
| Arrive   |      | Belt Moves  |      | Arm (Pre-       |      |
Station   |      | Goods      |
|          |      | Goods       |      | programmed      |      |
(Fixed Box) |      | Depart    |
+----------+        +-------------+      | movements)      |      +---
----------+        +----------+
                                         +----------------+
```

Understanding Artificial Intelligence (AI):

- **Concept:** Artificial Intelligence, as we've discussed, involves creating systems that can mimic human cognitive functions such as learning, problem-solving, and decision-making. AI systems use algorithms and data [1] to learn patterns, adapt to new situations, and make intelligent choices without being explicitly programmed for every possibility.
- **Key Characteristics:**
    - **Intelligent Algorithms:** Uses complex algorithms, including machine learning and deep learning.
    - **Adaptive and Flexible:** Can adjust behavior based on new data and changing circumstances.
    - **Learning Capability:** Learns from data, identifies patterns, and improves performance over time.
    - **Human-like Decision-Making:** Can make decisions based on reasoning and learned knowledge.
    - **Handles Complexity and Uncertainty:** Better equipped to deal with dynamic and unpredictable environments.
- **Example in Detail: Robotic Arm Adjusting Packaging Style Based on Object Shape**
    - **Process:** Goods of varying shapes and sizes move along a conveyor belt. A robotic arm equipped with sensors and an AI vision system identifies the shape of each item. The AI algorithm then determines the optimal way to grasp and place

the item into a suitable container, potentially adjusting the orientation or the type of packaging used.

- o **Operation:** The AI system learns from a large dataset of object shapes and successful packaging methods. It uses computer vision to analyze the shape of the incoming item, its AI algorithm to decide on the best grasping and placement strategy, and controls the robotic arm to execute these actions.
- o **Adaptability:** If a new, previously unseen object shape appears, the AI system can attempt to classify it based on learned features and apply a suitable packaging strategy. Over time, with more data, it can learn the optimal way to handle even novel shapes.
- o **Diagram:**

```
+---------+        +------------+        +----------------+        +---
---------------+      +------------+      +----------+
| Goods   | --> | Conveyor   | --> | Robotic Arm with| --> | AI
Algorithm    | --> | Packaging  | --> | Packaged |
| (Various |     | Belt Moves |     | Sensors & AI    |     |          |
(Analyzes shape, |     | Station    |     | Goods    |
| Shapes) |     | Goods      |     | Vision          |     |          |
decides grasp &  |     | (Adapts to |     | Depart   |
+---------+      +------------+     | System          |     |          |
placement)       |     | shape)     |     +----------+
                                          +----------------+      +--
-----------------+      +------------+
```

Comparative Table (Expanded):

Feature	Automation	Artificial Intelligence (AI)
Definition	Use of rules-based systems to perform tasks	Use of intelligent algorithms to mimic human behavior
Adaptability	Fixed rules; limited flexibility	Learns and adapts from data
Decision-Making	Pre-programmed; no independent decisions	Can make human-like decisions based on learning
Learning Capability	No learning from data	Yes (Machine Learning, Deep Learning)
Handling Novelty	Struggles with new or unexpected situations	Can often handle and learn from new situations
Complexity	Best for simple, repetitive tasks	Capable of handling complex and dynamic tasks
Human Intervention	Requires human intervention for changes	Can operate more autonomously
Goal	Efficiency, speed, accuracy	Intelligence, problem-solving, autonomy
Examples	- Assembly line robots (fixed tasks)	- Self-driving cars
	- Automated email responses (simple rules)	- Medical diagnosis systems
	- Vending machines	- Fraud detection systems

Export to Sheets

Diagram: AI vs. Automation Comparison (More Detailed)

```
                                    AI vs. Automation

    +--------------------------+                    +------------------
-----------+
    | **Automation** |                         | **Artificial
Intelligence** |
    +--------------------------+                    +------------------
-----------+
    | - Rule-Based            |                    | - Algorithm-Based
(ML, DL)       |
    | - Fixed Logic           |                    | - Learning &
Adaptive        |
    | - Repetitive Tasks      |                    | - Complex Problem
Solving        |
    | - Limited Flexibility   |                    | - Intelligent
Decision-Making |
    | - No Learning           |                    | - Handles Novelty
|
    | - Focus: Efficiency     |                    | - Focus:
Intelligence & Autonomy|
    +--------------------------+                    +------------------
-----------+
                 |                                                |
|                               v
v
    +--------------------------+                    +------------------
-----------+
    | **Example:** |                          | **Example:** |
    | - Factory conveyor belt |                     | - Robotic arm
adjusting       |
    |   packaging fixed-shape|                      |   packaging based
on shape   |
    |   items                 |                     | - Self-driving
car navigating|
    +--------------------------+                    +------------------
-----------+
```

50 multiple choice questions (MCQs) with **answers** based on the topics:

- 1.1 What is AI?
- 1.2 Historical Background
- 1.3 Types of AI: Narrow, General, and Superintelligent AI
- 1.4 AI vs. Automation

🔍 Topic: 1.1 What is AI? (15 MCQs)

1. **What does AI stand for?**
   a) Automated Interface
   b) Artificial Intelligence
   c) Advanced Integration
   d) Analog Input
   ✅ **Answer: b) Artificial Intelligence**

2. **AI primarily aims to simulate which human ability?**
   a) Physical strength
   b) Intelligence
   c) Respiration
   d) Digestion
   ✅ **Answer: b) Intelligence**

3. **Which of the following is NOT a component of AI?**
   a) Learning
   b) Reasoning
   c) Sleeping
   d) Problem-solving
   ✅ **Answer: c) Sleeping**

4. **Which of the following is a real-world application of AI?**
   a) Electric fan
   b) Siri
   c) Flashlight
   d) Water pump
   ✅ **Answer: b) Siri**

5. **Which field is NOT directly related to AI?**
   a) Psychology
   b) Neuroscience
   c) Agriculture
   d) Computer Science
   ✅ **Answer: c) Agriculture**

6. **AI is used to build systems that can:**
   a) Only store data
   b) Only operate machinery
   c) Perform tasks that require human intelligence
   d) Cook food automatically
   ✅ **Answer: c) Perform tasks that require human intelligence**

7. **Which of these is NOT an AI feature?**
   a) Natural Language Processing
   b) Image Recognition
   c) Electrical Circuit Tuning
   d) Machine Learning
   ✅ **Answer: c) Electrical Circuit Tuning**

8. **An example of AI in daily life is:**
   a) Solar panel
   b) Washing machine
   c) Google Assistant
   d) Light bulb
   ✅ **Answer: c) Google Assistant**

9. **The main goal of AI is to build machines that can:**
   a) Sleep and eat
   b) Learn from experience
   c) Rotate automatically
   d) Convert AC to DC
   ✅ **Answer: b) Learn from experience**

10. **Which subfield allows AI to learn from data?**
    a) Mechanical Learning
    b) Manual Programming
    c) Machine Learning
    d) Logical Networking
    ✅ **Answer: c) Machine Learning**

11. **Which of the following is the best definition of AI?**
    a) Making machines efficient
    b) Making machines act like humans
    c) Using code for automation
    d) Developing fast processors
    ✅ **Answer: b) Making machines act like humans**

12. **AI can improve:**
    a) Manual labor only
    b) Cognitive tasks
    c) Only computer speed
    d) Internal computer temperature
    ✅ **Answer: b) Cognitive tasks**

13. **Which of these is NOT an example of AI?**
    a) Spam email filter
    b) Self-driving car
    c) Chess-playing robot
    d) Electric water heater
    ✅ **Answer: d) Electric water heater**

14. **Which of the following helps AI in decision-making?**
    a) Algorithms
    b) Magnets
    c) Fuel cells
    d) Hard disks
    ✅ **Answer: a) Algorithms**

15. **The ability of a system to improve its performance based on previous experiences is called:**
    a) Memorization

b) Supervision
c) Learning
d) Programming
✅ **Answer: c) Learning**

📕 Topic: 1.2 Historical Background (10 MCQs)

16. **Who proposed the Turing Test?**
a) Marvin Minsky
b) Alan Turing
c) John McCarthy
d) Geoffrey Hinton
✅ **Answer: b) Alan Turing**

17. **The term "Artificial Intelligence" was first coined in:**
a) 1956
b) 1960
c) 1945
d) 1997
✅ **Answer: a) 1956**

18. **The Dartmouth Conference is considered the birthplace of AI. When did it take place?**
a) 1943
b) 1956
c) 1979
d) 1983
✅ **Answer: b) 1956**

19. **Who developed the first artificial neuron model in 1943?**
a) McCarthy and Hinton
b) McCulloch and Pitts
c) Minsky and Turing
d) Tesla and Einstein
✅ **Answer: b) McCulloch and Pitts**

20. **Which game did IBM's Deep Blue defeat a world champion in?**
a) Poker
b) Go
c) Chess
d) Ludo
✅ **Answer: c) Chess**

21. **IBM Watson became famous after winning which TV quiz show?**
a) Kaun Banega Crorepati
b) Wheel of Fortune
c) Jeopardy!

d) The Chase

✅ **Answer: c) Jeopardy!**

22. **Which AI defeated Go champion Lee Sedol in 2016?**
    a) Watson
    b) AlphaGo
    c) Sophia
    d) ELIZA

    ✅ **Answer: b) AlphaGo**

23. **ELIZA was an early example of a:**
    a) Robot vacuum
    b) Chatbot
    c) Translation tool
    d) Game engine

    ✅ **Answer: b) Chatbot**

24. **In the 1980s, expert systems were used in:**
    a) Animation
    b) Medical diagnosis
    c) Fitness tracking
    d) Farming tools

    ✅ **Answer: b) Medical diagnosis**

25. **Who is NOT a contributor to early AI development?**
    a) Alan Turing
    b) John McCarthy
    c) Andrew Ng
    d) Marvin Minsky

    ✅ **Answer: c) Andrew Ng**

☐ Topic: 1.3 Types of AI (15 MCQs)

26. **Narrow AI is also known as:**
    a) Weak AI
    b) Fake AI
    c) Lazy AI
    d) Smart AI

    ✅ **Answer: a) Weak AI**

27. **General AI is expected to:**
    a) Perform only one task
    b) Outperform humans in driving only
    c) Match human intelligence across all areas
    d) Work like a calculator

    ✅ **Answer: c) Match human intelligence across all areas**

28. **Superintelligent AI refers to machines that:**
    a) Can be programmed easily

b) Are faster than desktops

c) Exceed human intelligence

d) Look like robots

✅ **Answer: c) Exceed human intelligence**

29. **Which is an example of Narrow AI?**

a) A robot that can perform surgery, drive, and sing

b) Google Translate

c) Human brain

d) None of these

✅ **Answer: b) Google Translate**

30. **Which type of AI currently exists in practical applications?**

a) General AI

b) Superintelligent AI

c) Narrow AI

d) Biological AI

✅ **Answer: c) Narrow AI**

31. **Which type of AI is still theoretical and not developed yet?**

a) Narrow AI

b) Expert AI

c) General AI

d) Weak AI

✅ **Answer: c) General AI**

32. **Superintelligent AI raises concern about:**

a) Storage devices

b) Water pollution

c) Control and ethics

d) Data speed

✅ **Answer: c) Control and ethics**

33. **Narrow AI is limited to:**

a) One specific task

b) Any human-level task

c) Emotional understanding

d) Social behavior

✅ **Answer: a) One specific task**

34. **General AI can:**

a) Only translate languages

b) Only play chess

c) Perform any intellectual task like a human

d) Only recognize faces

✅ **Answer: c) Perform any intellectual task like a human**

35. **Sophia the Robot is an example of:**

a) Super AI

b) Narrow AI with human-like features

c) Hardware AI

d) Cloud AI

✅ **Answer: b) Narrow AI with human-like features**

36. **Which type of AI can evolve and improve beyond human control?**
    a) Weak AI
    b) General AI
    c) Super AI
    d) Rule-based AI

    ✅ **Answer: c) Super AI**

37. **In AI hierarchy, which type comes first?**
    a) Super AI
    b) Narrow AI
    c) General AI
    d) Cloud AI

    ✅ **Answer: b) Narrow AI**

38. **Which is a risk associated with Superintelligent AI?**
    a) High electricity bills
    b) Global warming
    c) Ethical and security threats
    d) Slow processing

    ✅ **Answer: c) Ethical and security threats**

39. **General AI is:**
    a) Highly specific
    b) Task-dependent
    c) Multi-domain capable
    d) Used in elevators

    ✅ **Answer: c) Multi-domain capable**

40. **The dream of AI researchers is to build:**
    a) Weak AI
    b) General AI
    c) Static AI
    d) Clean AI

    ✅ **Answer: b) General AI**

⚙ Topic: 1.4 AI vs. Automation (10 MCQs)

41. **Automation is mainly based on:**
    a) Manual control
    b) Rules and logic
    c) Intelligent systems
    d) DNA programming

    ✅ **Answer: b) Rules and logic**

42. **AI systems are capable of:**
    a) Only repetitive tasks

b) Learning and adapting

c) Washing clothes

d) Sleeping during work

✓ **Answer: b) Learning and adapting**

43. **Which of these is an example of automation but not AI?**

a) Self-driving car

b) Fan controlled by temperature sensor

c) Chatbot

d) Facial recognition

✓ **Answer: b) Fan controlled by temperature sensor**

44. **Which feature is unique to AI and not in basic automation?**

a) Learning from data

b) Following fixed rules

c) Speed of processing

d) Circuit design

✓ **Answer: a) Learning from data**

45. **Automation usually lacks:**

a) Energy

b) Logic

c) Learning ability

d) Efficiency

✓ **Answer: c) Learning ability**

46. **AI requires which of the following to work effectively?**

a) Predefined logic only

b) Data and learning algorithms

c) Only manual input

d) Direct user supervision

✓ **Answer: b) Data and learning algorithms**

47. **A robot that learns how to pick up different objects is using:**

a) Automation

b) AI

c) Mechanical arms only

d) Physical sensors only

✓ **Answer: b) AI**

48. **Which of the following tasks is best handled by automation?**

a) Customer interaction

b) Fixed time-based switching

c) Complex diagnosis

d) Facial detection

✓ **Answer: b) Fixed time-based switching**

49. **AI is suitable for tasks that require:**

a) Rigid workflows

b) Static responses

c) Dynamic thinking and decisions

d) Periodic maintenance

✅ **Answer: c) Dynamic thinking and decisions**

50. **Difference between AI and automation lies in:**

a) AI's learning and decision-making ability

b) Automation's internet usage

c) AI's dependence on temperature

d) Automation being wireless

✅ **Answer: a) AI's learning and decision-making ability**

Chapter 2: Introduction to Robotics

2.1 What is a Robot? A Detailed Exploration

Definition: A Programmable Autonomous Machine

As you've stated, a robot is fundamentally a **programmable machine**. This means its actions are dictated by a set of instructions, or a program, that a human engineer or programmer has designed. The crucial aspect is its ability to carry out a **complex series of actions automatically**. This implies a level of autonomy – once initiated, the robot can perform its tasks without continuous direct human control. Furthermore, robots often draw inspiration from the natural world, aiming to **replicate or simulate human or animal behavior** in their form, movement, or capabilities.

Key Characteristics of a Robot: The Sense-Think-Act Cycle

The functionality of a robot can be elegantly summarized by a fundamental cycle: **Sensing - Computation - Action**. Let's explore each of these in detail:

- **Sensing: Perceiving the Environment**
    - **Explanation:** Robots need to be aware of their surroundings to interact effectively. This awareness comes through **sensors**, which are devices that detect and measure physical properties of the environment and convert them into signals that the robot's computational unit can understand.
    - **Types of Sensors (with examples):**
        - **Vision Sensors (Cameras):** Capture visual information, allowing the robot to "see" objects, recognize patterns, read labels, and navigate.
            - **Example:** A robot arm in a warehouse uses a camera to identify the correct product to pick from a shelf.
        - **Proximity Sensors (Infrared, Ultrasonic):** Detect the presence and distance of objects without physical contact.
            - **Example:** A robot navigating a crowded space uses ultrasonic sensors to avoid collisions with people and obstacles.
        - **Tactile Sensors (Force, Pressure):** Provide a sense of touch, allowing the robot to measure forces and pressures exerted on it.
            - **Example:** A robotic hand uses tactile sensors in its fingertips to grasp delicate objects without crushing them.
        - **Audio Sensors (Microphones):** Capture sound, enabling voice recognition, understanding commands, or detecting specific noises.
            - **Example:** A social robot uses microphones to understand spoken instructions from a user.
        - **Environmental Sensors (Temperature, Humidity, Light):** Measure ambient conditions.
            - **Example:** A robot in a greenhouse monitors temperature and humidity levels to optimize plant growth.

- **Position and Orientation Sensors (GPS, Encoders, IMUs):** Determine the robot's location, orientation, and movement.
  - **Example:** A delivery drone uses GPS to navigate to its destination, while wheel encoders on a mobile robot track its movement and distance traveled.
  - **Analogy to Human Body: Eyes/Ears = Sensors** Just as our eyes and ears gather information about the world around us, a robot's sensors are its primary means of perceiving its environment.
- **Computation: Processing Data and Making Decisions**
  - **Explanation:** Once the sensors gather data, this information needs to be processed to make sense of the environment and decide on the appropriate actions. This is the role of the **computation** unit, which typically involves a **microcontroller** or a more powerful **processor** (essentially the robot's "brain").
  - **Process:**

    0. **Data Acquisition:** Receiving signals from the sensors.
    1. **Data Processing:** Filtering, analyzing, and interpreting the sensor data. This might involve running algorithms to identify objects, map the environment, or detect changes.
    2. **Decision-Making:** Based on the processed information and its pre-programmed instructions or AI algorithms, the robot decides what action to take. This could involve planning a path, choosing a grasping strategy, or responding to a voice command.
    3. **Control Signal Generation:** Sending commands to the actuators to execute the decided action.
  - **Role of AI:** In more advanced robots, Artificial Intelligence plays a crucial role in the computation phase. AI algorithms enable the robot to learn from data, adapt to new situations, make more complex decisions, and even exhibit a degree of autonomy in unpredictable environments.
  - **Analogy to Human Body: Brain = Microcontroller/Processor** Similar to how our brain processes sensory input, interprets it, and decides on our actions, the robot's computational unit performs the crucial task of information processing and decision-making.
- **Action: Interacting with the World**
  - **Explanation:** The final step is for the robot to physically interact with its environment. This is achieved through **actuators**, which are devices that convert energy (usually electrical, pneumatic, or hydraulic) into motion or force.
  - **Types of Actuators (with examples):**

    - **Motors (Electric, Servo, Stepper):** Used for rotational motion, powering wheels, joints in robotic arms, and other movements.
      - **Example:** The wheels of a mobile robot are driven by electric motors. Servo motors control the precise angle of joints in a robotic arm.
    - **Pneumatic and Hydraulic Cylinders:** Use compressed air or fluid to create linear motion and exert significant force.

- **Example:** Industrial robots often use hydraulic cylinders for heavy lifting tasks.
  - **Solenoids:** Electromagnetic devices that produce linear motion when an electric current is passed through them.
    - **Example:** Used in robotic grippers for opening and closing mechanisms.
  - **Artificial Muscles (Electroactive Polymers):** Emerging technology that can contract or expand in response to electrical stimulation, mimicking biological muscles.
    - **Example:** Used in research for more lifelike and flexible robot movements.
  - **Speakers:** Used for generating sound and interacting verbally.
    - **Example:** Social robots use speakers to communicate with humans.
  - **Display Screens:** Used for visual communication and displaying information.
    - **Example:** Some robots have touchscreens for user interaction.
  - **Analogy to Human Body: Hands/Legs = Actuators** Just as our hands and legs allow us to manipulate objects and move around, a robot's actuators are its "muscles" and "limbs" that enable it to act upon its environment.

Example in Detail: A Robotic Vacuum Cleaner (Roomba)

You've provided an excellent example:

- **Sensing:** Roomba uses various sensors, including:
  - **Cliff Sensors:** To detect drops and prevent falling down stairs.
  - **Bump Sensors:** To detect collisions with walls and obstacles.
  - **Optical and Acoustic Dirt Detectors:** To identify areas with more dirt.
- **Computation:** Its internal processor analyzes the sensor data to:
  - **Map the room:** Create a virtual map of the cleaning area.
  - **Plan cleaning paths:** Decide on the most efficient way to cover the floor.
  - **Make decisions:** Change direction upon encountering obstacles or detecting a dirty area.
- **Action:** Actuators enable it to:
  - **Move:** Wheels allow it to navigate the room.
  - **Clean:** A motor-driven brush system sweeps up dirt and debris, which is then suctioned into a collection bin.

Suggested Diagram: A Labeled Diagram of a Simple Robot

Here's a more detailed version of the diagram you suggested, incorporating the sense-think-act cycle:

```
Simple Robot Diagram

+-------------+
```

```
                              | Power Source|
                              | (Battery)   |
                              +-------------+
                                    |
                                    | (Powers all components)
                                    v
        +-----------------+      +----------------------+      +--------------
---+
        | **1. Sensing** | --> | **2. Computation** | --> | **3. Action** |
        | - Sensors       |      | - Microcontroller/   |      | - Actuators
|
        |   (e.g., front  |      |   Processor (Brain)  |      |   (e.g.,
Wheels/ |
        |    proximity,   |      | - Algorithms         |      |
Arms/Grippers) |
        |    dirt         |      | - Memory             |      | - Motors
|
        |    detector)    |      | - AI (Optional)      |      | - Cylinders
|
        +-----------------+      +----------------------+      +--------------
---+
              ^                              |                          |
        | (Environmental Data)       | (Control Signals)        |
(Physical Interaction)
        +----------------------------------------------------------+
                          **The Sense-Think-Act Cycle**
```

2.2 Categories of Robots

Robotic systems exhibit a wide range of forms and capabilities, primarily determined by their intended function and the environments in which they operate. The following categories illustrate this diversity:

1. Robots in Industry:

These machines are integral to manufacturing processes, performing tasks with precision and consistency.

- **Function:** Automation of repetitive, hazardous, or intricate tasks within production lines.
- **Characteristics:** Typically robust construction, high accuracy and repeatability in their movements, often fixed in their operational area, and equipped with specialized tools tailored to the task.
- **Example:** Articulated robotic arms, such as those utilized in automotive assembly for welding operations. These arms follow pre-programmed paths to join components with consistent quality and speed, enhancing production efficiency.
- **Diagram Element:** An illustration of a robotic arm engaged in a manufacturing task, like welding a car chassis.

2. Robots for Domestic Use:

These robots are designed to assist with chores and provide convenience within residential settings.

- **Function:** Automation of household tasks, entertainment, or companionship.
- **Characteristics:** User-friendly interfaces, often operate autonomously with minimal supervision, and focus on making domestic life easier.
- **Example:** Autonomous vacuum cleaners that navigate and clean floors without direct human control, utilizing sensors to map rooms and avoid obstacles. Similarly, robotic lawnmowers can maintain lawns within defined boundaries on a programmed schedule.
- **Diagram Element:** Icons representing a robot vacuum cleaner and a robotic lawnmower.

3. Robots in Service Industries:

These robotic systems support human workers and interact with the public in various professional environments.

- **Function:** Assisting with tasks in sectors such as healthcare, hospitality, and logistics, often involving direct human interaction.
- **Characteristics:** Designed for collaboration with people, adaptable to specific tasks within their service domain, and aimed at improving efficiency, safety, or service quality.
- **Example:** Surgical robots that provide surgeons with enhanced dexterity and precision during minimally invasive procedures, controlled remotely by the surgeon. Additionally, robots in hotels can autonomously deliver amenities to guest rooms, navigating hallways and using elevators.
- **Diagram Element:** Illustrations of a surgical robot arm and a robot delivering items in a hotel setting.

4. Robots for Military Applications:

These robots are employed in defense and security for a variety of critical tasks.

- **Function:** Surveillance, reconnaissance, explosive ordnance disposal, and logistical support in challenging and dangerous environments.
- **Characteristics:** Often built to withstand harsh conditions, capable of remote operation or autonomous function to minimize risk to personnel, and equipped with specialized sensors, manipulators, or other mission-specific payloads.
- **Example:** Unmanned aerial vehicles (drones) used for aerial reconnaissance and surveillance. Also, remotely operated vehicles designed for the safe inspection and neutralization of explosive devices.
- **Diagram Element:** Icons depicting a military drone and a bomb disposal robot.

5. Robots for Space Exploration:

These robots are engineered to operate in the extreme conditions of outer space, performing tasks vital to exploration and research.

- **Function:** Exploration of celestial bodies, satellite maintenance, in-orbit construction, and astronaut assistance.
- **Characteristics:** Radiation-hardened components, resistance to vacuum and extreme temperatures, often require a high degree of autonomy due to communication delays, and equipped with specialized scientific instruments and tools.
- **Example:** Planetary rovers deployed by space agencies to explore the surfaces of other planets, equipped with sensors, cameras, and robotic arms for sample collection and analysis.
- **Diagram Element:** An illustration of a Mars rover exploring the Martian surface.

6. Humanoid Robots:

These robots are characterized by their physical resemblance to the human form.

- **Function:** Research in human-robot interaction, potential for companionship, entertainment, and assistance in human-centric environments.
- **Characteristics:** Anthropomorphic design including a torso, head, arms, and legs; require complex systems for movement and balance; and often incorporate AI for natural language processing and social interaction.
- **Example:** Robots designed with human-like features and the ability to engage in conversations and mimic facial expressions, serving as platforms for studying social robotics.
- **Diagram Element:** A representation of a humanoid robot.

7. Swarm Robots:

These systems involve a large number of small, simple robots working collectively.

- **Function:** Achieving complex tasks through the coordinated actions of many individual units.
- **Characteristics:** Decentralized control where each robot operates based on local information, scalability and robustness through redundancy, and the emergence of complex behaviors from simple individual rules.
- **Example:** Conceptual robots designed to mimic the pollination behavior of bees, with numerous small units working together to pollinate crops in a distributed manner.
- **Diagram Element:** An illustration of multiple small robots interacting with flowers.

Suggested Diagram Structure:

A mind map titled "Categories of Robots" at the center. Branches extending to each of the seven types (Industrial, Domestic, Service, Military, Space, Humanoid, Swarm). Sub-branches from each type could include key characteristics and visual icons representing the examples provided.

2.3 Essential Components: Sensors, Actuators, and Control Systems in Robotics

A robot's ability to interact with its environment and perform tasks hinges on three fundamental components: sensors for perception, actuators for action, and a control system to orchestrate these processes.

1. Sensors: The Robot's Perception of Its Surroundings

Sensors are devices that enable a robot to gather information about its environment by detecting various physical properties and converting them into electrical signals that the robot's control system can interpret. The type of sensor employed depends on the specific tasks the robot needs to perform and the environment in which it operates.

Type	Example	Function
Infrared (IR)	Line-following robot	Detects distance to objects or a designated path by measuring reflected infrared light.
Ultrasonic	Obstacle-avoiding robot	Measures the distance to objects by emitting sound waves and measuring the time it takes for the echo to return.
Camera	Surveillance robot	Captures visual information, enabling image processing for object recognition, navigation, and monitoring.
Touch Sensor	Collision detection system	Detects physical contact with objects, often used for safety or interaction.
Temperature Sensor	Industrial monitoring robot	Measures the temperature of objects or the surrounding environment, crucial for process control and safety.

Export to Sheets

2. Actuators: Enabling Physical Movement and Interaction

Actuators are the components that translate electrical signals from the robot's control system into physical motion or force, allowing the robot to interact with its environment. The choice of actuator depends on the type of movement and the force required for the robot's tasks.

Type	Example	Action
DC Motor	Wheeled robots	Produces continuous rotational movement, used for locomotion.
Servo Motor	Arm robots	Provides precise control over angular position, essential for controlled movements in robotic joints.
Pneumatic	Industrial robots	Generates linear motion and force using compressed air, often used for tasks requiring speed and moderate force.
Hydraulic	Heavy-duty robots	Generates significant linear force using pressurized fluid, suitable for lifting heavy loads and high-power applications.

Export to Sheets

3. Control System: The Robot's Brain

The control system serves as the central processing unit of the robot. It receives data from the sensors, processes this information according to its programmed algorithms or AI models, and then sends commands to the actuators to execute the desired actions.

- **Examples of Control Systems:**
  - **Microcontrollers (e.g., Arduino, Raspberry Pi):** Small, low-cost computers that can be programmed to control various electronic components, ideal for prototyping and simpler robotic applications.
  - **Embedded Computer Systems:** More powerful and complex computing platforms integrated directly into the robot, capable of handling more sophisticated sensor data processing and control algorithms, often used in advanced robots with AI capabilities.

Working Example: A Line-Following Robot

Consider a basic robot designed to follow a black line on a white surface:

1. **Sensor (Infrared Sensor):** An infrared sensor mounted on the bottom of the robot emits infrared light and detects the reflected light. Black surfaces absorb more infrared light than white surfaces. The sensor outputs a signal indicating the intensity of the reflected light, thus allowing it to "see" the line.
2. **Controller (Microcontroller - e.g., Arduino):** The microcontroller receives the signal from the infrared sensor. If the sensor detects a strong reflection (indicating it's over a white surface), the microcontroller determines that the robot is deviating from the black line.
3. **Actuator (DC Motors):** Based on the sensor input, the microcontroller sends signals to the DC motors that drive the robot's wheels. If the robot is veering to the right of the line, the microcontroller might decrease the speed of the right wheel and increase the speed of the left wheel (or even reverse the right wheel briefly) to steer the robot back onto the black line. Similarly, if it veers to the left, the opposite adjustment would be made.

Suggested Diagram: Block Diagram of a Robot System

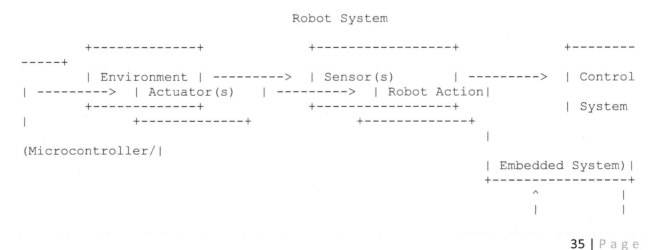

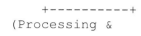
Commands)

This diagram illustrates the flow of information and control within a robotic system, highlighting the crucial roles of sensors in perceiving the environment, the control system in processing information and making decisions, and actuators in executing those decisions through physical action.

2.4 Understanding Human-Robot Interaction (HRI)

Human-Robot Interaction (HRI) is a multidisciplinary field dedicated to understanding, designing, and evaluating robotic systems for use by or with humans. It encompasses how people interact and communicate with robots, considering both the robot's capabilities and the human's needs and expectations.

Types of Interaction:

The way humans and robots work together can be categorized based on the level of autonomy the robot possesses and the degree of human involvement in its actions.

- **Remote-controlled (Teleoperation):** In this mode, a human operator exerts direct, real-time control over the robot's actions from a distance. The robot essentially acts as an extension of the human operator.
  - **Process:** A human uses an interface, such as a joystick, keyboard, or specialized control suit, to send commands to the robot, which then executes these commands in its environment. Sensory feedback from the robot (e.g., video feed, tactile information) is often provided to the operator to facilitate control.
  - **Example:** Bomb disposal robots are frequently teleoperated by trained personnel who can remotely navigate the robot, manipulate objects, and neutralize threats from a safe distance.
  - **Diagram Element:** An illustration of a person using a control console to operate a robot arm in a hazardous environment.
- **Shared Control:** This type of interaction involves a collaborative effort where both the human and the robot contribute to the control of the robot's actions. The robot may have some level of autonomy but relies on human input for high-level guidance or intervention in complex situations.
  - **Process:** The human provides overall goals or specific instructions, while the robot uses its sensors and processing capabilities to execute these commands, potentially offering suggestions or adjusting its actions based on its perception of the environment. The human can often override the robot's autonomous actions if necessary.
  - **Example:** Surgical robots used in minimally invasive surgery exemplify shared control. The surgeon controls the robot's instruments with high precision, while

the robot provides stability, tremor filtering, and enhanced visualization, effectively augmenting the surgeon's skills.

- o **Diagram Element:** A depiction of a surgeon using a console to guide a robotic surgical arm.
- **Autonomous Interaction:** In this mode, the robot operates independently, making decisions and taking actions based on its programming, sensors, and AI algorithms, with minimal or no real-time human intervention.
  - o **Process:** The robot is given high-level goals or tasks and then uses its onboard intelligence to plan and execute the necessary actions to achieve those goals. It perceives its environment, reasons about it, and acts accordingly without requiring continuous human commands.
  - o **Example:** Robots in warehouses that navigate autonomously to locate and retrieve items for order fulfillment. These robots use sensors and mapping technologies to understand their surroundings and plan efficient routes.
  - o **Diagram Element:** An illustration of a robot navigating autonomously through a warehouse aisle.
- **Collaborative Robots (Cobots):** These are specifically designed to work safely and directly alongside human workers in shared workspaces, typically in industrial or manufacturing settings.
  - o **Process:** Cobots are equipped with advanced safety features, such as force and torque sensors, that allow them to detect collisions with humans and react by stopping or moving away. They are often designed to assist humans with physically demanding or repetitive tasks, enhancing productivity and reducing the risk of injury.
  - o **Example:** Robotic arms, like the UR3 or Baxter, used in assembly lines to hand parts to human workers, hold items in place, or perform tasks that require consistent force or awkward positioning, working in close proximity to their human colleagues.
  - o **Diagram Element:** A depiction of a robotic arm working alongside a human on a factory assembly line.

Modes of Communication:

Effective HRI relies on clear and intuitive communication between humans and robots. Various modalities are used for this purpose:

- **Voice Commands:** Humans can communicate with robots using spoken language, which the robot processes using speech recognition technology and natural language understanding.
  - o **Example:** Interacting with virtual assistants like Alexa or Siri to ask questions, set reminders, or control smart devices.
  - o **Diagram Element:** A person speaking to a robot.
- **Gestures:** Robots can be designed to understand and respond to human body movements and hand signals. Conversely, robots can also use gestures to convey information or intent.

- o **Example:** Robots that can interpret sign language to communicate with hearing-impaired individuals.
  - o **Diagram Element:** A person making a hand gesture towards a robot.
- **Touch:** Physical contact can be a mode of interaction, either through direct manipulation of the robot or via touch-sensitive interfaces on the robot itself (e.g., touchscreens).
  - o **Example:** Using a touchscreen on a robot to give commands or access information.
  - o **Diagram Element:** A person touching a display screen on a robot.
- **Facial Expressions:** Some robots are designed with the ability to display facial expressions to convey emotions or indicate their internal state, aiming to make interactions more natural and intuitive for humans.
  - o **Example:** Emotional robots like Pepper that can display a range of expressions to respond to human emotions or indicate their own "mood."
  - o **Diagram Element:** A robot with a discernible facial expression.

Challenges in HRI:

Despite significant advancements, several challenges remain in creating seamless and effective human-robot interactions:

- **Trust:** Building trust is crucial for humans to effectively collaborate with and rely on robots. This involves ensuring the robot's reliability, predictability, and transparency in its actions. If humans do not trust a robot, they may be hesitant to work with it or accept its decisions.
- **Safety:** Ensuring the safety of humans interacting with robots is paramount. Robots, especially those with physical capabilities, must be designed and programmed to avoid causing harm, even in unexpected situations. This includes implementing safety mechanisms and robust error handling.
- **Ethics:** As robots become more autonomous and capable of making decisions, ethical considerations arise, particularly in situations where robot actions can significantly affect humans. Questions about responsibility, bias in algorithms, and the appropriate level of robot autonomy need careful consideration.

Suggested Diagram:

A central figure of a human interacting with a robot. Arrows extending from the human towards the robot could indicate different modes of communication: a speech bubble for voice, a hand symbol for gesture, and a finger touching a screen on the robot's chest for touch.

✅ Summary

Concept	Key Points
What is a Robot?	Machine that senses, thinks, acts
Types of Robots	Industrial, service, military, humanoid, etc.
Components	Sensors (input), Controller (processing), Actuators (output)
HRI	Interaction modes: remote, collaborative, autonomous

50 multiple-choice questions with answers covering the topics in (2.1 What is a Robot?, 2.2 Types of Robots, 2.3 Sensors, Actuators, and Control Systems, 2.4 Human-Robot Interaction (HRI)):

2.1 What is a Robot?

1. A robot is best defined as a: a) Human-like machine b) Remotely controlled device c) Programmable machine capable of carrying out complex actions automatically d) Simple automated tool **Answer: c)**
2. Which of the following is a key characteristic commonly found in robots? a) Biological reproduction b) Independent consciousness c) Ability to sense the environment d) Need for constant human input **Answer: c)**
3. The "brain" of a robot, responsible for processing data and making decisions, is analogous to which human body part? a) Eyes b) Hands c) Brain d) Legs **Answer: c)**
4. Actuators in a robot are primarily responsible for: a) Perceiving the environment b) Processing information c) Generating physical motion d) Storing data **Answer: c)**
5. Sensors enable a robot to: a) Move around its environment b) Understand and process human language c) Detect and measure physical properties of its surroundings d) Execute pre-programmed tasks repeatedly **Answer: c)**
6. A robotic vacuum cleaner (like Roomba) utilizes sensors to: a) Display information to the user b) Generate movement for cleaning c) Detect dirt, obstacles, and map the room d) Communicate with other smart devices **Answer: c)**
7. The ability of a robot to perform a series of actions without continuous direct human control is known as: a) Automation b) Teleoperation c) Autonomy d) Manipulation **Answer: c)**
8. Which of the following is NOT typically considered a key characteristic of a robot? a) Sensing b) Computation c) Action d) Emotional response **Answer: d)**
9. The microcontroller or processor in a robot performs the function of: a) Powering the actuators b) Interpreting sensor data and sending commands c) Physically interacting with the environment d) Storing the robot's physical design **Answer: b)**
10. Which human sense is most closely related to the function of a camera on a robot? a) Touch b) Hearing c) Sight d) Smell **Answer: c)**

2.2 Types of Robots

11. Robots used in manufacturing for tasks like welding and painting are classified as: a) Domestic robots b) Industrial robots c) Service robots d) Military robots **Answer: b)**

12. A robot vacuum cleaner is an example of a: a) Industrial robot b) Domestic robot c) Service robot d) Space robot **Answer: b)**

13. Surgical robots that assist surgeons in performing operations fall under the category of: a) Military robots b) Humanoid robots c) Service robots d) Industrial robots **Answer: c)**

14. Unmanned aerial vehicles (drones) used for surveillance are a type of: a) Domestic robot b) Service robot c) Military robot d) Space robot **Answer: c)**

15. NASA's Mars Rovers (like Curiosity) are examples of: a) Industrial robots b) Domestic robots c) Service robots d) Space robots **Answer: d)**

16. Robots designed to resemble and act like humans are known as: a) Swarm robots b) Humanoid robots c) Collaborative robots d) Teleoperated robots **Answer: b)**

17. A system where multiple simple robots work together to achieve a common goal, like robot bees for pollination, is called: a) Humanoid robotics b) Autonomous robotics c) Swarm robotics d) Teleoperation **Answer: c)**

18. Robots that are specifically designed to work alongside humans in a shared workspace are called: a) Industrial arms b) Humanoid assistants c) Collaborative robots (cobots) d) Autonomous mobile robots **Answer: c)**

19. Which type of robot is primarily designed for high precision and repeatability in tasks? a) Domestic robots b) Industrial robots c) Service robots d) Military robots **Answer: b)**

20. Robots that assist in hospitals with tasks like medication delivery are categorized as: a) Domestic robots b) Industrial robots c) Service robots d) Military robots **Answer: c)**

2.3 Sensors, Actuators, and Control Systems

21. An infrared (IR) sensor is commonly used in a line-following robot to: a) Measure temperature b) Detect the presence of a line c) Avoid obstacles d) Recognize voice commands **Answer: b)**

22. Ultrasonic sensors primarily function to: a) Detect colors b) Measure distance c) Sense touch d) Recognize images **Answer: b)**

23. In a surveillance robot, a camera acts as a: a) Proximity sensor b) Temperature sensor c) Vision sensor d) Tactile sensor **Answer: c)**

24. A touch sensor on a robot is typically used for: a) Measuring speed b) Detecting collisions c) Identifying objects d) Navigating autonomously **Answer: b)**

25. Which type of actuator is commonly used to provide rotational movement in wheeled robots? a) Pneumatic cylinder b) Hydraulic cylinder c) DC Motor d) Servo Motor **Answer: c)**

26. Servo motors are preferred in robotic arms for achieving: a) High speed linear motion b) Precise angular movement c) High force lifting d) Continuous high-power rotation **Answer: b)**

27. Pneumatic actuators utilize which medium to generate linear motion? a) Electricity b) Hydraulic fluid c) Compressed air d) Magnetic fields **Answer: c)**

28. Heavy-duty robots that need to lift very heavy objects often use which type of actuator? a) DC Motors b) Servo Motors c) Pneumatic actuators d) Hydraulic actuators **Answer: d)**

29. The "brain" of a robot that processes sensor input and sends commands to actuators is the: a) Power source b) End-effector c) Control system d) Transmission mechanism **Answer: c)**
30. Arduino and Raspberry Pi are examples of: a) Actuators b) Sensors c) Microcontrollers used in control systems d) Types of robot programming languages **Answer: c)**

2.4 Human-Robot Interaction (HRI)

31. The study of how people interact and communicate with robots is known as: a) Robot kinematics b) Artificial intelligence c) Human-Robot Interaction (HRI) d) Robot dynamics **Answer: c)**
32. Controlling a bomb disposal robot using a joystick is an example of: a) Autonomous interaction b) Collaborative control c) Remote-controlled (teleoperation) d) Shared control **Answer: c)**
33. In a surgical robot where the surgeon controls the instruments while the robot provides stability, this is an example of: a) Teleoperation b) Autonomous interaction c) Shared control d) Direct manipulation **Answer: c)**
34. Robots navigating autonomously in a warehouse to fulfill orders demonstrate: a) Teleoperation b) Shared control c) Autonomous interaction d) Collaborative robotics **Answer: c)**
35. Robots designed to work alongside humans in factories, like a UR3 arm, are known as: a) Industrial robots b) Humanoid robots c) Service robots d) Collaborative robots (cobots) **Answer: d)**
36. Interacting with a robot by giving spoken instructions is an example of communication through: a) Gestures b) Touch c) Voice commands d) Facial expressions **Answer: c)**
37. A robot that understands and responds to sign language utilizes communication through: a) Voice commands b) Gestures c) Touch d) Facial expressions **Answer: b)**
38. Using a touchscreen on a robot to provide input is an example of communication via: a) Voice commands b) Gestures c) Touch d) Facial expressions **Answer: c)**
39. Robots like Pepper that display emotions through their faces utilize which mode of communication? a) Voice commands b) Gestures c) Touch d) Facial expressions **Answer: d)**
40. A significant challenge in HRI is ensuring that humans can rely on the robot's actions, which relates to: a) Safety b) Ethics c) Trust d) Efficiency **Answer: c)**
41. Preventing robots from causing harm to people is a primary concern in HRI related to: a) Trust b) Ethics c) Safety d) Autonomy **Answer: c)**
42. Questions about whether robots should make decisions that affect humans fall under the ethical considerations of: a) Robot design b) Human-robot interaction c) Sensor accuracy d) Actuator limitations **Answer: b)**
43. Which of the following is NOT a common mode of communication in HRI? a) Voice commands b) Gestures c) Taste d) Touch **Answer: c)**
44. In shared control, the robot typically provides assistance by leveraging its: a) Emotional intelligence b) Superior physical strength c) Sensors and processing capabilities d) Ability to mimic human speech perfectly **Answer: c)**

45. The level of human involvement is minimal in which type of human-robot interaction? a) Teleoperation b) Shared control c) Autonomous interaction d) Collaborative robotics **Answer: c)**
46. Cobots are specifically designed for: a) High-speed, repetitive tasks without human intervention b) Safe and direct work alongside human workers c) Operation in hazardous and remote environments d) Mimicking human-like social interactions **Answer: b)**
47. Providing sensory feedback to a human operator in teleoperation aims to improve: a) The robot's autonomy b) The operator's control and awareness c) The robot's processing speed d) The robot's physical strength **Answer: b)**
48. Ethical considerations in HRI become increasingly important as robots gain more: a) Physical size b) Processing power c) Autonomy d) Number of sensors **Answer: c)**
49. Building trust in robots often involves making their actions more: a) Complex and unpredictable b) Opaque and difficult to understand c) Transparent and predictable d) Dependent on constant human oversight **Answer: c)**
50. Force and torque sensors are important safety features commonly found in: a) Teleoperated robots b) Autonomous mobile robots c) Collaborative robots (cobots) d) Humanoid robots **Answer: c)**

Chapter 3: The Intersection of AI and Robotics

3.1 The Role of Artificial Intelligence in Enhancing Robot Capabilities

Artificial Intelligence (AI) represents a significant advancement in the field of robotics, endowing machines with the capacity to perceive their surroundings, engage in reasoning, acquire knowledge through learning, and adapt their behavior in response to environmental changes. In contrast to conventional robots that execute pre-programmed sequences of actions along fixed pathways, AI-powered robots exhibit a degree of intelligence that allows for autonomous decision-making, continuous improvement based on experience, and effective operation within complex and unpredictable settings.

Key Components of AI-Driven Robotics:

The integration of AI into robotic systems involves several crucial components working in concert:

- **Perception:** AI algorithms enable robots to interpret sensory data obtained from various sensors, including cameras. A prime example is the application of **computer vision**, a field of AI that allows robots to "see" and understand visual information. Through computer vision, robots can identify different objects within their field of view, detect obstacles in their path, and recognize human presence and even their gestures or facial expressions. This sophisticated perception allows robots to build a detailed understanding of their operational environment.
    - **Example:** A delivery robot navigating a sidewalk uses computer vision to identify pedestrians, traffic signals, and potential hazards like potholes or construction barriers. This visual understanding informs its movement and decision-making.
- **Planning and Decision Making:** AI, particularly through **machine learning** models, provides robots with the ability to analyze data and determine the most effective course of action to achieve a specific goal. These models learn from vast amounts of data, allowing the robot to choose optimal paths for navigation, decide on the best manipulation strategies for objects, or respond appropriately to dynamic situations.
    - **Example:** A warehouse robot tasked with retrieving an item can use a machine learning model trained on warehouse layouts and past retrieval times to plan the most efficient route, avoiding congestion and minimizing travel distance.
- **Actuation:** Following the decision-making process driven by AI, the robot executes its chosen actions using its physical components, primarily **motors** and **servos**. These actuators translate the AI's instructions into precise physical movements, enabling the robot to navigate, manipulate objects, and interact with its environment in a controlled manner.
    - **Example:** An AI-powered robotic arm on an assembly line, having identified a specific part through computer vision and planned the grasping motion, uses its servo motors to precisely move its joints and grip the component.

- **Learning:** A key aspect of AI is the ability to learn and improve over time. **Reinforcement learning** is a powerful AI technique that allows robots to learn through trial and error. By interacting with their environment and receiving feedback (rewards or penalties) for their actions, robots can refine their behavior to achieve better performance in their tasks.
  - **Example:** A robot learning to walk might initially stumble and fall. Through reinforcement learning, it receives negative feedback for falling and positive feedback for stable movement. Over time, it adjusts its motor controls and learns a robust and efficient gait.

Illustrative Case: AI in Industrial Robotics

Consider an advanced assembly-line robot equipped with a **neural network**, a sophisticated type of machine learning model. This robot's task is to assemble complex products with various components.

- **Traditional Approach:** A traditional robot would be programmed with precise, step-by-step instructions for each assembly operation. If a component was slightly misaligned or presented in an unexpected orientation, the robot would likely fail or require manual intervention and reprogramming to handle the new scenario.
- **AI-Powered Approach:** The AI-equipped robot, using computer vision, can visually inspect each incoming component. If the neural network has been trained on data that includes examples of misaligned components, it can **detect the misalignment automatically**. Furthermore, the AI system can then analyze the degree and nature of the misalignment and **autonomously adjust the robot's movements** to correctly pick up and place the component, compensating for the variation. This flexibility, learned from data rather than explicitly programmed for every possible error, significantly enhances the robot's adaptability and reduces downtime.

Diagram: Integration of AI in a Robotic System

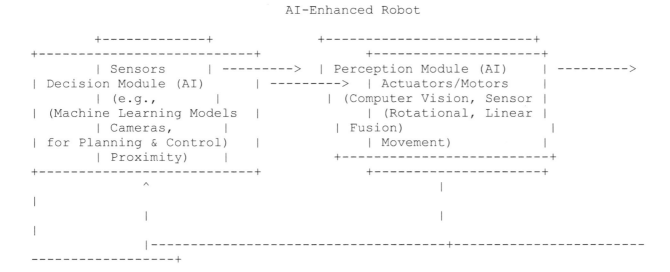

```
                                        [ Learning from Feedback
(Reinforcement Learning)  ]

                                                     ↑
                                                     |
                                        [ Environment Interaction & Task
Execution  ]
```

This diagram illustrates how sensor data flows into the AI-powered perception module, which interprets the environment. The decision module then uses this information, along with learned patterns, to determine the appropriate actions, which are translated into physical movements by the actuators. The robot's interactions with the environment provide feedback that can be used by the AI to learn and improve its performance over time.

3.2 The Pivotal Role of Artificial Intelligence in Contemporary Robotics

Artificial Intelligence (AI) has become an indispensable component of modern robotics, fundamentally altering the potential and application of these machines. By integrating AI, robots transcend the limitations of traditional pre-programmed automation, evolving into intelligent agents capable of operating effectively in complex, real-world scenarios and engaging with humans in more intuitive ways.

Significant Advantages of AI Integration:

The incorporation of AI into robotics yields several key benefits that dramatically enhance their utility and versatility:

- **Enhanced Autonomy:** AI empowers robots to perform tasks with significantly reduced or even complete independence from direct human control. Through sophisticated perception and decision-making algorithms, AI-driven robots can navigate environments, manipulate objects, and execute complex sequences of actions autonomously, adapting to unforeseen circumstances without requiring constant human guidance.
  - **Example:** An autonomous mobile robot (AMR) in a logistics center uses AI-powered navigation to move through dynamic warehouse layouts, avoiding obstacles like forklifts and personnel, to pick up and deliver goods efficiently, all without pre-defined paths or continuous human input.
- **Increased Adaptability:** AI enables robots to exhibit a high degree of adaptability to novel data and changing environments. Machine learning algorithms allow robots to learn from new experiences and adjust their behavior accordingly. This adaptability is crucial for operating in unstructured or unpredictable settings where pre-programmed responses would be insufficient.
  - **Example:** A cleaning robot deployed in a large office building can use AI to learn the building's layout over time, identify frequently cluttered areas, and adjust its

cleaning routes and intensity based on real-time sensor data about dirt levels and human activity.

- **Advanced Cognitive Abilities:** AI equips robots with cognitive capabilities that were previously unattainable. They can engage in reasoning to solve problems, make predictions based on learned patterns, and recognize complex patterns in data. These abilities allow robots to perform tasks that require a level of "understanding" and intelligence.
  - o **Example:** An AI-powered inspection robot in a manufacturing plant can analyze visual data from its cameras to identify subtle anomalies or defects in products that might be missed by human inspectors or traditional rule-based systems. It can learn what constitutes a "normal" product and flag deviations for further review.
- **Improved Human-Robot Interaction (HRI):** AI is fundamental to creating more natural and intuitive interactions between humans and robots. Natural Language Processing (NLP) allows robots to understand and respond to voice commands. Computer vision enables them to interpret facial expressions and gestures, facilitating more seamless and human-like communication.
  - o **Example:** A social robot designed to assist elderly individuals can use AI to understand their spoken requests, recognize their emotional state through facial expressions, and respond in a contextually appropriate and empathetic manner, fostering a more natural and helpful interaction.

Real-World Applications Demonstrating the Importance of AI in Robotics:

The transformative impact of AI on robotics is evident in a wide range of applications across various sectors:

- **Healthcare Robots:** AI-driven robots are revolutionizing healthcare. In surgery, AI assists surgeons with enhanced precision and control. In elderly care, robots equipped with AI can monitor vital signs, detect falls or other emergencies, and provide timely alerts or assistance, enhancing patient safety and well-being.
  - o **Example:** A robotic arm used in surgery can be guided by AI to perform intricate movements with millimeter-level accuracy, potentially improving surgical outcomes. An AI-powered home care robot can learn a patient's daily routines and detect deviations that might indicate a health issue, prompting a check-up or emergency response.
- **Agricultural Robots:** AI is transforming agricultural practices. Robots with AI-powered vision systems can identify ripe crops ready for harvesting, differentiate weeds from crops for targeted removal, and analyze data from sensors to optimize irrigation and fertilization, leading to increased efficiency and reduced resource consumption.
  - o **Example:** An autonomous harvesting robot can navigate a field, use AI to identify ripe strawberries based on their color and size, and pick them gently without damaging the fruit. A drone equipped with AI can fly over a field, analyze images to detect areas with weed infestation, and create a precise map for targeted herbicide spraying.
- **Exploration Robots:** In environments too hazardous or remote for humans, such as the surface of Mars, AI is crucial for enabling robots to operate effectively. Rovers like

Curiosity and Perseverance utilize AI for autonomous navigation over rugged terrain, obstacle avoidance, and decision-making regarding scientific investigations, allowing them to explore and gather data independently.

       o **Example:** The Perseverance rover on Mars uses AI-powered auto-navigation to plan its routes across the Martian surface, analyzing images from its cameras to identify safe paths and avoid obstacles like rocks and dunes, maximizing its exploration range and scientific productivity.

In conclusion, AI is no longer a supplementary feature in robotics but rather a fundamental driving force behind its evolution. The ability of AI to imbue robots with autonomy, adaptability, cognitive abilities, and enhanced interaction capabilities is unlocking a vast array of new applications and transforming industries across the globe, paving the way for a future where intelligent machines play an increasingly integral role in our lives.

3.3 Illustrative Example: The AI-Powered Autonomous Vacuum Cleaner

A common and readily accessible example of AI integration in consumer robotics is the autonomous vacuum cleaner, exemplified by popular models from manufacturers like iRobot and Xiaomi. These devices demonstrate how AI algorithms enable robots to perform complex tasks intelligently within dynamic household environments.

Operational Principles:

The functionality of an AI-powered autonomous vacuum cleaner relies on a sophisticated interplay of sensing, mapping, planning, and learning:

- **Sensing and Environmental Mapping:** These robots are equipped with a suite of sensors to perceive their surroundings. These can include **LiDAR (Light Detection and Ranging)**, which uses laser beams to create precise distance measurements; **infrared sensors**, which detect obstacles and edges; and **cameras**, which provide visual information about the environment. The data gathered from these sensors allows the robot to "see" and understand the layout of the room.
- **SLAM Algorithm (Simultaneous Localization and Mapping):** A core AI-driven algorithm employed by these vacuum cleaners is **SLAM**. This advanced technique enables the robot to simultaneously build a map of an unknown environment while also determining its own location within that map, all in real-time. By continuously processing sensor data, the SLAM algorithm allows the vacuum to understand its position relative to walls, furniture, and other obstacles, creating a dynamic and updating map of the cleaning area.
- **Intelligent Path Planning:** Once the robot has a map of the room and knows its location, AI algorithms are used to determine the most efficient cleaning path. These algorithms take into account factors such as the size and shape of the room, the location of obstacles,

and areas that have already been cleaned. The robot can plan its cleaning route to ensure comprehensive coverage while minimizing redundant movements and optimizing battery usage. Furthermore, the AI allows the robot to autonomously navigate around obstacles and even return to its charging dock when its battery is low.

- **Adaptive Learning:** Over time, AI enables these vacuum cleaners to learn from their experiences. They can identify areas that tend to accumulate more dirt based on sensor data from previous cleaning cycles. Consequently, the robot can adapt its future cleaning routes to focus more attention on these high-dirt areas, ensuring a more thorough cleaning over time. Some advanced models can even allow users to designate specific "no-go zones" or target specific areas for cleaning via a smartphone app, further enhancing the robot's adaptability to user needs.

Scenario Illustration:

Consider a living room with various obstacles such as scattered chairs, a coffee table with items on it, and children's toys on the floor.

- **Traditional Robot Vacuum:** A basic, non-AI-powered robot vacuum would typically follow a pre-set pattern (e.g., random bouncing or spiral movements). It would likely collide with the chairs and toys repeatedly, potentially getting stuck or inefficiently cleaning around these obstacles. Its cleaning path would be static and would not adapt to the specific layout or dirt distribution in the room.
- **AI-Powered Vacuum Cleaner:** The AI-equipped vacuum cleaner, upon entering the room, would use its LiDAR and other sensors to create a detailed map, identifying the chairs, table legs, and toys as obstacles. The SLAM algorithm would ensure it knows its precise location within this map. The AI path planning algorithm would then generate an efficient cleaning route that navigates around these obstacles, ensuring that the entire floor area is covered without excessive bumping. Furthermore, if its sensors detect a particularly dirty area (e.g., near a doorway), the AI might instruct the robot to increase its suction power or make multiple passes over that specific spot. Over subsequent cleaning cycles, the robot might learn that the area under the coffee table tends to accumulate crumbs and adjust its cleaning pattern accordingly.

Diagram: Operational Flow of an AI-Powered Vacuum Cleaner

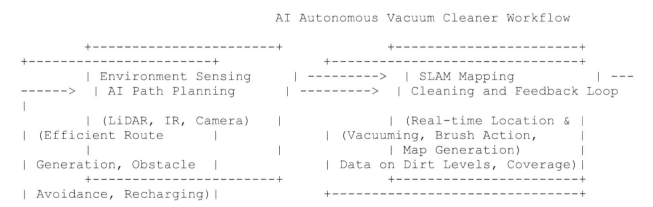

```
----------------+                              ^                           +------
               |                              |                           |
               v                              |                           
----------------+                              |                           +------
Obstacle Detection    |  -------------------------------------+           |
                                                              |           |
(Real-time Sensor     |                                       |           |
                                                              |           |
Input)                |                                       |           +------
----------------+
```

This diagram illustrates the cyclical process of an AI-powered vacuum cleaner. It begins with sensing the environment, which feeds into the SLAM algorithm for mapping and localization. The AI then plans an efficient cleaning path based on this map. During the cleaning process, the robot continuously detects obstacles and provides feedback on dirt levels and coverage, which can further refine future path planning and cleaning strategies through adaptive learning.

40 multiple-choice questions (MCQs) with answers based on The Intersection of AI and Robotics, covering the topics of how AI powers robots, the importance of AI in modern robotics, and a case study of AI-powered autonomous vacuum cleaners.

3.1 How AI Powers Robots

1. **What is the main role of AI in robotics?**
   - a) To provide a physical body to robots
   - b) To enhance the robot's decision-making ability
   - c) To make robots aesthetically pleasing
   - d) To provide fuel efficiency
   - **Answer: b) To enhance the robot's decision-making ability**
2. **Which of the following is NOT a key area where AI is used in robotics?**
   - a) Path planning
   - b) Object recognition
   - c) Data storage
   - d) Machine learning
   - **Answer: c) Data storage**
3. **Which AI technique helps robots to learn from past experiences?**
   - a) Supervised learning
   - b) Reinforcement learning
   - c) Natural language processing
   - d) Genetic algorithms
   - **Answer: b) Reinforcement learning**

4. **Which component allows a robot to perceive its environment in AI-powered robotics?**
   - a) Sensors
   - b) Actuators
   - c) CPU
   - d) Battery
   - **Answer: a) Sensors**
5. **What is the primary purpose of deep learning in robotics?**
   - a) To optimize speed
   - b) To enable robots to recognize patterns and objects
   - c) To control movements
   - d) To increase battery life
   - **Answer: b) To enable robots to recognize patterns and objects**
6. **Which of these algorithms is commonly used in AI-powered robots for navigation?**
   - a) A* algorithm
   - b) Linear regression
   - c) Decision trees
   - d) K-means clustering
   - *Answer: a) A algorithm**
7. **What does the term "robot perception" refer to?**
   - a) A robot's ability to learn
   - b) A robot's ability to understand and react to its environment
   - c) A robot's physical appearance
   - d) A robot's processing power
   - **Answer: b) A robot's ability to understand and react to its environment**
8. **Which of the following sensors are commonly used in AI-driven robots?**
   - a) Cameras
   - b) GPS
   - c) LiDAR
   - d) All of the above
   - **Answer: d) All of the above**
9. **Which area of AI helps robots to understand and generate human language?**
   - a) Natural Language Processing (NLP)
   - b) Machine learning
   - c) Computer vision
   - d) Expert systems
   - **Answer: a) Natural Language Processing (NLP)**
10. **What role does computer vision play in robotics?**
    - a) It helps robots navigate terrain
    - b) It allows robots to see and interpret visual information
    - c) It helps robots detect temperature
    - d) It controls robot speech
    - **Answer: b) It allows robots to see and interpret visual information**

3.2 Importance of AI in Modern Robotics

11. **Why is AI considered essential for modern robotics?**
    - o a) It simplifies the design of robots
    - o b) It allows robots to operate autonomously
    - o c) It makes robots smaller in size
    - o d) It makes robots more affordable
    - o **Answer: b) It allows robots to operate autonomously**
12. **How does AI improve robot adaptability?**
    - o a) By automating the manufacturing process
    - o b) By allowing robots to learn from interactions and adjust to new situations
    - o c) By increasing battery capacity
    - o d) By making robots faster
    - o **Answer: b) By allowing robots to learn from interactions and adjust to new situations**
13. **Which of the following is a key advantage of integrating AI with robots?**
    - o a) Increased weight and power consumption
    - o b) Robots can function without human input
    - o c) Robots will be unable to perform complex tasks
    - o d) Robots become less expensive
    - o **Answer: b) Robots can function without human input**
14. **AI-powered robots can be used to assist in which of the following industries?**
    - o a) Manufacturing
    - o b) Healthcare
    - o c) Agriculture
    - o d) All of the above
    - o **Answer: d) All of the above**
15. **What is a significant challenge when combining AI and robotics?**
    - o a) Excessive power consumption
    - o b) Limited computational power
    - o c) Complexity in programming and training the robots
    - o d) Lack of hardware availability
    - o **Answer: c) Complexity in programming and training the robots**
16. **Which of these AI technologies is essential for robotic automation?**
    - o a) Rule-based systems
    - o b) Machine learning algorithms
    - o c) Cryptography
    - o d) Internet of Things (IoT)
    - o **Answer: b) Machine learning algorithms**
17. **How does AI contribute to robot safety?**
    - o a) By avoiding obstacles in real-time
    - o b) By monitoring battery levels
    - o c) By increasing robot speed
    - o d) By reducing the size of the robot
    - o **Answer: a) By avoiding obstacles in real-time**
18. **Which of the following is a common application of AI in robotics?**

- a) Autonomous vehicles
- b) Automated manufacturing systems
- c) Surgical robots
- d) All of the above
- **Answer: d) All of the above**

19. **Which of the following is a key benefit of AI in healthcare robotics?**
- a) Reduced healthcare costs
- b) Improved accuracy in surgeries
- c) Increased hospital staff
- d) Less need for human involvement in decision-making
- **Answer: b) Improved accuracy in surgeries**

20. **What kind of learning allows robots to adapt to new environments without being explicitly programmed for each situation?**
- a) Unsupervised learning
- b) Reinforcement learning
- c) Supervised learning
- d) Deep learning
- **Answer: b) Reinforcement learning**

3.3 Case Study: AI-Powered Autonomous Vacuum Cleaner

21. **What is the primary function of an AI-powered autonomous vacuum cleaner?**
- a) To wash clothes automatically
- b) To clean floors autonomously
- c) To assist in cooking
- d) To monitor temperature changes
- **Answer: b) To clean floors autonomously**

22. **Which AI technology is mainly used in autonomous vacuum cleaners for navigation?**
- a) Computer vision
- b) Reinforcement learning
- c) Natural language processing
- d) Object detection
- **Answer: a) Computer vision**

23. **How does an AI-powered vacuum cleaner map its surroundings?**
- a) Using GPS
- b) Through 3D imaging
- c) By using LiDAR and sensors
- d) By mapping through sound waves
- **Answer: c) By using LiDAR and sensors**

24. **What helps an AI vacuum cleaner detect obstacles?**
- a) Weight sensors
- b) Proximity sensors
- c) Gyroscopes

- o   d) All of the above
- o   **Answer: b) Proximity sensors**

25. **Which AI feature enables an autonomous vacuum cleaner to adjust its cleaning patterns?**
    - o   a) Dynamic path planning
    - o   b) Pre-programmed routines
    - o   c) Manual control
    - o   d) Limited area scanning
    - o   **Answer: a) Dynamic path planning**

26. **How does an AI-powered vacuum cleaner improve its performance over time?**
    - o   a) By reducing its cleaning speed
    - o   b) By learning the layout of the house through machine learning algorithms
    - o   c) By operating in one cleaning mode
    - o   d) By ignoring smaller objects
    - o   **Answer: b) By learning the layout of the house through machine learning algorithms**

27. **Which sensor helps the AI vacuum cleaner to avoid falling down stairs?**
    - o   a) LiDAR
    - o   b) Infrared sensor
    - o   c) Ultrasonic sensor
    - o   d) Optical sensor
    - o   **Answer: b) Infrared sensor**

28. **In AI-powered vacuum cleaners, what does path optimization ensure?**
    - o   a) Reduced cleaning time and energy usage
    - o   b) Increased time spent on each floor
    - o   c) Higher cost of cleaning
    - o   d) Limited coverage of the cleaning area
    - o   **Answer: a) Reduced cleaning time and energy usage**

29. **Which aspect of AI allows the vacuum cleaner to operate based on a predefined schedule?**
    - o   a) Deep learning
    - o   b) Machine vision
    - o   c) Scheduling algorithms
    - o   d) Object recognition
    - o   **Answer: c) Scheduling algorithms**

30. **How does an AI-powered vacuum cleaner learn to optimize its cleaning path?**
    - o   a) By using sensors that detect dirt
    - o   b) By using feedback from users
    - o   c) By processing data about obstacles and room layout
    - o   d) By cleaning the same area multiple times
    - o   **Answer: c) By processing data about obstacles and room layout**

31. **Which is a primary benefit of AI in vacuum cleaning robots?**
    - o   a) It reduces human labor and time required for cleaning
    - o   b) It makes cleaning slower and more inefficient
    - o   c) It increases the cost of the vacuum cleaner
    - o   d) It can only clean one room at a time

o **Answer: a) It reduces human labor and time required for cleaning**
32. **What is one of the challenges of AI-powered vacuum cleaners?**
    o a) They require constant supervision
    o b) They cannot navigate around obstacles
    o c) They can be costly
    o d) They clean only carpeted surfaces
    o **Answer: c) They can be costly**
33. **Which of the following features do AI-powered vacuum cleaners often include?**
    o a) Voice control
    o b) Wi-Fi connectivity
    o c) Scheduled cleaning times
    o d) All of the above
    o **Answer: d) All of the above**
34. **How does an AI vacuum cleaner ensure efficient use of battery life?**
    o a) By cleaning all rooms at once
    o b) By charging itself after cleaning one room
    o c) By adjusting cleaning patterns based on the room's layout
    o d) By avoiding large areas
    o **Answer: c) By adjusting cleaning patterns based on the room's layout**
35. **What type of AI algorithm helps autonomous vacuum cleaners to avoid getting stuck in corners or obstacles?**
    o a) Pathfinding algorithms
    o b) Sorting algorithms
    o c) Compression algorithms
    o d) Sorting algorithms
    o **Answer: a) Pathfinding algorithms**
36. **Which of the following is an important feature in the AI system of a vacuum cleaner for obstacle avoidance?**
    o a) GPS integration
    o b) Audio signals
    o c) Real-time object detection and avoidance
    o d) Lack of any sensors
    o **Answer: c) Real-time object detection and avoidance**
37. **What is the role of AI in autonomous vacuum cleaner's cleaning efficiency?**
    o a) It makes the cleaning robot work faster but less effectively
    o b) It helps optimize cleaning by intelligently mapping and adapting
    o c) It only helps the robot to move randomly
    o d) It has no effect on cleaning efficiency
    o **Answer: b) It helps optimize cleaning by intelligently mapping and adapting**
38. **What is one reason AI-powered vacuum cleaners are more efficient than traditional models?**
    o a) They require less maintenance
    o b) They use machine learning to optimize cleaning routes
    o c) They are cheaper
    o d) They only clean one area at a time
    o **Answer: b) They use machine learning to optimize cleaning routes**

39. What can a user do with the AI-powered vacuum cleaner's companion mobile app?
- o a) Monitor cleaning progress and set schedules
- o b) Control cleaning speed
- o c) View the battery's charge level
- o d) All of the above
- o **Answer: d) All of the above**

40. How do AI-powered vacuum cleaners create a cleaning map of the home?
- o a) Using camera-based visual mapping
- o b) Using ultrasonic sensors
- o c) By recording users' movements
- o d) By storing old cleaning patterns
- o **Answer: a) Using camera-based visual mapping**

Chapter 4: Machine Learning in Robotics

4.1 Fundamental Approaches to Robot Learning: Supervised, Unsupervised, and Reinforcement Learning

Machine learning is a cornerstone of modern robotics, providing robots with the ability to acquire skills and perform tasks by extracting knowledge from data. Within machine learning, three primary paradigms exist: Supervised Learning, Unsupervised Learning, and Reinforcement Learning. Each of these approaches offers a distinct methodology for training robots and is particularly suited for different types of tasks and learning scenarios. Understanding these distinctions is crucial for appreciating the diverse ways in which robots are taught to interact with and operate within their world.

Supervised Learning: Learning from Labeled Examples

In **supervised learning**, the robot's learning model is trained using a **labeled dataset**. This means that for each piece of input data provided to the model, there is a corresponding "correct" output or label associated with it. The learning algorithm analyzes these input-output pairs to discover the underlying relationship between the inputs and the desired outputs. The robot then uses this learned relationship to make predictions or decisions when presented with new, unseen input data. The fundamental objective of supervised learning is to learn a function that accurately maps inputs to their corresponding outputs.

- **Illustrative Scenario:** Consider a robotic arm designed to sort items on a conveyor belt into two categories: "pickable" and "not pickable." To train this robot using supervised learning, it would be presented with numerous images of items (the input data). Each image would be accompanied by a label indicating whether the robot should pick up that specific item ("pick") or leave it ("no pick") (the output). Through exposure to a large number of these labeled examples, the robot's learning model would learn to identify visual features and patterns that distinguish pickable items from non-pickable ones. Once trained, when the robot encounters a new item on the conveyor belt, it can use its learned knowledge to predict whether it should pick up that item or not.
- **Diagram for Supervised Learning:**

```
+--------------------------+      +--------------------------+      +---------
--------------+
| Input Data               | --> | Supervised Learning Model| --> | Output
|
| (e.g., Images of Objects |      | (Learns from Labeled     |      | (e.g.,
"Pick" or        |
| with Labels)             |      | Input-Output Pairs)      |      | "No
Pick" Decision)    |
+--------------------------+      +--------------------------+      +---------
--------------+
```

Unsupervised Learning: Discovering Hidden Structures in Unlabeled Data

In **unsupervised learning**, the robot's learning model is provided with data that lacks explicit labels. The primary goal in this paradigm is to discover inherent patterns, structures, or groupings within the unlabeled data. In the context of robotics, unsupervised learning can be particularly valuable when a robot needs to explore and make sense of a new environment or identify similarities among objects or features without prior knowledge or pre-defined categories.

- **Illustrative Scenario:** Imagine a mobile robot tasked with exploring an unfamiliar warehouse environment. It is equipped with various sensors that collect data about its surroundings, such as images from its camera and readings from its proximity sensors. Using unsupervised learning algorithms, the robot can analyze this raw, unlabeled sensory data to identify clusters of similar objects or recurring spatial patterns within the warehouse. For instance, it might group together areas with tall, rectangular shapes (likely shelves) or identify regions with frequent movement (potential pathways). This ability to autonomously discover the underlying structure of the environment helps the robot build an understanding of the space even without being explicitly told what different objects are or how the space is organized.

- **Diagram for Unsupervised Learning:**

```
+-----------------------------------+        +----------------------------+
+-----------------------------------+
| Input Data                     | -->  | Unsupervised Learning Model  | -->
| Output                         |
| (e.g., Sensory Data from a New |      | (Finds Hidden Patterns &   |
| (e.g., Clusters of Similar Objects |
| Environment without Labels)    |      | Structures in Unlabeled Data)|
| or Identified Features)        |
+-----------------------------------+        +----------------------------+
+-----------------------------------+
```

Reinforcement Learning: Learning Through Interaction and Feedback

Reinforcement learning is a distinct type of machine learning where a robot learns optimal behavior by interacting with its environment and receiving feedback in the form of rewards or penalties. Unlike supervised learning, it does not rely on labeled input-output pairs. Instead, the robot takes actions within its environment, and based on the consequences of those actions (whether they lead to a reward or a penalty), it adjusts its strategy over time to maximize the cumulative reward it receives. This trial-and-error process allows the robot to learn complex behaviors without needing explicit instructions for every possible situation.

- **Illustrative Scenario:** Consider a robotic arm learning to navigate a maze. Initially, the robot might make random movements. If a movement leads it closer to the exit or helps it avoid a wall, it receives a positive reward. Conversely, if it moves into a dead end or collides with a wall, it receives a negative penalty. Through numerous trials and the associated rewards and penalties, the robot's reinforcement learning algorithm gradually learns a strategy (a policy) that dictates which actions to take in different situations to efficiently navigate the maze and reach the exit while minimizing penalties.

- **Diagram for Reinforcement Learning:**

```
+------------------+        +---------------------------------------+        +--------
------------------+        +-----------------------+
| Robot's Actions  | -->  | Environment Interaction               | -->  |
Environment Feedback       | --> | Robot Updates Strategy |
| (Exploration &   |        | (Robot Executes a Movement or Task)|        | (Reward
for Desirable     |        | (Adjusts its Policy   |
| Exploitation)    |        |                                       |        |
Outcomes, Penalty for      |        | Based on Feedback)     |
+------------------+        +---------------------------------------+        +--------
------------------+        +-----------------------+
```

In summary, Supervised Learning trains robots based on explicit examples of correct behavior, Unsupervised Learning enables robots to discover patterns in unlabeled data for exploration and understanding, and Reinforcement Learning allows robots to learn optimal actions through trial-and-error interaction with their environment. These three fundamental approaches provide a powerful toolkit for endowing robots with a wide range of intelligent capabilities.

4.2 Imparting Skills to Robots: The Process of Data-Driven Training

A fundamental aspect of enabling robots to execute tasks intelligently and adapt to diverse situations lies in the process of training them through data. This involves providing robots with substantial amounts of information that they can learn from, allowing them to make informed decisions and enhance their performance over time. This data-centric approach is crucial for equipping robots with the flexibility required to operate in dynamic environments and handle a variety of tasks. The information used for training can originate from numerous sources, including the robot's own sensors and cameras, as well as direct input from human users or pre-existing datasets.

The typical procedure for training a robot through data encompasses several key stages:

- **Data Acquisition:** The initial step involves gathering relevant data that the robot will learn from. Robots are equipped with various sensors, such as cameras, lidar, infrared sensors, and tactile sensors, to collect information from their operational environment. This raw data can take many forms, including visual images, depth maps, distance readings, force measurements, and even records of the robot's own past actions and their outcomes.
    - **Example:** A robot designed for autonomous navigation in a warehouse would collect data from its cameras and lidar sensors, capturing images of the aisles, locations of shelves, and distances to obstacles.
- **Data Preprocessing:** The raw data collected by robots is often characterized by noise, inconsistencies, or incompleteness. To make this data suitable for effective training, a preprocessing stage is essential. This involves cleaning the data by removing irrelevant noise or outliers, handling missing values, and transforming the data into a consistent

format. For instance, sensor readings might be filtered to reduce random fluctuations, or images might be resized and normalized to ensure uniformity for the learning model.

- o **Example:** The images of warehouse aisles collected by the navigation robot might be preprocessed by adjusting their brightness and contrast, resizing them to a standard resolution, and masking out irrelevant background elements to focus on the structural features of the environment.

- **Model Training:** Once the data has been preprocessed, it is used to train machine learning models. The specific type of learning employed (supervised, unsupervised, or reinforcement learning) depends on the nature of the task the robot is intended to perform and the characteristics of the available data. The training process involves feeding the preprocessed data into the chosen learning algorithm, allowing the model to identify underlying patterns, relationships, or optimal strategies within the data.

  - o **Example:** To train the navigation robot to recognize navigable paths and obstacles, a supervised learning model might be used. Preprocessed images of the warehouse environment (input) would be paired with labels indicating whether a particular area is a valid path or an obstacle (output). The model would learn to associate visual features with these labels.

- **Validation:** After the machine learning model has been trained on a portion of the data, its performance is evaluated using a separate, unseen dataset known as the validation set. This step is crucial to ensure that the trained model can generalize well to new, data it has not encountered during training and that it has not simply memorized the training data (a phenomenon known as overfitting). The validation process helps to fine-tune the model's parameters and assess its real-world applicability.

  - o **Example:** After training the navigation model, its ability to correctly identify paths and obstacles would be tested using new images of different parts of the warehouse that were not part of the training data. The accuracy of its predictions on this validation set would indicate how well it is likely to perform in the actual warehouse environment.

- **Deployment:** The final stage involves integrating the trained and validated machine learning model into the robot's control system. Once deployed, the robot can utilize the learned knowledge to perform its tasks autonomously. The model processes real-time data from the robot's sensors and makes decisions or predictions that guide the robot's actions in its environment.

  - o **Example:** The validated navigation model would be deployed on the warehouse robot's onboard computer. As the robot moves through the warehouse, it continuously captures images, which are then processed by the deployed model to identify paths and avoid obstacles, enabling autonomous navigation.

Illustrative Example: Training a Robot for Object Identification and Manipulation

Consider a robotic arm tasked with identifying and picking specific objects from a table. To train this robot:

1. **Data Collection:** A camera mounted on the robot captures numerous images of various objects placed on the table. These images form the initial dataset.

2. **Preprocessing:** The captured images are preprocessed. This might involve labeling each object in the images with its shape, size, and a designation of whether the robot should pick it up (e.g., "pick_cylinder," "no_pick_cube"). The images might also be cropped to focus on the individual objects and resized for consistency.
3. **Model Training:** A supervised learning model, such as a convolutional neural network (CNN), is trained using these labeled images. The CNN learns to extract relevant visual features from the images and associate them with the corresponding labels (shape, size, pick/no-pick). Over time, the model learns to distinguish between different objects and determine which ones should be picked up based on the provided labels.
4. **Validation:** After training, the CNN's performance is evaluated using a separate set of labeled object images that the model has never seen before. The accuracy of the model in correctly identifying the objects and predicting whether to pick them up is assessed.
5. **Deployment:** Once the model achieves satisfactory performance on the validation set, it is deployed on the robotic arm's control system. When the robot encounters a new object on the table, its camera captures an image, which is then processed by the deployed CNN. The CNN identifies the object and determines whether the robot should pick it up based on its learned knowledge, guiding the arm's movements to grasp the object if necessary.

Through this data-driven training process, robots acquire the ability to perceive, understand, and interact with their environment in increasingly sophisticated and adaptable ways.

4.3 Case Study: Acquiring Dexterity for Pick and Place Operations

The "pick and place" task stands as a fundamental challenge in the realm of robotics, requiring a robot to identify an object, securely grasp it, and then relocate it to a designated target position. This seemingly simple operation serves as an excellent illustration of how various machine learning techniques can be integrated to imbue a robot with the necessary skills and adaptability.

Stages of Learning for Pick and Place:

The process of enabling a robot to perform the pick and place task through machine learning typically involves a sequence of interconnected steps:

- **Input Data Acquisition:** The robot begins by gathering information about its surrounding environment using its sensory apparatus. This often includes visual data captured by cameras, providing images of the objects present, as well as data from other sensors like tactile sensors, which can provide information about contact forces during grasping. Additionally, data regarding the robot's own state, such as the current position and orientation of its arm, is also collected.
  - **Example:** A robot arm equipped with a camera captures an image of a table containing a cup, a ball, and a book. The robot also records the initial joint angles of its arm.

- **Object Recognition:** To interact effectively with different items, the robot must first be able to identify them. This is commonly achieved through **supervised learning**. The robot is trained on a dataset of labeled images, where each image of an object (the input) is paired with a label indicating the type of object (e.g., "cup," "ball," "book"). By analyzing these labeled examples, the robot's object recognition model learns to extract distinctive visual features associated with each object category, enabling it to differentiate between them when presented with a new, unseen object.
    - **Example:** The robot is shown thousands of labeled images of cups, balls, and books from various angles and under different lighting conditions. Its supervised learning model learns to recognize the unique visual characteristics of each object type. When a new image of a cup appears, the model can accurately identify it as a "cup."
- **Grasp Planning:** Once an object has been identified, the robot needs to determine the optimal way to grasp it securely. This often involves **reinforcement learning**. The robot explores different grasping strategies, such as approaching the object from various angles and applying different amounts of force with its gripper. For each attempted grasp, it receives feedback in the form of rewards (e.g., a positive reward if the grasp is successful and the object is lifted securely) or penalties (e.g., a negative reward if the object slips or is knocked over). Through numerous trials and the associated feedback, the robot gradually learns the most effective and robust grasping strategies for each type of object it encounters.
    - **Example:** The robot attempts to grasp a ball using different gripper configurations and approach angles. If a particular approach consistently results in a stable grasp, it receives a positive reward, strengthening that strategy. If another approach causes the ball to slip, it receives a penalty, discouraging that action in the future.
- **Action Execution:** After identifying the object and planning the grasp, the robot executes the pick-and-place action. The precise movements of the robot's arm to reach for, grasp, lift, and then place the object at the desired location are typically controlled by algorithms. While the initial learning of fundamental motor control might involve other techniques, the fine-tuning and adaptation of these movements to specific object properties and placement locations can involve elements of learning. The goal is to achieve smooth and adaptive motions without requiring explicit, step-by-step instructions for every single pick and place instance.
    - **Example:** Having identified a cup and determined a suitable grasping point, the robot's control system coordinates the movement of its arm joints to reach the cup, close its gripper with the appropriate force, lift the cup, move its arm to the designated placement area, and then release the cup.
- **Feedback and Improvement:** Following each pick and place attempt, the robot receives feedback on the outcome. This could be a simple binary indication of success or failure (e.g., the object was placed correctly, or it was dropped). More sophisticated feedback might involve information about the stability of the grasp, the precision of the placement, or the efficiency of the movement. This feedback is then used to further refine the robot's object recognition, grasp planning, and action execution strategies through continuous learning, allowing it to improve its overall pick and place performance over time and adapt to variations in object properties or environmental conditions.

- **Example:** If the robot frequently drops a particular type of object, its learning algorithms will analyze the sensor data and the grasping parameters used in those failures. It might then adjust its grasp planning strategy for that object type, perhaps by increasing the gripping force or changing the contact points, to improve the success rate in future attempts.

Diagram for Pick and Place Learning:

```
+---------------------------------------+          +------------------------------
---------------+
| Input Data (Object Image + Position)  | --> | Object Recognition
(Supervised Learning -      |
|                                           |          | Identifies Object Type)
|
+---------------------------------------+          +------------------------------
---------------+
                                                                 |
                                                                 v
+---------------------------------------+          +------------------------------
---------------+
| Object Type Information                   | --> | Grasp Planning (Reinforcement
Learning -       |
|                                           |          | Determines Optimal Grasp
Strategy)            |
+---------------------------------------+          +------------------------------
---------------+
                                                                 |
                                                                 v
+------------------------------------------------------------------------------
---------------+
|                                Robot Grasping and Placement Action
|
|                                (Controlled by learned motor skills)
|
+------------------------------------------------------------------------------
---------------+
                                                                 |
                                                                 v
+------------------------------------------------------------------------------
---------------+
| Feedback (Success/Failure, Grasp Stability, Placement Accuracy) ---->
Learning and Improvement |
| (Updates Object Recognition, Grasp Planning, and Action Execution
Strategies)              |
+------------------------------------------------------------------------------
---------------+
```

This diagram illustrates the flow of information and learning within a robotic pick and place system. Supervised learning enables object identification, reinforcement learning guides grasp planning, and feedback from the robot's actions drives continuous improvement across all stages of the task.

40 multiple-choice questions (MCQs) with answers based on **Machine Learning in Robotics**:

4.1 Supervised, Unsupervised, and Reinforcement Learning

1. **Which type of learning involves training the robot with labeled data?**
   a) Unsupervised Learning
   b) Supervised Learning
   c) Reinforcement Learning
   d) None of the above
   Answer: b) Supervised Learning

2. **What is the primary goal of unsupervised learning in robotics?**
   a) To predict the output from the given input
   b) To find hidden patterns in data
   c) To maximize rewards
   d) To learn from labeled data
   Answer: b) To find hidden patterns in data

3. **In reinforcement learning, how does the robot learn?**
   a) By learning from labeled data
   b) By receiving feedback from the environment
   c) By clustering data
   d) By supervised examples
   Answer: b) By receiving feedback from the environment

4. **Which of the following is a key feature of supervised learning?**
   a) No labeled data is required
   b) The algorithm learns from labeled data
   c) The model learns by trial and error
   d) It uses clustering techniques
   Answer: b) The algorithm learns from labeled data

5. **What type of learning is most suitable for teaching robots to navigate through unknown environments?**
   a) Supervised Learning
   b) Unsupervised Learning
   c) Reinforcement Learning
   d) None of the above
   Answer: c) Reinforcement Learning

6. **Which of the following is a major advantage of reinforcement learning?**
   a) It requires labeled data
   b) It helps the robot learn by making mistakes and adjusting actions
   c) It groups similar data points
   d) It does not need any data to train the robot
   Answer: b) It helps the robot learn by making mistakes and adjusting actions

7. **Which learning type does not require any predefined labels for input data?**
   a) Supervised Learning
   b) Unsupervised Learning
   c) Reinforcement Learning
   d) All of the above
   Answer: b) Unsupervised Learning
8. **In which learning type is the robot rewarded for performing the correct action?**
   a) Supervised Learning
   b) Unsupervised Learning
   c) Reinforcement Learning
   d) None of the above
   Answer: c) Reinforcement Learning
9. **What is the primary difference between supervised and unsupervised learning?**
   a) Supervised learning uses unlabeled data, while unsupervised uses labeled data
   b) Unsupervised learning is based on feedback, while supervised learns from examples
   c) Supervised learning uses labeled data, while unsupervised does not
   d) There is no difference
   Answer: c) Supervised learning uses labeled data, while unsupervised does not
10. **Which of the following is most commonly used in robotics for learning control policies?**
    a) Supervised Learning
    b) Reinforcement Learning
    c) Unsupervised Learning
    d) Clustering
    Answer: b) Reinforcement Learning

4.2 Training Robots through Data

11. **Which step comes first in the process of training robots through data?**
    a) Model Training
    b) Data Collection
    c) Validation
    d) Preprocessing
    Answer: b) Data Collection
12. **What is the main purpose of preprocessing data for robot training?**
    a) To make the data readable
    b) To clean and transform data for better learning
    c) To reduce the size of the data
    d) To store data efficiently
    Answer: b) To clean and transform data for better learning
13. **Which of the following is an example of data collected from a robot's sensors?**
    a) Camera images of objects
    b) Audio data
    c) Video clips from the robot's environment

d) All of the above

Answer: d) All of the above

14. **What does the model training step involve?**

    a) Collecting data

    b) Cleaning data

    c) Feeding data to the robot's learning algorithm

    d) None of the above

    Answer: c) Feeding data to the robot's learning algorithm

15. **What is the purpose of model validation in robot training?**

    a) To check if the model performs well on unseen data

    b) To collect more data

    c) To modify the robot's sensors

    d) To label the data correctly

    Answer: a) To check if the model performs well on unseen data

16. **Which method is used to improve robot performance after model training?**

    a) Data augmentation

    b) Data collection

    c) Feedback loops

    d) None of the above

    Answer: c) Feedback loops

17. **Why is preprocessing important in machine learning for robotics?**

    a) It reduces the data size

    b) It makes data suitable for learning models

    c) It helps robots learn faster

    d) It removes unnecessary features from the data

    Answer: b) It makes data suitable for learning models

18. **Which type of data is most commonly used for training robots in object recognition tasks?**

    a) Time-series data

    b) Image data

    c) Audio data

    d) Text data

    Answer: b) Image data

19. **In training robots, what is meant by "labeling" data?**

    a) Giving the data a specific name

    b) Tagging data with relevant information like class or category

    c) Reducing data size

    d) Collecting data in batches

    Answer: b) Tagging data with relevant information like class or category

20. **How does data collection help in training robots?**

    a) It provides labeled data for supervised learning

    b) It helps improve robot performance

    c) It ensures better model validation

    d) All of the above

    Answer: d) All of the above

4.3 Example: Learning to Pick and Place

21. **Which task is the robot trying to perform in the "pick and place" example?**
    a) Identify objects
    b) Classify objects
    c) Pick up objects and place them at specific locations
    d) Navigate through a maze
    Answer: c) Pick up objects and place them at specific locations

22. **In the pick and place task, what data does the robot need to perform the action?**
    a) Object size and shape
    b) Object color
    c) Object position
    d) All of the above
    Answer: d) All of the above

23. **What learning method is commonly used for the pick and place task?**
    a) Supervised Learning
    b) Unsupervised Learning
    c) Reinforcement Learning
    d) Clustering
    Answer: c) Reinforcement Learning

24. **In the learning process of a robot performing pick and place, what is crucial for its success?**
    a) Trial and error through reinforcement learning
    b) Supervision from humans
    c) Labeling of the objects
    d) Using unsupervised learning only
    Answer: a) Trial and error through reinforcement learning

25. **What is the first step in the pick and place task for a robot?**
    a) Planning the grasp
    b) Recognizing objects
    c) Executing the action
    d) Receiving feedback
    Answer: b) Recognizing objects

26. **In the pick and place task, which machine learning technique helps the robot to determine the best way to pick an object?**
    a) Supervised Learning
    b) Unsupervised Learning
    c) Reinforcement Learning
    d) Clustering
    Answer: c) Reinforcement Learning

27. **Why does the robot in the pick and place task require continuous feedback?**
    a) To adapt its behavior and improve over time
    b) To receive instructions from humans
    c) To reduce the complexity of the task

d) To make decisions in a random manner

Answer: a) To adapt its behavior and improve over time

28. **What is the purpose of feedback in the pick and place task?**

    a) To measure the robot's efficiency

    b) To correct errors and adjust future actions

    c) To increase the robot's speed

    d) To decrease the data collection requirement

    Answer: b) To correct errors and adjust future actions

29. **What type of sensors would a robot use for the pick and place task?**

    a) Camera for object detection

    b) Proximity sensors for measuring distance

    c) Tactile sensors for grasping

    d) All of the above

    Answer: d) All of the above

30. **What type of data is needed to teach a robot to pick up an object in the pick and place task?**

    a) Shape and weight of the object

    b) Object color

    c) Object texture

    d) Object size and shape, along with location

    Answer: d) Object size and shape, along with location

31. **What role does supervised learning play in the pick and place task?**

    a) It helps the robot decide the best action without errors

    b) It provides the robot with labeled images for object recognition

    c) It helps the robot navigate autonomously

    d) It adjusts the robot's movements based on feedback

    Answer: b) It provides the robot with labeled images for object recognition

32. **How does reinforcement learning benefit the pick and place task in robotics?**

    a) It enables the robot to make decisions without human input

    b) It allows the robot to learn from mistakes and improve its actions

    c) It helps the robot move faster

    d) It reduces the need for data collection

    Answer: b) It allows the robot to learn from mistakes and improve its actions

33. **What does the robot need to learn in the pick and place task?**

    a) Which object to pick

    b) The best way to grasp each object

    c) How to place the object correctly

    d) All of the above

    Answer: d) All of the above

34. **In reinforcement learning, what does the robot receive after performing an action?**

    a) Data

    b) Reward or penalty

    c) Labeled data

    d) Instructions

    Answer: b) Reward or penalty

35. **Which of the following is an example of feedback in the pick and place task?**
    a) The robot being told whether it has picked up the object correctly
    b) The robot receiving more training data
    c) The robot adjusting the speed of its movements
    d) The robot's arm position being corrected
    Answer: a) The robot being told whether it has picked up the object correctly
36. **Which of the following is a real-world application of the pick and place task?**
    a) Automated assembly lines in manufacturing
    b) Autonomous vacuum cleaning
    c) Object classification in robotics
    d) Object clustering for inventory management
    Answer: a) Automated assembly lines in manufacturing
37. **What challenge does the robot face in a dynamic environment during the pick and place task?**
    a) Constantly adjusting to new objects and layouts
    b) Reducing the speed of its movements
    c) Dealing with sensor inaccuracies
    d) Memorizing object positions
    Answer: a) Constantly adjusting to new objects and layouts
38. **What role do cameras play in the pick and place task for robots?**
    a) They provide the robot with feedback
    b) They help recognize objects and their location
    c) They monitor the robot's internal state
    d) They improve the robot's movement speed
    Answer: b) They help recognize objects and their location
39. **Which of the following would make the pick and place task easier for a robot?**
    a) A fixed and predictable environment
    b) Randomization of objects
    c) Complex object shapes
    d) Unclear object positions
    Answer: a) A fixed and predictable environment
40. **What is the benefit of using reinforcement learning in robotics for pick and place?**
    a) It allows robots to make autonomous decisions based on feedback
    b) It requires minimal training data
    c) It simplifies object detection
    d) It eliminates the need for sensors
    Answer: a) It allows robots to make autonomous decisions based on feedback

Chapter 5: Computer Vision for Robots

5.1 Enabling Robotic Vision: Image Processing and Object Recognition

A fundamental capability for robots operating in the physical world is the ability to "see" and interpret their surroundings. This is achieved through **computer vision**, a field that empowers robots to understand and extract meaningful information from visual data. The processes of **image processing** and **object recognition** are crucial components of computer vision, allowing robots to perceive their environment, identify specific items of interest, and make informed decisions based on what they "see."

Image Processing: Preparing Visual Data for Analysis

Image processing is the initial stage in computer vision. It involves taking raw image data, typically captured by cameras or other imaging sensors, and manipulating it to enhance its quality and extract relevant features. The primary objective of image processing is to make the image more suitable for subsequent analysis, such as object recognition or tracking movements. Several key image processing techniques are commonly employed:

- **Filtering:** This category of techniques involves modifying the pixel values within an image to emphasize certain characteristics while suppressing unwanted noise or irrelevant details. Common filtering methods include:
    - **Edge Detection:** Algorithms like Sobel and Canny are used to identify significant changes in pixel intensity, effectively highlighting the boundaries and outlines of objects within an image. This is crucial for segmenting objects from the background and understanding their shapes.
    - **Blurring:** Techniques such as Gaussian blur are applied to smooth out an image, reducing high-frequency noise and softening sharp edges. This can be useful for preparing an image for feature extraction or for reducing the impact of minor imperfections.
    - **Thresholding:** This process converts a grayscale image into a binary image (containing only black and white pixels) by setting all pixels with an intensity value above a certain threshold to white and all pixels below it to black. Thresholding is often used to isolate objects with distinct intensity levels from the background.
- **Segmentation:** This process aims to partition an image into multiple distinct regions or segments, with the goal of isolating individual objects of interest from the background or separating different parts of a scene. Various techniques are used for segmentation:
    - **Region Growing:** This method starts with a seed pixel and iteratively adds neighboring pixels to the region based on predefined criteria, such as color or intensity similarity.
    - **K-means Clustering:** This algorithm groups pixels into a specified number (k) of clusters based on their color or intensity values, effectively segmenting the image into regions with similar characteristics.

- Contour Detection: Algorithms like Canny edge detection followed by contour tracing can identify the boundaries of objects, allowing them to be isolated as distinct segments.

Object Recognition: Identifying Items Within an Image

Once an image has been processed to enhance its features and potentially segment objects, the next critical step is **object recognition**. This refers to the robot's ability to identify specific objects present within the image by comparing the visual data to a database or model of known objects. Several approaches are used for object recognition:

- **Template Matching:** This is a relatively straightforward technique where the system searches the processed image for a predefined template or a small image representing the object of interest. The system slides the template across the image and calculates a similarity score at each position to find the best match.
- **Feature-Based Matching:** This approach relies on identifying and extracting distinctive features from objects, such as corners, edges, or local intensity patterns. Algorithms like SIFT (Scale-Invariant Feature Transform) and SURF (Speeded-Up Robust Features) are popular for extracting robust features that are invariant to changes in scale, rotation, and illumination. Once features are extracted from the unknown object in the image, they are compared to the features of known objects stored in a database to find the best match.
- **Deep Learning:** Modern, high-accuracy object recognition often leverages **Convolutional Neural Networks (CNNs)**. These are complex neural network architectures that are trained on vast datasets of labeled images. CNNs learn hierarchical representations of visual features, allowing them to recognize and classify objects with remarkable accuracy, even in complex scenes with variations in lighting, viewpoint, and occlusion. Once trained, a CNN can take an input image and output the probability of different objects being present in the image.

Illustrative Example: Robotic Box Handling in a Warehouse

Consider a robot operating in a warehouse tasked with identifying and picking up specific types of boxes.

1. **Image Acquisition:** The robot's camera captures a live video feed of its surroundings, showing various boxes on shelves.
2. **Image Processing:** The robot first processes these images. It might apply **edge detection** algorithms (like Canny) to clearly outline the edges of the boxes, making them distinct from the background and each other. This helps in determining the boundaries and shapes of potential objects.
3. **Object Recognition:** Next, the robot employs object recognition techniques. If using **template matching**, it might have predefined templates of the different types of boxes it needs to handle. It would then search the processed image for regions that closely match these templates. If using **feature-based matching**, it would extract key features (like corners and edges) from the outlined boxes and compare them to a database of features associated with known box types (e.g., a specific arrangement of corners for "Type A

Box"). If using **deep learning**, the captured image would be fed into a pre-trained CNN. The CNN would analyze the image and output classifications for the objects present, identifying which boxes are of the desired type ("Type A Box," "Type B Box," etc.) and their locations within the image.

4. **Action Planning:** Based on the identified box types and their positions (obtained through the bounding boxes provided by the object recognition algorithm), the robot can then plan its picking task. It can determine which box to approach, the optimal grasping points, and the sequence of movements required to pick up the box and place it in the designated location.

In this way, the integration of image processing and object recognition empowers the warehouse robot to "see" and understand its environment, enabling it to perform complex tasks like identifying and manipulating specific objects efficiently and autonomously.

5.2 Autonomous Navigation in Uncharted Spaces: Visual SLAM

Visual Simultaneous Localization and Mapping (Visual SLAM) is a sophisticated technique that empowers robots to navigate autonomously in previously unknown environments. This method enables a robot to concurrently construct a map of its surroundings while simultaneously determining its own position and orientation within that generated map. Visual SLAM is particularly advantageous in scenarios where global positioning systems (GPS) are unreliable or unavailable, such as indoor settings, underground environments, or terrains obstructed from satellite signals. The process relies on the analysis of visual data acquired from cameras, often integrated with data from other sensors like Inertial Measurement Units (IMUs), to achieve robust and accurate localization and mapping.

The operation of Visual SLAM can be decomposed into two tightly coupled primary tasks:

- **Localization:** This aspect focuses on the robot's ability to ascertain its precise position and orientation (its pose) within a given environment. Visual SLAM achieves this by processing the stream of images captured by its cameras. From these images, distinctive visual features, such as corners, edges, and other salient points, are extracted. By tracking how these features move and change across successive images, and by comparing them to previously observed landmarks, the robot can estimate its current position and orientation relative to these known points in the environment.
  - **Example:** As a robot moves through a room, its camera captures a sequence of images. Visual SLAM algorithms identify unique corners of furniture, the intersection of walls, and other stable visual features in these images. By observing how these features shift in the image plane from one frame to the next, and by using techniques like feature matching and triangulation, the robot can calculate its own motion and thus estimate its current location and orientation within the room.

- **Mapping:** Concurrently with localization, the robot builds a representation of its environment by observing it through the continuous stream of images from its cameras. This map is constructed incrementally as the robot moves and gathers more visual information. The mapping process involves identifying and tracking the same visual feature points over multiple viewpoints. By understanding the relative positions of these features from different camera perspectives, the robot can create a consistent and increasingly accurate map of its surroundings. This map can be represented in various forms, such as a collection of 3D points (a point cloud) or a more structured representation including surfaces and objects.
  - **Example:** While the robot is localizing itself by tracking the corners of a table, it is also adding these corners as landmarks to its internal map of the room. As it moves and views the table from different angles, it refines the estimated 3D position of these corners on its map, making the map more accurate over time.

Illustrative Scenario: Visual SLAM in a Robot Vacuum Cleaner

A robot vacuum cleaner navigating within a home provides a practical example of Visual SLAM in action.

As the robot moves across the floor, its onboard cameras continuously capture images of the room. Visual SLAM algorithms within the robot process these images in real-time.

1. **Feature Extraction:** The robot identifies distinctive visual features within the images, such as the corners of walls, the edges of furniture legs, and unique patterns on the floor or objects.
2. **Localization:** By tracking how these features move across successive frames, the robot estimates its own movement (how far it has traveled and in what direction) and thus determines its current position and orientation within the room relative to the features it has already observed.
3. **Mapping:** Simultaneously, the robot uses the observed features and its estimated motion to build a map of the room. It records the 3D positions of the identified walls, obstacles (like furniture), and other persistent visual landmarks. As it explores further, it adds new features to the map and refines the positions of existing ones based on new observations.
4. **Continuous Operation:** This process of capturing images, extracting features, estimating its pose (localization), and updating the map continues as the robot moves throughout the room. This allows the robot to clean the entire area efficiently, knowing where it has already been and avoiding obstacles, all without relying on external beacons or pre-programmed paths.

Diagram: Simplified Workflow of Visual SLAM

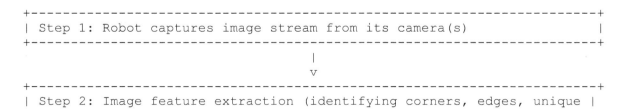

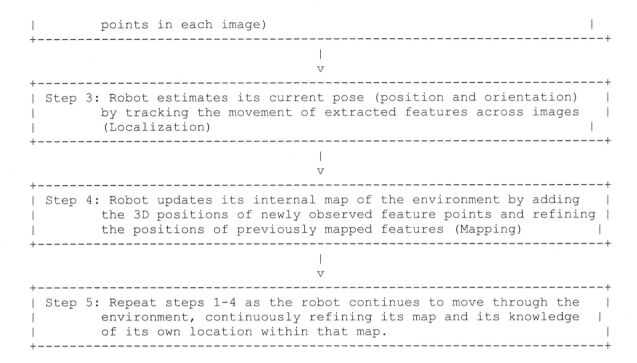

```
|         points in each image)                                      |
+--------------------------------------------------------------------+
                                  |
                                  v
+--------------------------------------------------------------------+
| Step 3: Robot estimates its current pose (position and orientation) |
|         by tracking the movement of extracted features across images |
|         (Localization)                                             |
+--------------------------------------------------------------------+
                                  |
                                  v
+--------------------------------------------------------------------+
| Step 4: Robot updates its internal map of the environment by adding |
|         the 3D positions of newly observed feature points and refining |
|         the positions of previously mapped features (Mapping)      |
+--------------------------------------------------------------------+
                                  |
                                  v
+--------------------------------------------------------------------+
| Step 5: Repeat steps 1-4 as the robot continues to move through the |
|         environment, continuously refining its map and its knowledge |
|         of its own location within that map.                       |
+--------------------------------------------------------------------+
```

Visual SLAM is a powerful technique that enables robots to achieve true spatial awareness in complex and unknown environments, paving the way for more autonomous and intelligent robotic systems.

5.3 Enabling Natural Interaction: Facial Recognition and Gesture Control in Robotics

Facial recognition and gesture control are prominent examples of how computer vision is employed to create more intuitive and natural interactions between humans and robots. By enabling robots to "understand" human faces and movements, these technologies pave the way for more seamless and user-friendly robotic systems.

Facial Recognition: Establishing Identity Through Visual Analysis

Facial recognition is a technology focused on identifying or verifying the identity of an individual by analyzing the unique characteristics of their facial features. In the context of robotics, this capability holds significant potential for applications such as enhancing security protocols, personalizing robot interactions, and creating more engaging social robots.

The typical process of facial recognition involves the following stages:

- **Face Detection:** The initial step is to locate and isolate any human faces present within an image or video stream. Several algorithms are commonly used for this purpose.

Traditional methods include the **Haar Cascade classifier**, which utilizes a series of simple features to identify face-like regions, and the **Histogram of Oriented Gradients (HOG)** algorithm, which captures the distribution of edge orientations in localized parts of an image to detect potential faces.

- **Feature Extraction:** Once a face has been detected and its location within the image determined, the system proceeds to extract key and distinctive facial features. These can include the relative position and size of the eyes, nose, mouth, and the contours of the face. Modern facial recognition systems often employ **Deep Learning** techniques, particularly **Convolutional Neural Networks (CNNs),** to automatically learn and extract more robust and discriminative facial features directly from the image data. These learned features are less susceptible to variations in lighting, pose, and expression.
- **Matching:** The extracted facial features are then compared against a database of facial features associated with known individuals. Various matching algorithms are used to calculate a similarity score between the extracted features and the features stored in the database. If the similarity score exceeds a predefined threshold, a match is declared, and the individual's identity is verified or recognized.
  - **Example:** In a healthcare setting, a robot might be equipped with facial recognition to identify patients as they approach. Upon detecting a face, it extracts the unique facial features and compares them to a database of registered patients. If a match is found, the robot can access the patient's records and provide personalized assistance, such as guiding them to their room or delivering their medication.

Gesture Control: Communicating Through Movement

Gesture control provides a means for humans to interact with robots using bodily movements, such as waving a hand, pointing, or making specific hand signs. This mode of interaction can be particularly advantageous in environments where voice commands might be noisy or impractical, or where physical contact is undesirable.

Gesture recognition typically involves the following steps:

- **Image Segmentation:** The first stage is to isolate the specific body part performing the gesture, usually the hand or arm, from the rest of the visual scene captured by the robot's camera. Techniques like background subtraction or skin color detection can be used to segment the relevant part of the image.
- **Feature Extraction:** Once the gesturing body part has been segmented, the system extracts relevant features that characterize the gesture. These features can include the position of the hand, the trajectory of its movement over time, the orientation of the hand, the shape of the hand (e.g., open, closed, pointing), and the speed of the movement.
- **Classification:** The extracted features are then fed into a classification algorithm, which has been trained on a dataset of labeled gestures. The algorithm compares the extracted features of the current gesture with the learned patterns of known gestures. Based on this comparison, the system classifies the performed gesture (e.g., "wave," "stop," "point").
- **Action Execution:** Once the gesture has been classified, the robot triggers the appropriate response that has been programmed to correspond to that specific gesture.

This response could be a physical movement of the robot, the initiation or termination of a task, or the execution of a specific command.

- o **Example:** A robot working in a manufacturing environment might use gesture control to allow human workers to control its actions without needing to touch a control panel. A simple wave of the hand could signal the robot to start a specific assembly process, while a closed fist could instruct it to stop.

Diagram for Gesture Recognition:

```
+-----------------------------------+
| Step 1: Capture Image from Camera |
+-----------------------------------+
              |
              v
+-----------------------------------+
| Step 2: Hand or body part segmentation|
+-----------------------------------+
              |
              v
+-----------------------------------+
| Step 3: Extract relevant features |
| (e.g., hand position, movement, shape)|
+-----------------------------------+
              |
              v
+-----------------------------------+
| Step 4: Classify gesture based on |
|         learned patterns          |
+-----------------------------------+
              |
              v
+-----------------------------------+
| Step 5: Execute robot response    |
| (e.g., start, stop, or move)      |
+-----------------------------------+
```

The integration of computer vision technologies such as image processing, object recognition, SLAM, facial recognition, and gesture control significantly enhances the capabilities of robots to perceive, understand, and interact with their environment and with humans in meaningful ways. These advancements are crucial for expanding the utility of robots across diverse fields, including healthcare, manufacturing, service industries, and personal robotics.

45 multiple-choice questions (MCQs) based on covering Image Processing, Object Recognition, Visual SLAM, Facial Recognition, and Gesture Control:

5.1 Image Processing and Object Recognition

1. **What is the primary goal of image processing in robotics?**
   - o a) To capture the image data

- o b) To enhance the image and prepare it for analysis
- o c) To move the robot
- o d) To display the image
- o **Answer**: b) To enhance the image and prepare it for analysis

2. **Which of the following is used for edge detection in image processing?**
   - o a) Sobel operator
   - o b) K-means clustering
   - o c) Gaussian blur
   - o d) Hough Transform
   - o **Answer**: a) Sobel operator

3. **What does image segmentation help with in object recognition?**
   - o a) Identifying objects
   - o b) Dividing an image into meaningful regions
   - o c) Enhancing image features
   - o d) Converting the image to black and white
   - o **Answer**: b) Dividing an image into meaningful regions

4. **Which technique is commonly used for object recognition in computer vision?**
   - o a) Template matching
   - o b) Fourier Transform
   - o c) Principal Component Analysis (PCA)
   - o d) Image Segmentation
   - o **Answer**: a) Template matching

5. **Which of the following algorithms is used for feature-based object recognition?**
   - o a) SIFT
   - o b) K-means
   - o c) KNN
   - o d) RANSAC
   - o **Answer**: a) SIFT

6. **What is the main advantage of using Convolutional Neural Networks (CNN) in object recognition?**
   - o a) It requires no image preprocessing
   - o b) It performs faster than traditional methods
   - o c) It can learn complex patterns and features from the data
   - o d) It uses less computational power
   - o **Answer**: c) It can learn complex patterns and features from the data

7. **Which image processing technique is used to remove noise from an image?**
   - o a) Edge detection
   - o b) Filtering
   - o c) Segmentation
   - o d) Feature extraction
   - o **Answer**: b) Filtering

8. **What does the term "thresholding" refer to in image processing?**
   - o a) Converting a color image to grayscale
   - o b) Detecting edges in an image
   - o c) Converting a grayscale image into a binary image
   - o d) Reducing the size of the image

- Answer: c) Converting a grayscale image into a binary image
9. **Which of the following is a characteristic of a good object recognition algorithm?**
    - a) Low computation time and high accuracy
    - b) High computation time and low accuracy
    - c) Inability to handle diverse lighting conditions
    - d) Only works on specific objects
    - **Answer**: a) Low computation time and high accuracy
10. **Which of the following is NOT typically used in object recognition?**
    - a) Histogram of Oriented Gradients (HOG)
    - b) Convolutional Neural Networks (CNN)
    - c) K-means clustering
    - d) Fourier Transform
    - **Answer**: d) Fourier Transform

5.2 Visual SLAM (Simultaneous Localization and Mapping)

11. **What is the main purpose of Visual SLAM in robotics?**
    - a) To enhance image quality
    - b) To help a robot navigate and map its environment
    - c) To recognize objects in the environment
    - d) To detect facial features
    - **Answer**: b) To help a robot navigate and map its environment
12. **Which of the following is typically used in Visual SLAM?**
    - a) Stereo vision
    - b) GPS data
    - c) Acoustic signals
    - d) LIDAR data
    - **Answer**: a) Stereo vision
13. **In SLAM, what does localization refer to?**
    - a) Mapping the environment
    - b) Tracking the robot's position within the map
    - c) Object recognition
    - d) Gesture recognition
    - **Answer**: b) Tracking the robot's position within the map
14. **What is the key feature of visual SLAM over traditional SLAM techniques?**
    - a) It does not require any sensors
    - b) It uses visual information from cameras for localization and mapping
    - c) It does not require a map
    - d) It uses sonar data
    - **Answer**: b) It uses visual information from cameras for localization and mapping
15. **Which of the following is a challenge faced by Visual SLAM systems?**
    - a) High computational cost
    - b) Low resolution cameras
    - c) Limited environment mapping

- o d) Limited usage of cameras
- o **Answer**: a) High computational cost
16. **In Visual SLAM, which of the following is used to improve the accuracy of localization?**
    - o a) Feature extraction from images
    - o b) GPS tracking
    - o c) Simple object recognition
    - o d) Sonar mapping
    - o **Answer**: a) Feature extraction from images
17. **Which technique is commonly used for feature extraction in Visual SLAM?**
    - o a) SIFT
    - o b) Edge detection
    - o c) K-means clustering
    - o d) Fourier transform
    - o **Answer**: a) SIFT
18. **Visual SLAM typically requires which of the following sensors for optimal performance?**
    - o a) Ultrasonic sensor
    - o b) Inertial Measurement Unit (IMU)
    - o c) Light sensor
    - o d) Microphone
    - o **Answer**: b) Inertial Measurement Unit (IMU)
19. **What does the term "mapping" refer to in the context of SLAM?**
    - o a) Determining the robot's position
    - o b) Creating a representation of the robot's surroundings
    - o c) Recognizing objects in the environment
    - o d) Analyzing environmental conditions
    - o **Answer**: b) Creating a representation of the robot's surroundings
20. **What is the primary advantage of using Visual SLAM over traditional SLAM methods?**
    - o a) It is more energy-efficient
    - o b) It can operate without any sensor data
    - o c) It provides more accurate and detailed maps using camera data
    - o d) It requires no preprocessing of image data
    - o **Answer**: c) It provides more accurate and detailed maps using camera data

5.3 Facial Recognition and Gesture Control

21. **What is the primary purpose of facial recognition in robotics?**
    - o a) To recognize objects in the environment
    - o b) To identify or verify a person's identity
    - o c) To navigate the environment
    - o d) To map the robot's surroundings
    - o **Answer**: b) To identify or verify a person's identity

22. **Which algorithm is commonly used for face detection in robotics?**
    - o a) Haar Cascade classifier
    - o b) K-means clustering
    - o c) PCA (Principal Component Analysis)
    - o d) FFT (Fast Fourier Transform)
    - o **Answer**: a) Haar Cascade classifier
23. **What is the main feature of deep learning-based facial recognition?**
    - o a) Requires no image preprocessing
    - o b) Performs face recognition with low accuracy
    - o c) Learns robust and complex facial features from large datasets
    - o d) Uses manual feature extraction
    - o **Answer**: c) Learns robust and complex facial features from large datasets
24. **Which of the following facial features is commonly used in recognition?**
    - o a) Eye color
    - o b) Nose shape
    - o c) Mouth curvature
    - o d) All of the above
    - o **Answer**: d) All of the above
25. **Which of the following is a common application of facial recognition in robotics?**
    - o a) To detect obstacles
    - o b) To interact with users in a personalized manner
    - o c) To map the environment
    - o d) To detect room temperature
    - o **Answer**: b) To interact with users in a personalized manner
26. **Gesture control in robotics involves recognizing which of the following?**
    - o a) Human hand movements
    - o b) Objects in the environment
    - o c) Robot's position
    - o d) Environmental changes
    - o **Answer**: a) Human hand movements
27. **Which technique is commonly used in gesture recognition?**
    - o a) Feature extraction from human movements
    - o b) K-means clustering
    - o c) Convolutional Neural Networks (CNN)
    - o d) Deep Q-learning
    - o **Answer**: a) Feature extraction from human movements
28. **Which of the following can be used to classify hand gestures?**
    - o a) Principal Component Analysis (PCA)
    - o b) Dynamic Time Warping (DTW)
    - o c) Linear Regression
    - o d) k-NN
    - o **Answer**: b) Dynamic Time Warping (DTW)
29. **What is the main advantage of gesture control for robot interactions?**
    - o a) It simplifies the robot's movement
    - o b) It allows the user to control the robot without physical contact
    - o c) It reduces the robot's processing power

- o d) It eliminates the need for facial recognition
- o **Answer**: b) It allows the user to control the robot without physical contact
30. **In facial recognition, what is the purpose of matching extracted facial features with a database?**
    - o a) To classify objects in the image
    - o b) To track facial expressions
    - o c) To identify or verify the person's identity
    - o d) To measure the distance between objects
    - o **Answer**: c) To identify or verify the person's identity

---

31. **What is one of the challenges of using Visual SLAM in robotics?**

    - a) It is too expensive for most robots.
    - b) It can only be used outdoors.
    - c) It requires real-time processing of large amounts of image data.
    - d) It cannot handle dynamic environments.
    - **Answer**: c) It requires real-time processing of large amounts of image data.

32. **Which of the following is NOT an advantage of using stereo vision in SLAM?**

    - a) Provides depth information
    - b) Increases the accuracy of localization
    - c) Works in all lighting conditions
    - d) Can be used for both mapping and localization
    - **Answer**: c) Works in all lighting conditions

33. **What is typically used for recognizing faces in low-light conditions?**

    - a) Infrared cameras
    - b) Standard cameras
    - c) GPS systems
    - d) LIDAR sensors
    - **Answer**: a) Infrared cameras

34. **Which of the following algorithms is used for real-time gesture recognition?**

    - a) Hidden Markov Models
    - b) Decision Trees
    - c) Convolutional Neural Networks (CNN)
    - d) K-means clustering
    - **Answer**: a) Hidden Markov Models

35. **What does a typical Visual SLAM system rely on for mapping?**

- a) LIDAR and GPS
- b) RGB images and depth information
- c) Facial recognition algorithms
- d) Gesture control sensors
- **Answer**: b) RGB images and depth information

36. How does image thresholding help in object recognition?

- a) Converts an image into a binary format for easier analysis
- b) Extracts object features
- c) Increases image resolution
- d) Detects edges in the image
- **Answer**: a) Converts an image into a binary format for easier analysis

37. Which of the following is a critical step for SLAM systems in robotic navigation?

- a) Localization and feature extraction
- b) Image smoothing and noise reduction
- c) Depth perception and gesture tracking
- d) Object segmentation and classification
- **Answer**: a) Localization and feature extraction

38. Which of the following is an example of a deep learning-based object recognition algorithm?

- a) Haar Cascade
- b) YOLO (You Only Look Once)
- c) Hough Transform
- d) K-means clustering
- **Answer**: b) YOLO (You Only Look Once)

39. In gesture recognition, what is the purpose of feature extraction?

- a) To detect the position of the robot
- b) To separate foreground from background
- c) To identify specific movements or actions
- d) To identify obstacles in the robot's path
- **Answer**: c) To identify specific movements or actions

40. Which type of camera is commonly used in facial recognition systems for robots?

- a) Depth camera
- b) RGB camera
- c) Infrared camera
- d) LIDAR
- **Answer**: b) RGB camera

41. What does the term "dynamic mapping" refer to in Visual SLAM?

- a) Updating the robot's map in real-time
- b) Identifying objects using machine learning
- c) Predicting the robot's path in the environment
- d) Creating a fixed map for robot navigation
- **Answer**: a) Updating the robot's map in real-time

42. What is the role of the IMU (Inertial Measurement Unit) in Visual SLAM systems?

- a) To detect obstacles
- b) To provide orientation and acceleration data to improve localization
- c) To perform object recognition
- d) To track gestures
- **Answer**: b) To provide orientation and acceleration data to improve localization

43. Which of the following technologies does NOT use image recognition for robot navigation?

- a) Visual SLAM
- b) Object recognition
- c) LIDAR-based mapping
- d) Gesture recognition
- **Answer**: c) LIDAR-based mapping

44. How does a robot benefit from gesture control?

- a) It increases its speed and efficiency
- b) It reduces the need for voice commands and physical controllers
- c) It helps the robot understand the environment better
- d) It allows the robot to perform more tasks simultaneously
- **Answer**: b) It reduces the need for voice commands and physical controllers

45. What is the main purpose of using deep learning in facial recognition systems?

- a) To increase the resolution of images
- b) To enhance the speed of recognition
- c) To identify complex patterns in facial features
- d) To simplify the recognition process
- **Answer**: c) To identify complex patterns in facial features

Chapter 6: Natural Language Processing (NLP)

6.1 Bridging the Communication Gap: Enabling Robots to Understand and Speak Through Natural Language Processing

Natural Language Processing (NLP) serves as a critical bridge between human communication and machine interaction, empowering robots to understand, interpret, and respond to human language. By integrating principles from linguistics, machine learning, and computational modeling, NLP enables a machine to process and comprehend the nuances of human languages in a meaningful way. For robots, the ability to understand and generate natural language is paramount for achieving effective human-robot interaction, allowing them to comprehend commands, execute tasks, and communicate seamlessly.

The Mechanism of NLP in Robots:

To equip robots with the capabilities of understanding and speaking, the system undergoes a series of crucial stages:

- **Speech Recognition (Automatic Speech Recognition - ASR):** The initial step involves enabling the robot to "hear" and interpret spoken language. This is achieved through Automatic Speech Recognition (ASR) systems, which are responsible for converting audio signals into textual representations. ASR systems analyze the sound waves captured by the robot's microphones and transcribe them into a sequence of words that can then be processed further by the NLP components.
  - **Example:** When a user says to a robot, "What is the weather like today?", the ASR system first converts this spoken query into the text string: "What is the weather like today?".
- **Syntactic Parsing:** Once the spoken input has been converted into text, the robot needs to understand the grammatical structure of the sentence. This is where syntactic parsing comes into play. Parsing involves breaking down the sentence into its constituent parts, such as nouns, verbs, adjectives, and adverbs, and identifying the grammatical relationships between these components. This analysis helps the robot understand the subject, verb, and object of the sentence, as well as the overall grammatical structure.
  - **Example:** For the sentence "Bring me the book on the table," the parsing stage would identify "Bring" as the verb (action), "me" as the indirect object (recipient), "book" as the direct object (item), and "on the table" as a prepositional phrase modifying "book" (location).
- **Semantic Analysis:** Semantics refers to the understanding of the meaning conveyed by the words and the overall sentence. This stage involves mapping words to their corresponding meanings and resolving any ambiguities in language. Human language often contains words with multiple meanings (homonyms) or context-dependent interpretations. Semantic analysis utilizes the surrounding words (context) and potentially information from previous interactions to determine the intended meaning.

- **Example:** In the sentence "The robot needs to run the program," semantic analysis understands that "run" in this context means "execute" and not the physical act of running. Similarly, if a user says "Put the bat down," the robot would need to rely on the context of the interaction (e.g., are they in a baseball game or a cave?) to determine whether "bat" refers to a piece of sports equipment or a flying mammal.
- **Speech Synthesis (Text-to-Speech - TTS):** After the robot has processed and understood the user's instruction or query, it often needs to generate a spoken response. This is the role of speech synthesis, also known as Text-to-Speech (TTS). TTS systems convert text-based responses generated by the robot's internal processing into audible speech. To make the robot's speech sound natural and engaging, TTS systems employ various prosody techniques, which involve controlling aspects like intonation (tone modulation), rhythm, speaking rate, and stress on specific syllables.
  - **Example:** If the robot has determined that the weather is sunny with a temperature of 25 degrees Celsius, its TTS system would take the text "The weather today is sunny with a temperature of twenty-five degrees Celsius" and generate an audible spoken version of this sentence with appropriate intonation and emphasis to sound natural to a human listener.

Illustrative Scenario: A Home Assistant Robot Interacting with Natural Language

Consider a home assistant robot equipped with a comprehensive NLP system.

If a user in the living room says, **"Turn off the lights,"** the following steps would occur:

1. **Speech Recognition (ASR):** The robot's microphones capture the audio of the user's command, and the ASR system converts it into the text string: "Turn off the lights."
2. **Syntactic Parsing:** The NLP system parses this text, identifying "Turn off" as a verb phrase indicating an action and "lights" as the noun representing the object of the action.
3. **Semantic Analysis:** The robot's semantic understanding component interprets "lights" in the context of a home environment as referring to the electrical lighting system in the current room. It also understands the meaning of the phrasal verb "turn off" as an instruction to deactivate something.
4. **Action Execution:** Based on this understanding, the robot sends a command to its internal control system to switch off the lights in the living room.

If the user then asks, **"What time is it?"**, the process would be similar:

1. **Speech Recognition (ASR):** The audio is converted to the text: "What time is it?".
2. **Syntactic Parsing:** The system identifies "What time" as an interrogative phrase and "is it" as the verb and subject.
3. **Semantic Analysis:** The robot understands the user is asking for the current time.
4. **Response Generation and Speech Synthesis (TTS):** The robot retrieves the current time from its internal clock and generates a textual response, such as "The current time is 3:45 PM." This text is then passed to the TTS system, which converts it into natural-sounding spoken language, which the robot then outputs through its speakers.

Through this intricate process of understanding and generating natural language, robots can engage in more meaningful and intuitive interactions with humans, making them more effective assistants and companions in various aspects of life.

6.2 Conversational Interfaces: Voice Assistants and Chatbots in Robotics

In the realm of modern robotics, particularly in applications designed for direct interaction with consumers, voice assistants and chatbots are gaining significant prominence. These AI-driven systems provide robots with the ability to engage in conversations with humans, fostering more natural and intuitive communication.

Voice Assistants Integrated into Robots:

The success and familiarity of voice assistants like Siri, Alexa, and Google Assistant in smartphones and smart home devices have paved the way for their integration into robotic platforms. By incorporating these technologies, robots can understand and respond to spoken commands, effectively allowing users to control them through voice. These systems leverage the power of Natural Language Processing (NLP) to decipher the meaning behind spoken instructions, process the requested information, and generate an appropriate verbal response.

Robots equipped with voice assistants can perform a diverse range of tasks based on user queries. This includes controlling smart home devices (e.g., "Turn on the living room lights"), providing real-time information (e.g., "What is the weather forecast for tomorrow?"), answering general knowledge questions (e.g., "Who painted the Mona Lisa?"), and setting reminders or alarms.

- **Illustrative Scenario:** Consider a robot designed to provide assistance to elderly individuals in their homes. This robot is integrated with a voice assistant. A user might say, "Remind me to take my medication at 8 PM." The robot's voice assistant would utilize NLP to understand the intent behind this command, extracting the action ("remind"), the object ("take my medication"), and the time ("8 PM"). The robot would then process this information to set an internal reminder, which it would audibly convey to the user at the specified time. Similarly, the user could ask the robot to play their favorite music ("Play some classical music") or to provide assistance with a daily task ("Where did I put my glasses?"), and the robot would use its perception capabilities and knowledge base to respond accordingly through voice.

Chatbots as Text-Based Interaction Interfaces for Robots:

Chatbots integrated into robots are software applications designed to simulate human-like conversation through text-based interactions. These systems employ NLP to understand and respond to textual input from users in real-time. In a robotic context, chatbots provide a conversational interface through which users can interact with the robot by typing questions or giving instructions via a screen or other text input method.

Chatbots in robots can be particularly useful in scenarios where a visual interface is available or preferred, or where a record of the interaction is beneficial. They can handle a wide variety of user queries, providing information, guiding users through processes, or troubleshooting issues.

- **Illustrative Scenario:** Imagine a robot deployed in a retail store to provide customer service. This robot is equipped with a chatbot interface accessible through a touchscreen on its display. A customer might interact with the robot by typing questions such as "What time does the store close today?" or "Where can I find the electronics section?". The chatbot would use NLP to interpret the user's question, access relevant information from the store's database, and respond with a textual answer displayed on the screen (e.g., "The store closes at 9 PM today" or "The electronics section is located on the second floor, aisle 5"). Similarly, a user could type a request like "Can I make a reservation for a product?", and the chatbot would guide them through the reservation process via a text-based dialogue.

In essence, both voice assistants and chatbots serve as crucial modalities for enabling more natural and accessible communication with robots. Voice assistants cater to spoken interactions, offering hands-free control and information retrieval, while chatbots facilitate text-based conversations, providing a visual and recordable means of communication. The integration of these conversational interfaces is making robots more user-friendly and enhancing their utility in a wide range of applications, particularly those involving direct engagement with human users.

6.3 Illustrative Case: The Pepper Robot in Customer Engagement

The Pepper robot, created by SoftBank Robotics, serves as a compelling illustration of how robots can leverage Natural Language Processing (NLP) and Artificial Intelligence (AI) to engage with humans in real-world scenarios. Pepper is specifically designed for deployment in customer-facing roles, particularly within retail environments, where it is capable of conducting conversations with customers, recognizing individuals, and responding to their emotional cues.

NLP as Pepper's Communication Foundation:

Pepper utilizes NLP as a core mechanism for understanding and responding to customer inquiries. When a customer poses a question or makes a statement, Pepper's system first listens to the spoken words and employs speech recognition to transcribe the audio into text. Subsequently, semantic processing techniques are applied to analyze the meaning and intent behind the words within the context of the conversation. Based on this understanding, Pepper generates a spoken response, which might involve providing requested information, offering directions to a specific area or staff member, or answering a query.

Beyond simply answering questions, Pepper is also programmed to engage in basic social interactions, often referred to as "small talk," which contributes to making the robot appear more personable and approachable to customers. Furthermore, its voice recognition capabilities enable it to remember returning customers, allowing for the potential to personalize their experience based on previous encounters.

Facial Recognition and Emotion Detection for Enhanced Interaction:

In addition to its NLP capabilities, Pepper is equipped with advanced facial recognition and emotion detection technologies. By analyzing the facial expressions and the tone of voice of the individuals it interacts with, Pepper can infer their emotional state. This ability allows Pepper to respond in a more contextually appropriate and empathetic manner. For instance, if Pepper detects that a customer appears upset or confused (indicated by facial cues like a frown or a furrowed brow, or a frustrated tone of voice), it can offer reassuring words or proactively alert a human staff member to provide further assistance.

Scenario Example:

Consider a customer entering a retail store and being greeted by Pepper, who says in a friendly tone, "Hello, welcome! How may I assist you today?"

The customer then asks, "Excuse me, where can I find the latest smartphones?"

Pepper's internal processing would proceed as follows:

1. **Speech Recognition:** Pepper's microphones capture the customer's spoken query, and the ASR system converts it into the text: "Where can I find the latest smartphones?"
2. **Semantic Processing:** The NLP system analyzes the sentence, understanding that the customer is asking for the location of a specific product category ("latest smartphones").
3. **Response Generation:** Pepper generates a spoken response, such as, "The latest smartphones are located in the aisle to your left. Would you like me to guide you there?"

Now, imagine the customer responds to Pepper's directions with a facial expression indicating confusion or frustration, perhaps accompanied by a hesitant tone of voice. Pepper's emotion detection system would analyze these cues.

1. **Facial Analysis:** Pepper's camera detects and analyzes the customer's facial expression, recognizing the signs of confusion or frustration (e.g., a frown, pursed lips).
2. **Voice Tone Analysis:** Pepper's audio processing analyzes the customer's tone of voice, detecting hesitation or uncertainty.
3. **Adaptive Response:** Based on this multimodal emotion detection, Pepper can adapt its interaction by offering further assistance. It might say something like, "I sense that you might be having some difficulty. Let me assist you further," and then potentially offer to physically guide the customer to the smartphone aisle or provide more detailed instructions.

This example highlights how the integration of NLP for understanding language and AI-powered perception for recognizing faces and emotions allows a robot like Pepper to engage in more nuanced and helpful interactions, ultimately enhancing the customer service experience.

Conclusion

Natural Language Processing enables robots to interact in a human-like manner, allowing them to understand and produce language effectively. Through speech recognition, semantic understanding, and speech synthesis, robots can communicate with humans seamlessly. Technologies like voice assistants and chatbots have enhanced robot capabilities, making them more useful in customer service, healthcare, and personal assistance. The Pepper robot serves as a prime example of how NLP can be leveraged to create robots that not only understand language but also react to human emotions, further enriching the interaction between robots and users.

50 multiple-choice questions with answers covering the topics in Chapter 6: Natural Language Processing (NLP) (6.1 Enabling Robots to Understand and Speak, 6.2 Voice Assistants and Chatbots in Robots, 6.3 Case Study: Pepper Robot in Customer Service):

50 multiple-choice questions with answers covering the topics in (6.1 Enabling Robots to Understand and Speak, 6.2 Voice Assistants and Chatbots in Robots, 6.3 Case Study: Pepper Robot in Customer Service):

6.1 Enabling Robots to Understand and Speak

1. What does NLP stand for in the context of robotics? a) Natural Language Programming b) Neural Linguistic Processing c) Natural Language Processing d) Network Language Protocol **Answer: c)**
2. The primary goal of NLP in robotics is to: a) Control the robot's physical movements b) Enable robots to understand and respond to human language [1] c) Process sensor data from the environment d) Recognize objects using computer vision **Answer: b)**
3. The process of converting audio signals into text is known as: a) Syntactic parsing b) Semantic analysis c) Speech synthesis d) Speech recognition **Answer: d)**
4. Which NLP stage focuses on understanding the grammatical structure of a sentence? a) Semantics b) Speech synthesis c) Syntactic parsing d) Speech recognition **Answer: c)**
5. Understanding the meaning behind words and interpreting ambiguous language is the focus of: a) Syntactic parsing b) Speech recognition c) Semantics d) Text-to-Speech **Answer: c)**
6. The process of converting text-based responses into audible speech is called: a) Speech recognition b) Natural language understanding c) Semantic analysis d) Speech synthesis **Answer: d)**
7. Breaking down a sentence into components like nouns and verbs is part of: a) Semantic analysis b) Speech synthesis c) Syntactic parsing d) Speech recognition **Answer: c)**

8. Mapping words to their meanings and resolving ambiguities relies on: a) Syntactic structure b) Semantic understanding c) Prosody techniques d) Phonetic analysis **Answer: b)**

9. Techniques like tone modulation and stress on syllables are used in: a) Speech recognition b) Syntactic parsing c) Semantic analysis d) Speech synthesis **Answer: d)**

10. What is the first step a robot takes when a human speaks to it? a) Semantic analysis b) Syntactic parsing c) Speech recognition d) Speech synthesis **Answer: c)**

6.2 Voice Assistants and Chatbots in Robots

11. Systems like Siri and Alexa integrated into robots are examples of: a) Text-based chatbots b) Voice recognition software c) Voice assistants d) Semantic parsers **Answer: c)**

12. Voice assistants in robots primarily use NLP to: a) Control the robot's movement b) Understand spoken commands and generate responses c) Process visual information d) Plan complex tasks **Answer: b)**

13. Robots with voice assistants can perform tasks like: a) Only physical manipulation b) Only navigation c) Controlling appliances, providing updates, answering questions d) Only complex calculations **Answer: c)**

14. Chatbots in robots simulate human conversation through: a) Physical gestures b) Spoken language c) Text-based interactions d) Emotional responses **Answer: c)**

15. Chatbots in robots use NLP to: a) Move the robot's limbs b) Understand and respond to text-based inputs c) Recognize objects in images d) Navigate using maps **Answer: b)**

16. A robot in customer service using a chatbot interface can handle queries like: a) Only technical specifications b) Store hours and reservations c) Only robot maintenance schedules d) Only weather information **Answer: b)**

17. What is a key difference between voice assistants and chatbots in robots? a) Voice assistants use NLP, chatbots do not b) Chatbots understand spoken language, voice assistants do not c) Voice assistants interact through speech, chatbots through text d) Chatbots are more advanced than voice assistants **Answer: c)**

18. Which of the following is NOT a typical function of a voice assistant in a robot? a) Answering questions b) Controlling physical actuators directly c) Providing information updates d) Setting reminders **Answer: b)**

19. Chatbots in robots are particularly useful when: a) Hands-free interaction is required b) A visual interface is available or preferred c) The environment is noisy d) The user is speaking from a distance **Answer: b)**

20. Both voice assistants and chatbots rely heavily on the capabilities of: a) Robot hardware b) Computer vision c) Natural Language Processing (NLP) d) Actuator control systems **Answer: c)**

6.3 Case Study: Pepper Robot in Customer Service

21. Pepper robot is developed by: a) Boston Dynamics b) iRobot c) SoftBank Robotics d) Hanson Robotics **Answer: c)**

22. Pepper is primarily designed for which application area? a) Industrial automation b) Space exploration c) Customer service d) Domestic cleaning **Answer: c)**

23. How does Pepper understand customer queries? a) Through physical touch b) By analyzing facial expressions only c) Using Natural Language Processing (NLP) d) Through pre-programmed keywords only **Answer: c)**

24. What process does Pepper use to convert spoken words into text? a) Semantic processing b) Syntactic parsing c) Speech synthesis d) Speech recognition **Answer: d)**

25. Understanding the context and intent behind customer words is achieved by Pepper through: a) Speech recognition b) Syntactic parsing c) Semantic processing d) Speech synthesis **Answer: c)**

26. How does Pepper respond to customer queries? a) Through text displayed on a screen only b) Using physical gestures only c) By generating a spoken response d) By sending an email to a human agent **Answer: c)**

27. Pepper's ability to engage in small talk makes it appear more: a) Efficient b) Powerful c) Personable and approachable d) Autonomous **Answer: c)**

28. What capability allows Pepper to remember returning customers? a) Advanced navigation b) Voice recognition c) Object recognition d) Gesture control **Answer: b)**

29. Besides NLP, what other AI capabilities does Pepper utilize for interaction? a) Only object manipulation b) Facial recognition and emotion detection c) Only path planning d) Advanced motor control **Answer: b)**

30. How does Pepper detect the emotional state of a person? a) By analyzing their clothing b) By reading their mind c) By analyzing facial expressions and voice tone d) By measuring their heart rate **Answer: c)**

31. If a customer appears upset, Pepper might: a) Ignore them b) Perform a dance c) Offer calming words or alert human staff d) Increase its speaking volume **Answer: c)**

32. When a customer asks Pepper for the location of smartphones, Pepper uses NLP to: a) Physically move to the smartphone aisle b) Display a map on its screen only c) Understand the query and provide directions d) Call a human employee **Answer: c)**

33. If Pepper interprets a customer's frown, it might offer: a) A discount coupon b) Technical specifications c) Additional help or clarification d) To end the interaction **Answer: c)**

34. Pepper's primary role in retail environments is to: a) Clean the store b) Stock shelves c) Interact with and assist customers d) Manage inventory **Answer: c)**

35. Pepper's ability to personalize experiences for returning customers is based on: a) Their purchasing history b) Remembering their voice c) Their facial features d) Their preferred language **Answer: b)**

36. Which of the following is NOT a typical way Pepper interacts with customers? a) Answering questions b) Providing directions c) Physically carrying items d) Engaging in small talk **Answer: c)**

37. Pepper's emotion detection primarily aims to: a) Understand the content of the conversation b) Respond appropriately to the customer's feelings c) Identify the customer's age d) Track the customer's movement in the store **Answer: b)**

38. The success of Pepper in customer service relies on the effective integration of: a) Only hardware components b) Only software applications c) NLP, facial recognition, and emotion detection d) Only navigation and manipulation skills **Answer: c)**

39. Pepper's design emphasizes making it a robot that is: a) Intimidating and authoritative b) Efficient but not interactive c) Personable and approachable d) Strictly functional and task-oriented **Answer: c)**

40. When Pepper provides directions to a product, it demonstrates its understanding of: a) Customer demographics b) Store layout and product locations c) Real-time inventory levels d) Competitor pricing **Answer: b)**
41. Pepper's ability to remember returning customers through voice recognition contributes to: a) Faster processing speeds b) More efficient navigation c) Personalized customer experience d) Enhanced security features **Answer: c)**
42. The analysis of facial expressions by Pepper falls under the domain of: a) Natural Language Understanding b) Computer Vision c) Robotics Kinematics d) Sensor Fusion **Answer: b)**
43. Pepper's spoken responses are generated using: a) Speech recognition b) Syntactic parsing c) Semantic analysis d) Speech synthesis **Answer: d)**
44. The primary purpose of Pepper's emotion detection is to improve: a) The robot's movement efficiency b) The quality of human-robot interaction c) The accuracy of object recognition d) The speed of speech processing **Answer: b)**
45. Pepper's NLP capabilities allow it to handle: a) Only simple, direct commands b) A wider range of natural language queries c) Only pre-programmed phrases d) Only text-based interactions **Answer: b)**
46. Recognizing a returning customer by their voice is an example of: a) Object permanence b) Pattern recognition c) Emotional intelligence d) Spatial awareness **Answer: b)**
47. Pepper's ability to guide a customer demonstrates its understanding of: a) The customer's purchase history b) The physical environment of the store c) The customer's emotional state d) The robot's own battery level **Answer: b)**
48. The combination of NLP and emotion detection allows Pepper to engage in more _____ interactions. a) Robotic and formal b) Human-like and empathetic c) Efficient and transactional d) Simple and repetitive **Answer: b)**
49. Pepper's success in customer service highlights the growing importance of _____ in robotics. a) Physical strength b) Dexterous manipulation c) Human-robot interaction d) High-speed processing **Answer: c)**
50. By understanding and responding to human language and emotions, robots like Pepper are making technology feel more: a) Complex b) Mechanical c) Intuitive and accessible d) Distant and impersonal **Answer: c)**

Chapter 7: Neural Networks and Deep Learning

7.1 Leveraging Convolutional Neural Networks (CNNs) for Robotic Vision

Convolutional Neural Networks (CNNs) represent a specialized category of deep learning algorithms specifically engineered to process data with a grid-like structure, such as images, video sequences, and even time-series data. These networks have demonstrated exceptional capabilities in various computer vision tasks, including the classification of images, the detection of objects within images, and the generation of new image content. The architecture of CNNs incorporates unique layers that enable them to automatically learn hierarchical patterns from data, making them particularly well-suited for tasks like visual recognition in robotic systems.

The Operational Mechanism of CNNs:

CNNs process an input image by passing it through a sequence of distinct layers: convolutional layers, pooling layers, and fully connected layers. The function of each layer is as follows:

- **Convolutional Layer:** This layer forms the core of a CNN. It applies a set of learnable filters, also referred to as kernels, to the input image. These filters are small spatial weight matrices that slide across the width and height of the input image, performing a mathematical operation called convolution at each spatial location. This process allows the filters to detect local features present in the image, such as edges, textures, and color gradients. Each filter is specifically designed to respond strongly to certain types of patterns within the image. The output of a convolutional layer is a set of feature maps, where each map highlights the presence and spatial location of a specific feature detected by its corresponding filter.
- **Pooling Layer:** Following one or more convolutional layers, a pooling layer is often inserted to reduce the spatial dimensions (width and height) of the feature maps generated by the convolutional layer. This downsampling process helps to retain only the most salient information while discarding redundant details. Common pooling operations include **max pooling**, which selects the maximum value from a small rectangular region of the input feature map, and **average pooling**, which computes the average value. By reducing the spatial size of the feature maps, pooling layers contribute to reducing the computational complexity of the network and also help to make the learned features more invariant to small shifts and distortions in the input image, thereby mitigating overfitting.
- **Fully Connected Layer:** After the convolutional and pooling operations have extracted a hierarchy of features from the input image, the resulting feature maps are typically flattened into a one-dimensional vector. This vector is then fed into one or more fully connected layers, which are similar to the layers in traditional multi-layer perceptron neural networks. Each neuron in a fully connected layer is connected to all the neurons in the preceding layer. These layers learn high-level relationships between the extracted features and are responsible for making the final predictions, such as identifying the class of an object present in the image. The last fully connected layer usually has an output size

equal to the number of classes in the classification task, with each output neuron representing the probability of the input image belonging to a particular class.

Illustrative Application in Robotic Vision:

In a robotic vision system, CNNs can be effectively employed for the task of identifying various objects within the robot's operational environment. For instance, a robot equipped with a camera can utilize CNNs to recognize different objects such as chairs, tables, or human beings by analyzing the visual data captured by its camera. The CNN processes the incoming image through its convolutional layers, which automatically detect fundamental visual patterns like edges, corners, and basic shapes. Subsequently, the pooling layers downsample these feature maps, retaining the most critical information. Finally, the flattened feature maps are passed through the fully connected layers, which, based on the patterns learned during the training phase, determine the identity of the object present in the image.

This object recognition capability is crucial for enabling robots to perceive and understand their surroundings. By accurately identifying obstacles, recognizing specific objects of interest, and even distinguishing between different individuals, robots can make informed decisions based on visual input. For example, a robot navigating a cluttered environment can use a CNN to identify and avoid obstacles like chairs and tables. A robot interacting with humans can use a CNN to recognize specific individuals. In manufacturing, a robot can use CNNs to identify and manipulate different parts on an assembly line. The ability of CNNs to automatically extract relevant visual features and perform accurate classification makes them a powerful tool for endowing robots with sophisticated visual intelligence.

7.2 Processing Sequences: Recurrent Neural Networks (RNNs) in Robotics

Recurrent Neural Networks (RNNs) are a class of neural networks specifically designed to handle sequential data. In contrast to traditional feedforward neural networks, RNNs incorporate feedback loops that enable information to persist across time steps. This inherent memory capability makes them particularly well-suited for tasks where the order and temporal dependencies within the data are crucial. Consequently, RNNs find significant utility in areas such as natural language processing, speech recognition, and any robotic application where the sequence of data points carries important meaning.

The Operational Principles of RNNs:

RNNs function by passing information derived from previous elements in a sequence to the processing of subsequent elements. This creates a form of "memory" that allows the network to learn from the order and context of the data. This characteristic makes RNNs effective for tasks involving time-series prediction, the interpretation of spoken language, and the generation of sequential outputs.

- **The Looping Mechanism:** At the core of a basic RNN is a feedback loop. The output of the network at a specific time step is fed back as part of the input to the network at the subsequent time step. This recurrent connection allows the network to maintain a state that reflects information from earlier parts of the sequence, effectively enabling it to "remember" prior inputs and use this memory to influence the processing of the current input.
- **The Vanishing Gradient Problem:** Standard RNN architectures can encounter challenges when dealing with long sequences of data. During the training process, the gradients used to update the network's weights can diminish significantly as they are propagated backward through time across many time steps. This phenomenon, known as the vanishing gradient problem, can hinder the network's ability to learn long-range dependencies within the sequence. To address this limitation, more advanced and sophisticated RNN architectures have been developed, most notably Long Short-Term Memory (LSTM) networks and Gated Recurrent Units (GRUs). These advanced RNNs incorporate specialized mechanisms, such as memory cells and gating units, that help to preserve and propagate important information over extended sequences, thus mitigating the vanishing gradient problem.

Illustrative Applications in Robotics:

RNNs can be employed in various robotic tasks that involve processing sequential data:

- **Generating Robot Movement Sequences from Speech Commands:** Consider a robot instructed to perform a series of actions based on a natural language command, such as, "Pick up the red block, move it to the blue table, and then place it gently." An RNN can be used to process this sequential instruction. The RNN would analyze the command word by word or phrase by phrase, taking into account the order and relationships between the words. Based on its training, the RNN would then generate an appropriate sequence of motor commands for the robot to execute the desired actions in the correct order: first, identify and grasp the red block, then move its arm to the location of the blue table, and finally release the block.
- **Predictive Maintenance for Robots:** RNNs can also be valuable in applications like predictive maintenance for robotic systems. Robots are often equipped with various sensors that continuously monitor their operational status, generating time-series data on parameters such as motor current, temperature, vibration levels, and joint angles. An RNN can be trained on historical time-series data that includes patterns of normal operation as well as patterns leading to failures or the need for maintenance. By analyzing the current sensor data in a sequential manner, the RNN can learn to recognize subtle anomalies and predict when a robot component is likely to require maintenance in the future, based on the learned patterns of wear and tear over time. This allows for proactive scheduling of maintenance, reducing downtime and increasing the overall lifespan and reliability of the robotic system.

In both of these examples, the ability of RNNs to process sequential data and learn temporal dependencies is crucial for enabling the robot to perform complex tasks based on ordered inputs or to make predictions based on sequences of sensor readings. Their capacity to maintain a form of memory over time distinguishes them as a powerful tool for a wide range of sequential tasks in robotics.

7.3 Real-World Deployments: Neural Networks Driving Robotic Capabilities

Neural networks, encompassing both Convolutional Neural Networks (CNNs) and Recurrent Neural Networks (RNNs), have become indispensable components in a multitude of robotics applications, fundamentally transforming the abilities of robots across diverse industries.

Applications of CNNs in Robotics:

CNNs, with their proficiency in processing visual data, have enabled significant advancements in robotic perception and interaction with the physical world:

- **Object Detection and Grasping:** Robots equipped with CNNs can analyze the visual information captured by their cameras to detect and identify objects within their operational space. In sectors such as manufacturing and warehouse automation, this capability is crucial. Robots utilize CNNs to recognize objects based on their shape, orientation, and spatial location, enabling them to precisely pick up and manipulate these items. This allows for automated sorting, assembly, and material handling tasks with increased efficiency and accuracy.
  - **Example:** A robotic arm in a factory uses a CNN to identify different types of components on a conveyor belt. The CNN analyzes the camera images to locate and classify each part, allowing the robot to grasp the correct component with the appropriate orientation for the next stage of the assembly process.
- **Autonomous Vehicles:** A critical application of CNNs lies in the perception systems of autonomous vehicles. These networks process the continuous stream of images from the vehicle's cameras, enabling it to identify crucial elements of the driving environment, such as pedestrians, traffic signs, other vehicles, lane markings, and obstacles on the road. This real-time visual understanding allows the autonomous vehicle to navigate complex environments, make informed driving decisions, and react safely to dynamic situations.
  - **Example:** The camera system of a self-driving car employs CNNs to analyze the video feed. The CNN can identify a pedestrian crossing the street, recognize a stop sign, and detect the presence and movement of other vehicles, allowing the car's control system to adjust its speed and trajectory accordingly.

Applications of RNNs in Robotics:

RNNs, with their ability to process sequential data, have empowered robots with enhanced capabilities in understanding and generating sequences, making them valuable in tasks involving language and predictive modeling:

- **Speech Recognition and Interaction:** In the domain of human-robot interaction, RNNs are frequently employed for speech recognition. This enables robots to understand spoken commands issued by humans and generate appropriate responses. The recurrent nature of RNNs allows them to process speech input as a sequence of sounds, maintaining context over the duration of a conversation. This contextual understanding significantly improves the robot's ability to engage with humans in a more natural and coherent manner.
    - **Example:** A social robot uses an RNN-based speech recognition system to understand a user's request, such as "Please tell me the news headlines." The RNN processes the sequence of spoken words, understands the user's intent, and then generates a spoken summary of the current news using a text-to-speech system.
- **Sequence Generation:** RNNs are also utilized in robotics for task planning and decision-making processes that involve generating a sequence of actions. For instance, in a robotic assembly line, an RNN can be trained to determine the optimal sequence of operations required to complete a specific assembly task. This might involve planning the order in which different parts need to be moved and assembled, or the step-by-step execution of a complex manipulation task.
    - **Example:** A robot assembling a product might use an RNN to plan the sequence of movements for its arm and end-effector. Based on the final product design, the RNN generates a series of joint angle commands that allow the robot to pick up parts in the correct order and perform the necessary assembly actions sequentially.
- **Behavior Prediction:** Robots can leverage RNNs to predict the future actions of humans based on observations of their past behavior as a sequence of movements. This predictive capability is particularly beneficial for improving collaboration between humans and robots in shared workspaces. By anticipating where a person is likely to move or what action they might take next, the robot can adjust its own movements and actions proactively to work alongside humans more safely and efficiently.
    - **Example:** A collaborative robot working with a human on an assembly task observes the human's hand movements using its sensors. An RNN trained on human motion data can predict the likely next step the human will take, allowing the robot to anticipate and prepare to assist with the subsequent part of the assembly process without causing collisions or delays.

Conclusion:

Neural networks, particularly CNNs and RNNs, are fundamental in empowering robots to perform a wide array of complex tasks. CNNs excel in analyzing visual information, enabling robots to "see" and comprehend their surroundings. RNNs, on the other hand, are adept at processing sequential data, facilitating capabilities like speech understanding and the generation of ordered actions. The synergistic integration of these deep learning techniques allows robots to not only interpret sensory input but also to make intelligent decisions, plan effective actions, and interact meaningfully with both their environment and the humans they encounter. As deep learning continues to advance, robots are becoming increasingly autonomous, efficient, and capable of tackling an ever-expanding range of applications across various industries.

45 MCQs with answers on Chapter 7: Neural Networks and Deep Learning.

7.1 CNNs for Vision

1. **What is the primary purpose of a Convolutional Neural Network (CNN)?**
   - o a) To perform image classification
   - o b) To handle sequential data
   - o c) To generate speech
   - o d) To train reinforcement learning agents
   - o **Answer:** a) To perform image classification
2. **Which layer of a CNN is responsible for reducing the spatial dimensions of the data?**
   - o a) Convolutional layer
   - o b) Fully connected layer
   - o c) Pooling layer
   - o d) ReLU layer
   - o **Answer:** c) Pooling layer
3. **Which of the following is NOT a typical operation performed in the convolutional layer of a CNN?**
   - o a) Feature extraction
   - o b) Weight sharing
   - o c) Spatial down-sampling
   - o d) Fully connected calculations
   - o **Answer:** d) Fully connected calculations
4. **What is the role of the activation function, such as ReLU, in a CNN?**
   - o a) To reduce overfitting
   - o b) To introduce non-linearity
   - o c) To optimize the model
   - o d) To increase computational speed
   - o **Answer:** b) To introduce non-linearity
5. **Which type of CNN layer is typically used to detect edges and textures in an image?**
   - o a) Pooling layer
   - o b) Convolutional layer
   - o c) Fully connected layer
   - o d) Dropout layer
   - o **Answer:** b) Convolutional layer
6. **In a CNN, what does the "filter" or "kernel" do?**
   - o a) Reduces the size of the image
   - o b) Performs a convolution operation to detect features
   - o c) Normalizes the image data
   - o d) Ensures faster training time
   - o **Answer:** b) Performs a convolution operation to detect features
7. **Which of the following is a common use of CNNs in robotics?**
   - o a) Object recognition
   - o b) Speech synthesis
   - o c) Predicting next actions

- o d) Reinforcement learning
- o **Answer:** a) Object recognition

8. **What is the typical outcome of the final layer in a CNN used for classification tasks?**
   - o a) A vector of class probabilities
   - o b) The original image
   - o c) A continuous value for regression
   - o d) The feature map of the image
   - o **Answer:** a) A vector of class probabilities

9. **Which CNN architecture is known for its success in image classification tasks?**
   - o a) ResNet
   - o b) AlexNet
   - o c) InceptionNet
   - o d) All of the above
   - o **Answer:** d) All of the above

10. **Which CNN technique helps reduce overfitting by randomly setting certain neuron outputs to zero during training?**
    - o a) Convolution
    - o b) Pooling
    - o c) Dropout
    - o d) Batch normalization
    - o **Answer:** c) Dropout

7.2 RNNs for Sequential Tasks

11. **What is the key feature of a Recurrent Neural Network (RNN) compared to a traditional neural network?**

- a) The ability to process sequential data
- b) The ability to handle large image data
- c) The ability to operate without data dependencies
- d) The ability to process unstructured data
- **Answer:** a) The ability to process sequential data

12. **Which problem is commonly faced when training long RNNs?**

- a) Vanishing gradient problem
- b) Overfitting
- c) Lack of data
- d) Data imbalance
- **Answer:** a) Vanishing gradient problem

13. **What modification to RNNs helps mitigate the vanishing gradient problem?**

- a) Using CNNs

- b) Using LSTM (Long Short-Term Memory) cells
- c) Using pooling layers
- d) Using dropout
- **Answer:** b) Using LSTM (Long Short-Term Memory) cells

14. **Which of the following is NOT an application of RNNs?**

- a) Speech recognition
- b) Time-series prediction
- c) Image classification
- d) Language translation
- **Answer:** c) Image classification

15. **What does an RNN typically use from the previous time steps to process the current time step?**

- a) External data
- b) Hidden state or memory
- c) A different set of weights
- d) A random input
- **Answer:** b) Hidden state or memory

16. **Which of the following RNN architectures is best suited for long-term memory?**

- a) Vanilla RNN
- b) LSTM
- c) GRU (Gated Recurrent Units)
- d) All of the above
- **Answer:** b) LSTM

17. **In an RNN, what is the purpose of the "hidden state"?**

- a) To store the final output
- b) To keep track of important information over time
- c) To preprocess the data
- d) To act as a filter for input data
- **Answer:** b) To keep track of important information over time

18. **Which of the following tasks could benefit from an RNN's ability to maintain context over time?**

- a) Sorting an image dataset
- b) Translating a sentence from one language to another
- c) Predicting the future stock prices without historical data
- d) Running image classification
- **Answer:** b) Translating a sentence from one language to another

19. **Which RNN-based model is commonly used for speech-to-text systems?**

- a) CNN
- b) LSTM
- c) GAN
- d) Autoencoder
- **Answer:** b) LSTM

20. **What is a common application of RNNs in robotics?**

- a) Object detection
- b) Motion planning
- c) Language understanding
- d) All of the above
- **Answer:** c) Language understanding

7.3 Robotics Applications

21. **Which neural network model is primarily used for processing images in robotics?**

- a) RNN
- b) CNN
- c) LSTM
- d) GAN
- **Answer:** b) CNN

22. **What is the role of neural networks in autonomous robots?**

- a) Image classification
- b) Decision-making based on sensory input
- c) Motion planning and control
- d) All of the above
- **Answer:** d) All of the above

23. **Which robot is an example of a robot using deep learning for vision tasks?**

- a) Baxter
- b) Pepper
- c) Boston Dynamics' Spot
- d) KUKA industrial robots
- **Answer:** c) Boston Dynamics' Spot

24. **In industrial robotics, neural networks help robots in:**

- a) Detecting objects
- b) Picking up objects
- c) Navigating complex environments
- d) All of the above
- **Answer:** d) All of the above

25. **In a robot that needs to learn a task from a human demonstration, which type of neural network is most commonly used?**

- a) CNN
- b) RNN
- c) LSTM
- d) Deep Reinforcement Learning (DRL)
- **Answer:** d) Deep Reinforcement Learning (DRL)

26. **Which of the following is NOT a real-world application of neural networks in robotics?**

- a) Facial recognition in social robots
- b) Object detection and tracking in autonomous vehicles
- c) Predicting the future price of cryptocurrencies
- d) Gesture control in human-robot interaction
- **Answer:** c) Predicting the future price of cryptocurrencies

27. **Which architecture is commonly used in robots for decision-making tasks?**

- a) CNN
- b) RNN
- c) DQN (Deep Q-Network)
- d) LSTM
- **Answer:** c) DQN (Deep Q-Network)

28. **Which of the following allows robots to interact with humans using natural language?**

- a) LSTM networks
- b) CNNs
- c) RNNs with attention mechanisms
- d) GANs
- **Answer:** c) RNNs with attention mechanisms

29. **Which deep learning technique is used in reinforcement learning for robotics?**

- a) Convolutional Neural Networks (CNNs)
- b) Generative Adversarial Networks (GANs)
- c) Q-Learning with Deep Neural Networks

- d) Long Short-Term Memory (LSTM)
- **Answer:** c) Q-Learning with Deep Neural Networks

30. Which type of neural network can enable robots to recognize speech commands?

- a) CNN
- b) RNN
- c) GAN
- d) LSTM
- **Answer:** b) RNN

---

31. Which deep learning model is most effective for motion planning in robotics?

- a) RNN
- b) CNN
- c) Deep Reinforcement Learning
- d) SVM
- **Answer:** c) Deep Reinforcement Learning

32. In a robot vision system, which technique is primarily used for detecting specific objects in images?

- a) Convolutional Neural Networks (CNNs)
- b) Recurrent Neural Networks (RNNs)
- c) Deep Q-Networks (DQN)
- d) Long Short-Term Memory (LSTM)
- **Answer:** a) Convolutional Neural Networks (CNNs)

33. Which of the following is an important feature of neural networks in autonomous vehicles?

- a) Predicting vehicle speed
- b) Object detection for navigation
- c) Reading road signs and interpreting traffic signals
- d) All of the above
- **Answer:** d) All of the above

34. Neural networks are crucial for robots working in dynamic environments because they enable:

- a) Real-time decision making
- b) Static programming
- c) Handling repetitive tasks
- d) Predictive text generation

- **Answer:** a) Real-time decision making

35. Which neural network architecture is designed for processing spatial data, especially in images?

- a) Recurrent Neural Networks (RNNs)
- b) Generative Adversarial Networks (GANs)
- c) Convolutional Neural Networks (CNNs)
- d) Support Vector Machines (SVMs)
- **Answer:** c) Convolutional Neural Networks (CNNs)

36. Which neural network architecture is most appropriate for sequence generation in robotics?

- a) CNN
- b) RNN
- c) LSTM
- d) GAN
- **Answer:** b) RNN

37. Which type of neural network is mainly used for solving tasks that involve long-term dependencies in sequences?

- a) CNN
- b) RNN
- c) LSTM
- d) GAN
- **Answer:** c) LSTM

38. Which of the following is a task that requires reinforcement learning in robotics?

- a) Object detection
- b) Motion control
- c) Language understanding
- d) Classification of images
- **Answer:** b) Motion control

39. Which deep learning approach is often used in autonomous robots for learning from exploration?

- a) Supervised learning
- b) Unsupervised learning
- c) Reinforcement learning
- d) Transfer learning

- **Answer:** c) Reinforcement learning

40. What does "training" a neural network in robotics typically involve?

- a) Teaching the robot to process sensor data
- b) Collecting large datasets to train models
- c) Implementing programming logic
- d) None of the above
- **Answer:** b) Collecting large datasets to train models

41. Which neural network method is often used in robotics for language processing and human-robot interaction?

- a) RNN with attention mechanism
- b) GAN
- c) CNN with spatial analysis
- d) Deep Q-Network (DQN)
- **Answer:** a) RNN with attention mechanism

42. Which network is typically used for generating 3D models or environments in robotics?

- a) GAN
- b) CNN
- c) LSTM
- d) RNN
- **Answer:** a) GAN

43. Which of the following is the major benefit of using neural networks in industrial robots?

- a) Flexibility to adapt to new tasks
- b) High-speed computation
- c) Reduced energy consumption
- d) Faster object recognition
- **Answer:** a) Flexibility to adapt to new tasks

44. What is the key advantage of using reinforcement learning in robotic systems?

- a) Ability to recognize images
- b) Ability to make decisions based on rewards and penalties
- c) Ability to control motion planning directly
- d) Ability to generate speech
- **Answer:** b) Ability to make decisions based on rewards and penalties

45. Which neural network method helps robots in predicting human actions and movements?

- a) CNN
- b) RNN
- c) Deep Q-Network
- d) GAN
- **Answer:** b) RNN

Chapter 8: Reinforcement Learning and Decision Making

8.1 Learning Through Exploration: The Trial-and-Error Approach

Trial-and-error learning describes a fundamental process by which an intelligent agent acquires knowledge and skills through direct interaction with its environment. In this paradigm, the agent lacks prior understanding of the consequences associated with its potential actions and must actively explore various choices to discover which ones lead to the most favorable outcomes. This method of learning forms the bedrock of reinforcement learning, where agents progressively refine their behavioral strategies over time based on the experiences gained.

Illustrative Scenario:

Consider a robotic agent tasked with navigating an unknown maze. The robot does not possess a map or any pre-programmed instructions on how to reach the exit. Consequently, it begins by attempting different paths and movements within the maze. Initially, its actions might be random, leading it into dead ends or causing collisions with walls. However, as the robot continues its exploration, it learns from each experience. Successful movements that lead it closer to the exit can be designated as positive outcomes, providing a form of "reward." Conversely, actions that result in hitting a wall or entering a dead end can be considered negative outcomes, imposing a form of "penalty." Over numerous attempts, the robot gradually adjusts its decision-making process, favoring actions that have historically yielded positive rewards and avoiding those associated with penalties. Through this accumulation of experience, the robot becomes increasingly adept at finding the solution to the maze, demonstrating a refined and efficient navigation strategy.

Diagrammatic Representation:

The following diagram illustrates the iterative process of trial-and-error learning. The agent initiates an action, which results in a transition to a new state within the environment. Associated with this transition is a reward signal that provides feedback on the outcome of the action. This reward then informs the agent's future decisions, influencing its selection of actions in subsequent interactions with the environment.

```
[Initial State] --> [Action Option 1] --> [Resulting State 1] -->
[Reward/Penalty]
                  ↘
                    --> [Action Option 2] --> [Resulting State 2] -->
[Reward/Penalty]
                  ↘
                    --> [Action Option 3] --> [Resulting State 3] -->
[Reward/Penalty]
```

Each time the agent undertakes an action, it transitions to a subsequent state in the environment and receives feedback in the form of rewards or penalties that are directly linked to the consequences of that action. Across multiple interactions and iterations, the agent progressively refines its internal decision-making process based on the accumulated knowledge derived from these rewards and penalties, learning to associate specific actions with their likely outcomes in different situations.

8.2 Formalizing Decision-Making: Markov Decision Processes (MDPs)

Markov Decision Processes (MDPs) provide a mathematical framework for modeling sequential decision-making in environments where the outcomes of an agent's actions are partly probabilistic and partly under its control. An MDP is formally defined by a tuple of five elements:

- **States (S):** This represents the complete set of all possible situations or configurations that the agent can find itself in within the environment. Each distinct arrangement or condition the agent can experience is considered a unique state.
- **Actions (A):** This is the set of all possible actions that the agent can take when it is in a particular state. The available actions might vary depending on the current state of the agent and the environment.
- **Transition Function (T):** This function defines the dynamics of the environment by specifying the probability of transitioning from one state to another when the agent takes a specific action in a given state. It essentially describes how the environment will evolve as a consequence of the agent's choices. The transition function is often denoted as $T(s'|s,a)=P(S_{t+1}=s'|S_t=s,A_t=a)$, which represents the probability of ending up in state s' at time $t+1$, given that the agent was in state s at time t and took action a at that time.
- **Rewards (R):** This function specifies the immediate reward that the agent receives after transitioning from one state to another as a direct result of taking a particular action. The reward signal provides feedback to the agent about the desirability of its actions and the resulting states. The reward function can be denoted as $R(s,a,s')$, representing the reward received for transitioning from state s to state s' after taking action a.
- **Discount Factor (γ):** This value, typically between 0 and 1 (i.e., $0 \leq \gamma \leq 1$), represents the agent's preference for immediate rewards versus future rewards. A discount factor closer to 0 makes the agent more focused on immediate gains, while a value closer to 1 makes it consider long-term rewards more significantly. It essentially determines the present value of future rewards.

Illustrative Scenario: Navigating a Grid World

Consider an intelligent agent situated in a grid-based environment. The agent's objective is to navigate from a designated starting position to a predefined goal position. Each cell within the grid represents a distinct state (S) that the agent can occupy. From any given non-terminal state, the agent can choose to perform one of four possible actions (A): move up, move down, move left, or move right (assuming no boundaries restrict these movements).

After each attempted move (action), the agent transitions to a new state (an adjacent cell in the grid). The **transition function (T)** in this case would typically be deterministic, meaning that if the agent chooses to move up from a certain cell, it will reliably end up in the cell directly above it (unless there's a boundary or obstacle).

Upon reaching a new state, the agent receives a **reward (R)**. For instance, reaching the goal position might yield a positive reward of +1. Colliding with an obstacle within the grid might result in a negative reward or penalty of -1. For all other normal movements between adjacent cells that do not lead to the goal or an obstacle, the agent might receive a neutral reward of 0.

In this scenario, the agent's ultimate goal is to learn a sequence of actions that maximizes its **cumulative reward** over time, effectively finding a path from the start to the goal while avoiding obstacles. The agent utilizes its knowledge of how its actions cause transitions between states (the transition function) and the immediate rewards associated with these transitions to make informed decisions about which action to take in each state. By considering the **discount factor (γ)**, the agent can weigh the immediate rewards of its actions against the potential for future rewards obtained by reaching the goal. The MDP framework provides the mathematical tools for the agent to analyze this environment and determine an optimal policy, which specifies the best action to take in each state to achieve its objective.

Diagrammatic Representation:

The following simplified MDP diagram illustrates a small segment of the grid-world scenario:

```
[Start State] --(Action: Right)--> [Intermediate State A] --(Action: Up)-->
[Goal State] (Reward: +1)
                        ↘
                  --(Action: Down)--> [Intermediate State B] --(Action:
Left)--> [Obstacle State] (Reward: -1)
```

Each arrow in this diagram represents a possible action that the agent can take from a particular state, leading to a subsequent state. The label on the arrow indicates the action performed, and the state it points to is the resulting state after the transition. The reward associated with reaching the "Goal State" and the "Obstacle State" is explicitly indicated. The agent's task within the MDP framework is to learn a strategy (a policy) that dictates which action to choose in each state to maximize its overall accumulated reward, taking into account the transition probabilities and the discount factor.

8.3 Enabling Independent Movement: Autonomous Navigation and Planning

Autonomous navigation and planning refer to the capabilities of intelligent agents, such as robots, drones, or autonomous vehicles, to move through their environments and determine the most effective paths from an initial location to a desired destination. This process involves utilizing reinforcement learning and decision-making frameworks, such as Markov Decision

Processes (MDPs), to enable these agents to navigate while avoiding obstacles and achieving their goals efficiently.

Within the context of reinforcement learning, autonomous navigation typically employs the principles of trial-and-error learning and MDPs to address the challenge of identifying the optimal route within a given environment. The agent must consider a multitude of factors relevant to its navigation task, including environmental conditions, the presence of obstacles, and even governing rules or constraints, to inform its decision-making process.

Illustrative Scenario:

Consider an autonomous vehicle operating on urban roadways. The vehicle's objective is to navigate complex scenarios, including intersections, pedestrian crossings, adherence to traffic signals, and ultimately reaching a specified destination. To achieve this, the vehicle is equipped with various sensors that provide real-time information about its surroundings. Based on the data gathered from these sensors, the vehicle must make continuous decisions regarding its movement.

The vehicle's decision-making process can be modeled using the components of an MDP:

- **States (S):** The vehicle's current location, speed, and the surrounding traffic conditions represent the state of the system at any given time.
- **Actions (A):** The actions available to the vehicle include accelerating, decelerating, steering left, steering right, stopping, and proceeding straight.
- **Rewards (R):** The vehicle receives positive rewards for making progress towards its destination in a timely manner and adhering to traffic regulations. Conversely, it receives negative rewards or penalties for actions that lead to collisions with obstacles (e.g., pedestrians, other vehicles, static objects) or violations of traffic laws (e.g., running a red light, exceeding speed limits).

Through continuous interaction with the dynamic environment, the autonomous vehicle employs reinforcement learning algorithms to learn which actions, taken in specific states, lead to better overall outcomes (i.e., maximizing the cumulative reward). Over time, the vehicle refines its control policies, adjusting its behavior to navigate efficiently, safely, and in compliance with traffic rules.

Diagrammatic Representation:

The process of autonomous navigation can be conceptualized as a Markov Decision Process, as illustrated below:

```
[Start Location] --(Action: Proceed Straight)--> [Intersection Approach] --
(Action: Turn Left)--> [Destination Reached] (Positive Reward)
                     ↘
                     --(Action: Apply Brakes)--> [Obstacle Encountered]
(Negative Reward)
```

In this simplified representation, the agent (autonomous vehicle) transitions from one state (e.g., its current location or a specific situation like approaching an intersection) to another based on the actions it chooses to take. The agent receives rewards or penalties based on the consequences of its actions at each step. For example, successfully navigating an intersection and progressing towards the goal yields a positive reward, while encountering an obstacle due to an incorrect action results in a negative reward. This continuous process of taking actions, observing the resulting states, and receiving feedback in the form of rewards enables the agent to learn the optimal sequence of actions required to reach its destination efficiently and safely.

Summary

Reinforcement learning empowers agents to learn from interaction, enabling them to make decisions that maximize long-term rewards. By using trial-and-error learning and frameworks like Markov Decision Processes (MDPs), agents can solve complex decision-making problems such as autonomous navigation. Whether it's a robot exploring a maze, a car driving through a city, or a drone flying through a field, reinforcement learning provides the foundation for decision-making in uncertain environments.

45 multiple-choice questions (MCQs) with answers covering the topics of Trial-and-Error Learning, Markov Decision Processes (MDPs), and Autonomous Navigation and Planning:

8.1 Trial-and-Error Learning

1. **What is the main concept behind trial-and-error learning?**
   - a) Learning through predefined rules
   - b) Learning by receiving feedback from actions
   - c) Learning through observation
   - d) Learning from fixed data
   - **Answer: b**
2. **In trial-and-error learning, which of the following is a key component?**
   - a) Repetition without feedback
   - b) Learning from experience and feedback
   - c) Random actions without any goal
   - d) Learning from others' experiences
   - **Answer: b**
3. **Which type of machine learning is trial-and-error learning most related to?**
   - a) Supervised learning
   - b) Unsupervised learning
   - c) Reinforcement learning
   - d) Semi-supervised learning
   - **Answer: c**
4. **What is the role of rewards in trial-and-error learning?**
   - a) They act as punishments for bad actions

- o b) They encourage exploration and optimal decision-making
- o c) They act as signals for future learning
- o d) They replace actions completely
- o **Answer: b**

5. **Trial-and-error learning is most effective in which kind of tasks?**
   - o a) Tasks that require immediate feedback
   - o b) Tasks that have predefined actions
   - o c) Tasks with high predictability
   - o d) Tasks that involve no learning
   - o **Answer: a**

6. **Which of the following is an example of trial-and-error learning?**
   - o a) A student reading textbooks
   - o b) A robot learning to navigate a maze by making mistakes
   - o c) A teacher explaining concepts
   - o d) A machine executing a fixed program
   - o **Answer: b**

7. **In trial-and-error learning, what happens after the agent makes a mistake?**
   - o a) The agent receives feedback and adjusts its behavior
   - o b) The agent continues to make the same mistake
   - o c) The agent forgets the mistake and repeats actions
   - o d) The agent gets no feedback
   - o **Answer: a**

8. **Trial-and-error learning in robotics typically involves:**
   - o a) Controlled environments only
   - o b) Random actions without consequences
   - o c) Gradual improvement based on outcomes
   - o d) Instantaneous perfect performance
   - o **Answer: c**

9. **Which of the following is a challenge of trial-and-error learning?**
   - o a) Slow exploration and learning
   - o b) Excessive learning speed
   - o c) Immediate feedback
   - o d) Lack of exploration
   - o **Answer: a**

10. **Trial-and-error learning is particularly useful for:**
    - o a) Theoretical tasks
    - o b) Tasks with uncertain outcomes
    - o c) Tasks with predictable results
    - o d) Simple tasks with fixed actions
    - o **Answer: b**

8.2 Markov Decision Processes (MDPs)

11. **What does a Markov Decision Process (MDP) model?**

- o a) The best decision based on past experience
- o b) The actions of agents in a deterministic environment
- o c) Decision-making in environments with uncertainty and rewards
- o d) Task automation in fixed scenarios
- o **Answer: c**

12. **Which of the following is a component of an MDP?**
    - o a) States, actions, rewards, and transitions
    - o b) Only rewards and transitions
    - o c) Only states and actions
    - o d) Actions and goals only
    - o **Answer: a**

13. **What does the 'state' in MDP represent?**
    - o a) The action taken by the agent
    - o b) The result of a particular action
    - o c) The environment or condition the agent is in
    - o d) The agent's future predictions
    - o **Answer: c**

14. **In an MDP, the transition function describes:**
    - o a) The possible rewards from a state
    - o b) The probability of moving between states based on actions
    - o c) The cost of actions
    - o d) The final goal state
    - o **Answer: b**

15. **What is the reward function in an MDP used for?**
    - o a) To calculate the transition probabilities
    - o b) To evaluate how good a state-action pair is
    - o c) To define the states
    - o d) To predict the agent's future actions
    - o **Answer: b**

16. **The discount factor in MDPs determines:**
    - o a) The value of current rewards relative to future rewards
    - o b) The discount on actions
    - o c) The transition between states
    - o d) The termination of learning
    - o **Answer: a**

17. **What is the primary objective of an agent in an MDP?**
    - o a) To maximize its actions
    - o b) To minimize transition probabilities
    - o c) To maximize cumulative rewards over time
    - o d) To ignore the rewards and focus on state transitions
    - o **Answer: c**

18. **Markov Property in MDP means:**
    - o a) The future state depends only on the current state, not past states
    - o b) The rewards are fixed for all states
    - o c) The actions are random and independent of the state
    - o d) The environment does not change over time

- o **Answer: a**

19. **Which of the following is true for an MDP with a deterministic environment?**
    - o a) Transition probabilities are not relevant
    - o b) Each action will always lead to the same state
    - o c) There are multiple possible rewards for each state
    - o d) The agent does not need to learn
    - o **Answer: b**

20. **What is the purpose of solving an MDP?**
    - o a) To maximize random actions
    - o b) To find the optimal policy for decision-making
    - o c) To reduce the number of states
    - o d) To increase computational complexity
    - o **Answer: b**

8.3 Autonomous Navigation and Planning

21. **Autonomous navigation refers to:**
    - o a) The ability of a robot to make decisions without human control
    - o b) The robot's ability to avoid obstacles
    - o c) The ability of a robot to follow predefined paths
    - o d) The ability of a robot to communicate with humans
    - o **Answer: a**

22. **Which of the following is NOT typically a goal of autonomous navigation?**
    - o a) Avoid obstacles
    - o b) Follow a specific path
    - o c) Maximize reward without feedback
    - o d) Reach a destination autonomously
    - o **Answer: c**

23. **Which of the following can be used in autonomous navigation to detect obstacles?**
    - o a) Cameras
    - o b) Lidar sensors
    - o c) Ultrasonic sensors
    - o d) All of the above
    - o **Answer: d**

24. **In autonomous navigation, the planning phase involves:**
    - o a) Deciding the optimal actions to take at each step
    - o b) Testing the system's reliability
    - o c) Collecting feedback from the environment
    - o d) Choosing random actions
    - o **Answer: a**

25. **Which of the following techniques is commonly used for path planning in autonomous systems?**
    - o a) Linear regression
    - o b) Dynamic programming

- o c) Genetic algorithms
- o d) Reinforcement learning
- o **Answer: b**

26. **Which environment condition is NOT typically considered in autonomous navigation?**
    - o a) Road conditions
    - o b) Environmental lighting
    - o c) Weather patterns
    - o d) Complete predictability of future events
    - o **Answer: d**

27. **Which type of sensor is commonly used in robots for obstacle detection during navigation?**
    - o a) GPS
    - o b) Lidar
    - o c) Thermal sensors
    - o d) Temperature sensors
    - o **Answer: b**

28. **Autonomous navigation relies heavily on:**
    - o a) Predefined routes only
    - o b) Real-time environmental perception and decision-making
    - o c) Simple task-based programming
    - o d) Random exploration
    - o **Answer: b**

29. **A robot learns the best path to navigate a maze using:**
    - o a) Dynamic pathfinding algorithms
    - o b) Repetitive looping without feedback
    - o c) Predefined static maps
    - o d) Fixed rules without interaction
    - o **Answer: a**

30. **Autonomous navigation systems can use which of the following approaches for decision-making?**
    - o a) Only supervised learning
    - o b) Rule-based decision-making
    - o c) Reinforcement learning
    - o d) Neural networks only
    - o **Answer: c**

31. **Markov Decision Processes (MDPs) are useful in autonomous navigation because they allow the agent to:**
    - o a) Precompute all possible actions
    - o b) Learn optimal actions based on rewards
    - o c) Avoid future predictions
    - o d) Always choose random actions
    - o **Answer: b**

32. **Which of the following is true regarding autonomous vehicles?**
    - o a) They are fully predictable with no uncertainties
    - o b) They cannot learn from past experiences

- c) They use a combination of sensors and decision-making algorithms
- d) They do not require navigation systems
- Answer: c

33. **In autonomous planning, what is the purpose of the reward function?**
    - a) To reduce the path cost
    - b) To measure how well an action leads to a desirable state
    - c) To perform random actions
    - d) To avoid obstacle collisions
    - Answer: b

34. **In autonomous systems, a robot's ability to make decisions based on previous experiences is known as:**
    - a) Supervised learning
    - b) Reinforcement learning
    - c) Unsupervised learning
    - d) Knowledge-based reasoning
    - Answer: b

35. **Which of the following is an essential part of autonomous navigation systems?**
    - a) Predefined maps
    - b) Environment perception and real-time decision-making
    - c) Pre-programmed actions
    - d) Random movement
    - Answer: b

36. **Autonomous planning requires the robot to consider:**
    - a) Only a fixed path
    - b) Dynamic interactions with its environment
    - c) Predefined obstacles only
    - d) None of the above
    - Answer: b

37. **Which of the following methods is used to improve autonomous navigation in real-time environments?**
    - a) Static decision-making
    - b) Dynamic adjustments based on environmental feedback
    - c) Pre-recorded training data only
    - d) Use of random actions
    - Answer: b

38. **In autonomous navigation, which factor is critical for decision-making?**
    - a) Random guessing
    - b) Experience with previous actions and rewards
    - c) Ignoring past failures
    - d) Predictable states
    - Answer: b

39. **In autonomous navigation, which of the following is used to calculate optimal actions?**
    - a) Static maps and fixed rules
    - b) Reward-based learning algorithms
    - c) Random decisions

- o d) Feedback loops
- o **Answer: b**
40. **Autonomous planning algorithms typically seek to:**
   - o a) Maximize immediate rewards only
   - o b) Find the shortest possible path
   - o c) Minimize the possibility of failure
   - o d) Minimize the learning process
   - o **Answer: b**

General Answers to MCQs

41. **What is the key benefit of reinforcement learning in autonomous navigation?**
   - o a) It allows the system to learn from past experiences
   - o b) It reduces the number of sensors required
   - o c) It guarantees success on the first try
   - o d) It eliminates the need for environment feedback
   - o **Answer: a**
42. **What does trial-and-error learning enable in autonomous systems?**
   - o a) Complete certainty about outcomes
   - o b) Ability to learn optimal actions through experience
   - o c) Immediate perfection in navigation
   - o d) Complete reliance on human guidance
   - o **Answer: b**
43. **In reinforcement learning, which process helps the robot decide between actions?**
   - o a) Random exploration
   - o b) Trial-and-error experience
   - o c) Decision trees
   - o d) Fixed reward system
   - o **Answer: b**
44. **Which framework is commonly used in autonomous vehicle navigation?**
   - o a) Markov Decision Processes
   - o b) Support Vector Machines
   - o c) Unsupervised learning
   - o d) Reinforcement learning
   - o **Answer: a**
45. **Which of the following best describes the transition function in an MDP?**
   - o a) A function that generates random rewards
   - o b) A function that determines state changes based on actions
   - o c) A function that initializes the environment
   - o d) A function that stores all possible actions
   - o **Answer: b**

Chapter 9: Industrial Robotics

9.1 The Apex of Manufacturing Intelligence: Deep Dive into Smart Factories

A smart factory signifies a paradigm shift in the landscape of manufacturing, moving beyond conventional automation towards a holistic ecosystem where interconnected systems, sophisticated data exchange mechanisms, and a suite of intelligent technologies operate in seamless synergy. The primary objective of this advanced manufacturing paradigm is to achieve unprecedented levels of productivity, operational efficiency, and stringent quality control across all stages of the production lifecycle. These future-forward facilities are characterized by a comprehensive integration of interconnected machinery and software systems, the pervasive application of Artificial Intelligence (AI) and Machine Learning (ML) algorithms, and the strategic deployment of advanced robotics. This confluence of technologies culminates in the creation of a highly adaptive, responsive, and self-optimizing production environment capable of meeting the dynamic demands of modern industry.

At the very core of a smart factory's intricate operational framework lies the **Internet of Things (IoT)**. The IoT serves as the critical nervous system, establishing a robust network that enables a vast and diverse array of physical devices, embedded sensors, industrial machines, and software applications to communicate and interact with one another over the internet. This pervasive connectivity facilitates the continuous and instantaneous sharing of real-time operational data across the entire manufacturing value chain. This wealth of information is then leveraged to gain deep insights into operational performance, identify areas for improvement, and ultimately drive optimization. Through the IoT infrastructure, intelligent machines acquire the ability to autonomously detect anomalies, predict potential failures, meticulously track the progress and status of production processes, continuously monitor crucial environmental parameters (such as temperature, humidity, and air quality), and dynamically adjust their operational parameters and processes in direct response to the real-time data they collect. This level of autonomous decision-making and process adaptation is a hallmark of the smart factory concept.

In the context of a smart factory, robots transcend their traditional role as isolated automation units performing repetitive tasks. Instead, they evolve into highly sophisticated and intelligent agents, equipped with a rich array of advanced sensors (including force sensors, proximity sensors, and tactile sensors), high-resolution cameras with advanced image processing capabilities, and powerful AI algorithms. This sophisticated sensory apparatus and cognitive processing power enable robots to collaborate seamlessly and safely with human workers, fostering a synergistic partnership that leverages the unique strengths of both humans and machines. The deep integration of advanced robotics within smart factories leads to a significant reduction in human-induced errors, which are often associated with fatigue or monotony, and a marked enhancement in the precision and consistency of manufacturing processes, particularly for intricate and delicate tasks. For instance, highly dexterous robotic arms deployed in a smart factory can perform complex assembly operations with unparalleled accuracy and speed. Furthermore, their integrated vision systems, powered by AI, enable them to meticulously inspect manufactured components for even the most minute flaws or deviations from quality standards. Based on the data acquired during these inspections, the robots can, in many cases, autonomously make real-time adjustments to the upstream manufacturing processes to rectify any detected imperfections, ensuring a consistently high level of product quality.

Illustrative Scenario: The Smart Automotive Manufacturing Plant

To vividly illustrate the principles of a smart factory in action, let us delve into a detailed scenario within the automotive industry. Consider a state-of-the-art automotive manufacturing plant that has fully embraced the smart factory paradigm. Within this facility, advanced robotic arms play a pivotal role in the critical process of welding together various components of car bodies. These sophisticated robots are not simply executing pre-programmed welding sequences; they are equipped with intelligent vision systems that continuously monitor the quality of each weld as it is being performed. The high-resolution cameras capture detailed images of the weld bead, and onboard AI algorithms analyze these images in real-time, looking for any signs of imperfections such as porosity, cracks, or incomplete fusion. If the vision system detects any such anomalies or deviations from the pre-defined quality standards, the robot can autonomously and instantaneously adjust the welding parameters. This might involve increasing or decreasing the welding current, altering the speed of the welding head, or modifying the shielding gas flow rate – all in direct response to the real-time feedback from the vision system. This closed-loop control system ensures that every weld meets the stringent quality requirements, significantly reducing the likelihood of defective car bodies moving further down the assembly line.

Furthermore, the smart automotive factory leverages the vast amounts of data generated by all its interconnected machines, including the welding robots, the conveyor systems, the painting booths, and the assembly line machinery. This data, collected through the IoT infrastructure, is continuously analyzed using sophisticated **predictive analytics** algorithms. These algorithms are designed to identify patterns and anomalies in the operational data that might indicate an impending equipment failure. For example, by monitoring the motor current, vibration levels, and operating temperature of a critical welding robot over time, the predictive analytics system can learn to recognize subtle deviations from normal operating parameters that might precede a breakdown. When such a pattern is detected, the system can automatically generate an alert, scheduling preventative maintenance for that specific robot before an actual failure occurs. This proactive approach to maintenance significantly minimizes unscheduled downtime, which can be incredibly costly in a high-volume automotive manufacturing environment. By ensuring that all critical machinery is maintained in optimal condition, the smart factory maintains a smooth and continuous flow of production, maximizing efficiency and output.

Beyond welding and predictive maintenance, a smart automotive factory would integrate numerous other intelligent systems. For instance, robots equipped with 3D vision systems could autonomously handle the kitting of parts for assembly, selecting the correct components from automated storage and retrieval systems and delivering them to the appropriate workstation just in time. AI-powered planning and scheduling systems would optimize the flow of materials and work orders throughout the factory, minimizing bottlenecks and maximizing throughput. Quality control would be enhanced through the use of AI-driven inspection systems at various stages of production, ensuring that every component and every assembled vehicle meets the highest standards. Human workers would be augmented by collaborative robots (cobots) that can assist with physically demanding or repetitive tasks, improving ergonomics and worker safety. The entire factory would be monitored and controlled through a centralized digital platform, providing real-time visibility into all aspects of the operation and enabling data-driven decision-making at every level. This comprehensive integration of smart technologies transforms the traditional automotive plant into a highly efficient, agile, and quality-focused smart factory of the future.

Diagrammatic Representation of a Smart Factory Ecosystem:

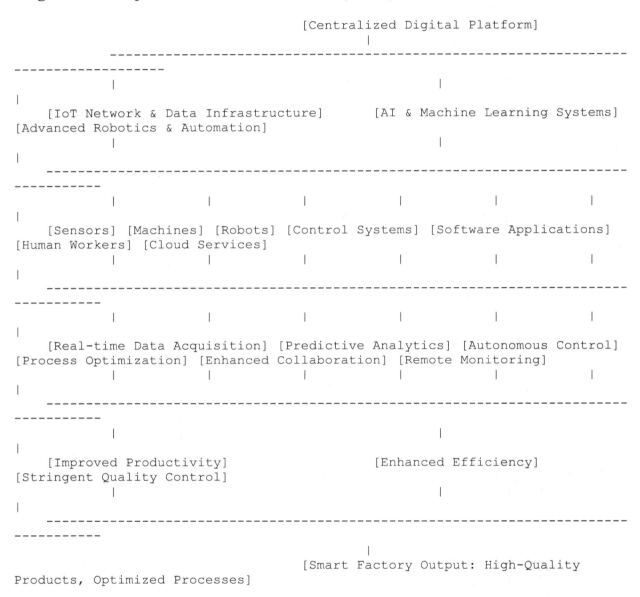

This diagram illustrates the interconnected nature of a smart factory. The central digital platform serves as the brain, orchestrating the flow of information and control. The IoT network provides the communication backbone, connecting various elements from sensors and machines to human workers and cloud services, enabling real-time data acquisition. AI and machine learning systems analyze this data, driving predictive analytics and autonomous control. Advanced robotics and automation execute physical tasks with precision and efficiency. The seamless integration of these components leads to significant improvements in productivity, enhanced efficiency across all operations, and the achievement of stringent quality control standards, ultimately resulting in the high-quality output that defines a smart factory.

9.2 Proactive Equipment Management and Intelligent Product Assurance: Predictive Maintenance and Quality Control in Advanced Robotics

Predictive maintenance and quality control represent two critical and increasingly sophisticated facets of modern industrial robotics, playing pivotal roles in optimizing operational efficiency, minimizing disruptions, and ensuring the consistent delivery of high-quality products. Predictive maintenance, a proactive approach to equipment upkeep, leverages the power of data analytics, machine learning algorithms, and an array of advanced sensors to forecast potential equipment failures before they occur. This foresight allows for timely and targeted maintenance interventions, enabling repairs or replacements to be scheduled strategically, thereby preventing unexpected breakdowns and the associated costly downtime. This methodology stands in stark contrast to traditional maintenance strategies, which often rely on fixed, time-based schedules for servicing equipment or, even less efficiently, on reactive repairs undertaken only after a complete equipment failure has already transpired.

In the dynamic landscape of a modern manufacturing environment, a diverse range of critical machinery, including intricate robotic arms, continuous conveyor belts, high-speed assembly lines, and precision machining tools, are continuously monitored for subtle indicators of wear, performance degradation, or potential malfunction. To facilitate this constant surveillance, these machines are often equipped with a network of embedded sensors that capture a wide spectrum of operational data, such as temperature fluctuations in critical components, vibration patterns indicative of mechanical stress or imbalance, pressure variations in hydraulic or pneumatic systems, electrical current draw signaling motor strain, acoustic emissions hinting at unusual friction, and lubricant condition reflecting wear and tear. The granular data streams generated by these sensors are then fed into sophisticated machine learning models. These models, trained on historical data encompassing both normal operational patterns and the precursors to past failures, are adept at identifying subtle anomalies, deviations from established baselines, and complex correlations within the sensor data that might signify the early stages of an impending failure. When the machine learning system detects patterns or anomalies that exceed predefined thresholds or indicate a heightened probability of future malfunction, it can automatically trigger a maintenance request. This alert allows maintenance personnel to schedule the necessary inspections, repairs, or component replacements in advance, during planned downtime or at a time that minimizes disruption to the overall production schedule. This proactive intervention avoids the costly consequences of unplanned equipment breakdowns, such as extended production halts, expedited and often more expensive emergency repairs, and potential damage to other parts of the system.

Illustrative Scenario: Intelligent Maintenance in Semiconductor Manufacturing Robots

Consider a highly specialized and sensitive semiconductor manufacturing facility, where intricate robots are entrusted with the delicate task of precisely placing microelectronic chips onto circuit boards. The accuracy and reliability of these robotic arms are paramount, as even the slightest deviation in their movements can lead to irreparable damage to the fragile chips, resulting in significant production losses. To ensure the continuous and flawless operation of these critical robots, a predictive maintenance system is implemented. Each robotic arm is equipped with a network of high-precision vibration sensors strategically placed on its motors, joints, and end-effector. These sensors continuously monitor the vibrational characteristics of the robot's movements, capturing even the most minute oscillations and frequencies. The real-time vibration data is then streamed to a sophisticated machine learning model that has been trained on extensive historical data, correlating specific vibration signatures with the onset of motor wear, joint looseness, or other mechanical issues. If the machine learning model detects a subtle but significant deviation in the robot's vibration patterns that indicates early signs of wear on a motor bearing, for example, the system can automatically generate a maintenance request. This alert provides maintenance technicians with ample lead time to inspect the affected robot, diagnose the specific issue, and schedule a replacement of the worn bearing during a planned maintenance window. This proactive intervention prevents the motor from failing catastrophically during production, which could lead to the robot malfunctioning, potentially damaging valuable semiconductor chips, and causing significant delays in the manufacturing process. The predictive maintenance system, therefore, ensures the high reliability and uptime of these critical robots, safeguarding the quality and efficiency of semiconductor production.

On the parallel front of **quality control**, advanced robotic systems are increasingly deployed to ensure that manufactured products consistently meet stringent quality specifications and adhere to industry standards. These intelligent robots are equipped with a diverse array of sophisticated sensors, high-resolution cameras with advanced image analysis capabilities, laser scanners for precise dimensional measurements, and AI algorithms for automated inspection and evaluation of finished products. This enables them to perform objective, consistent, and high-speed quality checks that often surpass the capabilities of human inspectors, particularly for tasks requiring meticulous attention to detail or the analysis of large volumes of products. For example, in the food production industry, robots equipped with advanced vision systems can meticulously inspect packaged food items for defects such as improper sealing, incorrect labeling, or products that fall outside the defined size or weight specifications. Similarly, in the electronics manufacturing sector, robots with high-precision cameras and AI-powered image recognition can examine circuit boards for missing components, misaligned parts, or soldering defects with far greater speed and accuracy than manual inspection.

Illustrative Scenario: Intelligent Packaging Inspection in a Food Processing Plant

Consider a state-of-the-art food processing plant that utilizes smart robotic arms to automate the packaging of its products. As each packaged food item moves along a conveyor belt, a smart robotic arm, equipped with a high-resolution camera and an integrated barcode scanner, performs a comprehensive quality check. The camera captures a detailed image of the packaging, and onboard AI algorithms analyze this image to assess the integrity of the seal, the correctness of the label placement, and the overall presentation of the package. Simultaneously, the barcode scanner verifies that the correct product barcode is present and legible. Furthermore, a highly accurate weight sensor integrated into the robotic arm's end-effector measures the weight of each packaged item. The quality control system is programmed with pre-defined acceptable limits for packaging quality, barcode accuracy, and product weight. If the AI-powered vision system detects a compromised seal, a misaligned label, or a missing barcode, or if the measured weight falls outside the defined upper and lower bounds, the system automatically identifies the non-conforming item. In such a case, the smart robotic arm can be programmed to gently but swiftly remove the rejected item from the production line. This rejected item can then be routed for further inspection, repackaging, or disposal, depending on the nature of the defect. This automated and intelligent quality control process ensures that only products that meet the stringent quality standards of the food processing plant and comply with industry regulations reach consumers, thereby safeguarding product quality, minimizing waste, and enhancing customer satisfaction.

The synergistic integration of predictive maintenance and quality control within advanced robotic systems in smart factories creates a powerful closed-loop system for optimizing both equipment performance and product quality. The data generated by sensors for predictive maintenance can also provide valuable insights into the health and performance of manufacturing processes, potentially revealing correlations between machine wear and product defects. This holistic view enables manufacturers to not only prevent costly downtime but also to continuously improve their production processes to minimize waste, enhance efficiency, and consistently deliver high-quality goods. As AI and machine learning algorithms become increasingly sophisticated and sensor technologies become more advanced and cost-effective, the role of predictive maintenance and quality control in industrial robotics will only continue to grow, driving further advancements in manufacturing excellence.

Diagrammatic Representation of Predictive Maintenance and Quality Control in Robotics:

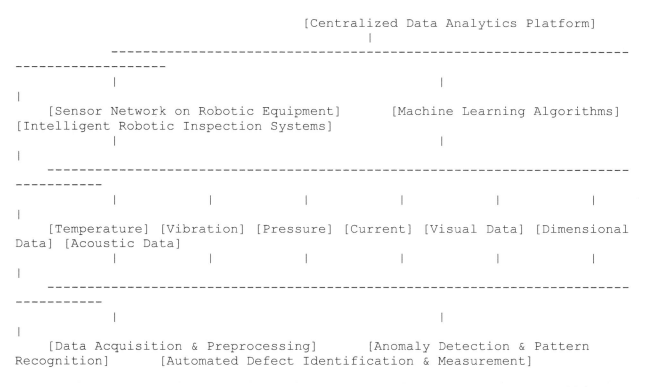

```
        |                                           |
|    ------------------------------------------------------------
------------
        |                                           |
|
    [Predictive Maintenance Alerts & Scheduling]    [Real-time Quality
Assessment & Feedback]
        |                                           |
|
|    ------------------------------------------------------------
------------
        |                                           |
|
    [Minimized Downtime & Optimized Lifespan]      [Enhanced Product Quality
& Reduced Waste]
        |                                           |
|
|    ------------------------------------------------------------
------------
                                    |
                        [Improved Operational Efficiency &
Product Excellence]
```

This diagram illustrates the interconnected processes of predictive maintenance and quality control driven by robotics and intelligent systems. Sensors embedded in robotic equipment continuously collect a variety of operational data. This data is then fed into machine learning algorithms that analyze it to detect anomalies and recognize patterns indicative of potential failures. The output of this analysis generates predictive maintenance alerts, enabling proactive scheduling of maintenance. Simultaneously, intelligent robotic inspection systems utilize sensors and AI to perform automated quality assessments on manufactured products, identifying defects and measuring critical dimensions in real-time. The feedback from these quality checks can be used to adjust production processes, reducing waste and enhancing product quality. The convergence of these two critical functions, facilitated by advanced robotics and data analytics, ultimately leads to improved operational efficiency and the consistent production of high-quality products.

9.3 The Vanguard of Automotive Manufacturing: A Detailed Examination of Tesla's Intelligent Production Ecosystem

Tesla, a prominent force in the global automotive industry, stands as a compelling and pioneering example of the transformative power of industrial robotics and intelligent automation applied at scale. Their state-of-the-art manufacturing lines, particularly within their Gigafactories, are characterized by a profound reliance on sophisticated automation technologies. This includes the extensive deployment of advanced robotic arms capable of intricate manipulations, intelligent conveyor belt systems that orchestrate the seamless flow of materials and components, and a suite of Artificial Intelligence (AI)-driven systems that oversee and optimize various aspects of the production process. All these disparate elements are intricately interconnected within a comprehensive smart factory model, creating a highly integrated and responsive manufacturing ecosystem.

At the heart of Tesla's manufacturing philosophy is a relentless pursuit of enhanced production efficiency, the maintenance of the most stringent quality standards across all vehicle components and finished products, and a strategic reduction in both human error and labor costs through the intelligent application of automation. Robotics plays a central and indispensable role in achieving these ambitious objectives by streamlining complex operational workflows, significantly improving the precision and consistency of manufacturing tasks, and dramatically increasing the overall throughput of their production lines.

Robotics at the Forefront of Tesla's Production Processes:

Within Tesla's Gigafactories, advanced robotics are strategically deployed across a multitude of production stages, spanning the initial assembly of individual vehicle parts and sub-assemblies to the final, meticulous inspection of fully manufactured cars before they leave the factory floor. This pervasive integration of robotics is evident in key areas such as:

- **Body Assembly and Welding:** Highly sophisticated robotic arms, often operating in coordinated teams, perform the intricate and precise welding operations required to join the various steel and aluminum components that form the structural skeleton of Tesla vehicles. These robots are equipped with advanced sensors and control systems that ensure the accuracy and strength of each weld, contributing significantly to the overall safety and durability of the vehicles. The speed and consistency of these robotic welding processes far surpass the capabilities of manual welding, leading to increased production rates and a more uniform quality of the vehicle body.
- **Painting and Finishing:** The application of paint and other protective coatings is another critical stage where Tesla leverages advanced robotics. Robotic painting arms ensure a consistent and uniform application of paint layers, resulting in a high-quality finish with optimal durability and aesthetic appeal. These robots can precisely control the spray patterns and coating thicknesses, minimizing material waste and ensuring a flawless exterior for each vehicle. Furthermore, automated systems are used for surface preparation and the application of sealants and adhesives, further enhancing the quality and longevity of the vehicle.
- **Component Assembly:** During the complex assembly stage, where numerous individual components are integrated into the vehicle, robotic arms play a crucial role in tasks such as attaching body panels, installing electrical wiring harnesses, mounting battery packs, and fitting interior trim pieces. These robots are often equipped with specialized end-effectors (the "hands" of the robot) designed for specific tasks, allowing them to handle a wide variety of parts with precision and care. While robots handle the more repetitive and high-precision assembly tasks, human workers often collaborate alongside them, focusing on more delicate or complex installations that require greater dexterity and adaptability. This human-robot collaboration optimizes the overall efficiency and flexibility of the assembly line.
- **Material Handling and Logistics:** Beyond direct manufacturing tasks, robots and automated guided vehicles (AGVs) play a vital role in the efficient movement of materials and components throughout Tesla's Gigafactories. These automated systems transport parts from storage areas to the production line and move sub-assemblies

between different workstations, ensuring a smooth and timely flow of materials, reducing manual handling, and minimizing the risk of damage to sensitive components.

Illustrative Scenario: Robotic Precision in Tesla's Model 3 Assembly Line:

A prime example of the application of robotics in Tesla's manufacturing process can be observed in the production line for the highly successful Model 3. During the critical assembly stage, numerous robotic arms are deployed to perform a wide range of tasks with remarkable speed and accuracy. For instance, large, multi-axis robotic arms are used to precisely position and attach the vehicle's body panels, such as doors, hoods, and trunk lids, ensuring perfect alignment and fit. These robots utilize advanced vision systems to identify the exact mounting points and apply the necessary force to securely fasten the panels. Similarly, other specialized robotic arms are responsible for the intricate task of installing the complex electrical wiring harnesses that run throughout the vehicle. These robots can navigate the intricate pathways within the car body and precisely connect numerous electrical connectors, ensuring the reliable operation of the vehicle's electrical systems. Furthermore, robots are employed to lift and position the heavy battery packs into the vehicle chassis, a task that requires significant strength and precision. While these robots handle the bulk of the assembly work with speed and consistency, human workers often work in close proximity, performing more delicate or complex tasks that require a higher degree of manual dexterity, problem-solving skills, and adaptability, such as the installation of intricate interior trim pieces or the final quality checks of assembled components. This collaborative approach, where robots handle repetitive and high-precision tasks and humans focus on more nuanced operations, maximizes both efficiency and quality on the Model 3 production line.

Proactive Equipment Management: Tesla's Predictive Maintenance System:

Tesla recognizes the critical importance of minimizing downtime and ensuring the continuous operation of its highly automated manufacturing lines. To achieve this, they have implemented a sophisticated predictive maintenance system that leverages the vast amounts of data generated by the robots and other machinery within their Gigafactories. This system employs a network of sensors embedded in the equipment to continuously monitor various operational parameters, such as motor current, vibration levels, operating temperatures, hydraulic pressures, and acoustic emissions. The real-time data streams from these sensors are then analyzed using advanced data analytics techniques and machine learning algorithms. These algorithms are trained to identify subtle patterns and anomalies in the data that might indicate the early stages of wear, performance degradation, or an impending malfunction of a specific component or machine.

For example, if a particular robotic arm begins to exhibit slightly elevated vibration levels or an increased motor current draw, the predictive maintenance system can detect these early warning signs. Based on its learned patterns and thresholds, the system can automatically generate a maintenance alert, notifying maintenance personnel about the potential issue. This proactive notification allows Tesla to schedule the necessary inspections, diagnostics, and repairs for that specific robot at an optimal time, ideally during planned downtime or before the issue escalates into a complete failure that could halt production. By addressing potential problems in their nascent stages, Tesla minimizes unscheduled downtime, reduces the risk of more extensive and costly repairs, and ensures the consistent and efficient operation of its highly automated manufacturing lines. This proactive approach to equipment management is crucial for maximizing production output and maintaining the high efficiency that Tesla strives for in its Gigafactories.

Intelligent Product Assurance: AI-Powered Quality Control Systems at Tesla:

Maintaining the highest quality standards for its vehicles is a paramount concern for Tesla. To achieve this, they have implemented advanced AI-powered quality control systems throughout their manufacturing process. A significant component of this system involves the deployment of vision-based robotic inspection systems at various stages of vehicle assembly. These robots are equipped with high-resolution cameras and sophisticated AI algorithms that continuously inspect vehicle parts and sub-assemblies as they move along the production line.

For instance, during the body assembly stage, robotic vision systems meticulously examine the welded seams for any imperfections, such as inconsistencies in the weld bead, gaps, or signs of inadequate fusion. These systems can quickly and objectively identify defects that might be difficult for human inspectors to consistently detect, ensuring the structural integrity and aesthetic quality of the vehicle body. Similarly, during the painting process, robotic vision systems inspect the painted surfaces for any flaws, such as scratches, dents, or inconsistencies in the paint application. The AI algorithms can analyze the visual data with remarkable speed and accuracy, identifying even minute imperfections that might otherwise be missed by manual inspection. When a defect is detected by these robotic inspection systems, the affected part or vehicle can be automatically flagged for rework or rejection, preventing substandard products from moving further down the assembly line.

This comprehensive and automated quality control process significantly enhances the speed and reliability of Tesla's quality assurance efforts. By leveraging the consistency and objectivity of robotic vision systems powered by AI, Tesla can maintain stringent quality standards across its high-volume production lines, ultimately ensuring that the vehicles delivered to customers meet the company's exacting specifications and contribute to high levels of customer satisfaction.

Diagram: Integrated Smart Factory Workflow at Tesla:

```
+-------------------------------+      +----------------------------------
-+      +-----------------------------------+
| IoT Sensors on Manufacturing  | --> | Data Analytics & Machine Learning
| --> | Predictive Maintenance System     |
| Equipment (Temperature,       |     | (Real-time Data Processing,
|     | (Anomaly Detection, Failure    |
| Vibration, Current, etc.)     |     | Pattern Recognition)
|     | Prediction, Maintenance Scheduling)|
+-------------------------------+      +----------------------------------
-+      +-----------------------------------+
         |                                        |
|
         v                                        v
|
+-------------------------------+                 |
|
```

```
| Real-time Data Acquisition &      |                              |
|                                                                  |
| Monitoring Platform               |                              |
|                                                                  |
+----------------------------------+                              |
|                                                                  |
|           |                                                      |
|                                                                  |
|           v                                         v
v
+----------------------------------+      +------------------------------------
-+        +------------------------------------+
| Advanced Robotics in Production  | --> | AI-Powered Vision Systems for
| --> | High-Quality Vehicle Output |     |
| (Welding, Assembly, Painting,    |     | Quality Control (Automated
|      | (Minimized Defects, Optimal |     |
| Material Handling)               |     | Inspection, Defect Detection)
|      | Performance & Reliability)  |     |
+----------------------------------+      +------------------------------------
-+        +------------------------------------+
```

This diagram illustrates a simplified representation of the integrated smart factory workflow at Tesla. IoT sensors embedded in the manufacturing equipment continuously collect operational data. This data is processed and analyzed by data analytics and machine learning systems to identify patterns and anomalies. This analysis feeds into the predictive maintenance system, enabling proactive maintenance scheduling and minimizing downtime. Simultaneously, advanced robotics perform the core manufacturing tasks, while AI-powered vision systems conduct continuous quality control inspections. The seamless integration of these systems ensures a high-quality vehicle output with minimized defects and optimized production efficiency.

Conclusion

Industrial robotics has revolutionized the manufacturing industry, making production faster, safer, and more efficient. Through smart factories, predictive maintenance, and real-time quality control, companies like Tesla are able to stay ahead of the curve. These systems not only reduce operational costs but also improve the reliability and quality of products, setting a new standard for the manufacturing industry.

40 multiple-choice questions (MCQs) with answers for **Industrial Robotics**, covering:

- **9.1 Smart Factories**
- **9.2 Predictive Maintenance and Quality Control**
- **9.3 Case Study: Tesla's Manufacturing Line**

Section 9.1 – Smart Factories

1. **What is the core technology behind a smart factory?**
   A) Steam engines
   B) IoT and AI
   C) Manual labor
   D) Fossil fuels
   ✓ **Answer:** B) IoT and AI
2. **Which term describes machines connected via the internet to share data in a smart factory?**
   A) LAN
   B) Blockchain
   C) IoT
   D) SCADA
   ✓ **Answer:** C) IoT
3. **A smart factory is also referred to as:**
   A) Fourth Industrial Lab
   B) Industry 4.0
   C) Mechanical Industry
   D) Data Hub
   ✓ **Answer:** B) Industry 4.0
4. **Which of these is *not* a characteristic of a smart factory?**
   A) Decentralized decision making
   B) Manual data recording
   C) Real-time monitoring
   D) Predictive analysis
   ✓ **Answer:** B) Manual data recording
5. **What helps smart factories adapt to changes in production requirements?**
   A) Static programming
   B) Flexible automation
   C) Rigid machinery
   D) Scheduled scripts
   ✓ **Answer:** B) Flexible automation
6. **What is the main advantage of using AI in smart factories?**
   A) Reduces the number of robots
   B) Improves energy consumption only
   C) Enables autonomous decision making
   D) Eliminates software use
   ✓ **Answer:** C) Enables autonomous decision making
7. **What is an example of real-time adjustment in a smart factory?**
   A) Human inspection
   B) Scheduled weekly updates
   C) Automated process correction using sensor data
   D) Monthly feedback sessions
   ✓ **Answer:** C) Automated process correction using sensor data
8. **Which of these is *most closely* associated with a smart production line?**
   A) Manual welding
   B) Assembly via conveyor belts
   C) Cyber-physical systems

D) Human inspection only

✓ **Answer:** C) Cyber-physical systems

9. **How do smart factories help in mass customization?**
   A) By increasing inventory
   B) By ignoring customer feedback
   C) Through flexible, data-driven systems
   D) By outsourcing production

   ✓ **Answer:** C) Through flexible, data-driven systems

10. **In smart factories, digital twins are used to:**
    A) Replace physical robots
    B) Simulate and monitor real-time processes
    C) Manufacture parts
    D) Store employee records

    ✓ **Answer:** B) Simulate and monitor real-time processes

Section 9.2 – Predictive Maintenance and Quality Control

11. **Predictive maintenance relies heavily on:**
    A) Guesswork
    B) Sensor data and analytics
    C) Daily inspections
    D) Annual overhauls

    ✓ **Answer:** B) Sensor data and analytics

12. **Which sensor is often used to detect vibration anomalies in machines?**
    A) Thermometer
    B) Accelerometer
    C) Photodiode
    D) Hydrometer

    ✓ **Answer:** B) Accelerometer

13. **What is the main benefit of predictive maintenance?**
    A) Increases downtime
    B) Prevents unexpected equipment failure
    C) Requires frequent shutdowns
    D) Depends on fixed schedules

    ✓ **Answer:** B) Prevents unexpected equipment failure

14. **Which technology is typically *not* used in predictive maintenance?**
    A) Machine learning
    B) Infrared imaging
    C) Real-time data analytics
    D) Typewriters

    ✓ **Answer:** D) Typewriters

15. **What is quality control in robotics most associated with?**
    A) Speed increase
    B) Profit margins
    C) Ensuring consistent product standards

D) HR decisions

✓ **Answer:** C) Ensuring consistent product standards

16. **Which of the following is used for robotic visual inspection?**
    A) Radio antenna
    B) Electric coil
    C) Machine vision cameras
    D) RFID tag

    ✓ **Answer:** C) Machine vision cameras

17. **Anomaly detection in quality control is performed using:**
    A) Syntax rules
    B) Visual AI inspection
    C) HR management software
    D) Static metrics

    ✓ **Answer:** B) Visual AI inspection

18. **Which approach leads to better long-term savings in maintenance?**
    A) Reactive maintenance
    B) Predictive maintenance
    C) Routine overhauls
    D) Emergency fixes

    ✓ **Answer:** B) Predictive maintenance

19. **In predictive maintenance, a sudden increase in machine temperature can indicate:**
    A) Improved performance
    B) Potential failure
    C) Scheduled shutdown
    D) Battery charging

    ✓ **Answer:** B) Potential failure

20. **Which system uses AI to spot defects during product inspection?**
    A) Payroll software
    B) Deep learning model
    C) Water-level sensor
    D) PLC controller

    ✓ **Answer:** B) Deep learning model

Section 9.3 – Case Study: Tesla's Manufacturing Line

21. **Tesla's factories are examples of:**
    A) Traditional assembly lines
    B) Smart factories
    C) Human-only workshops
    D) Oil-based factories

    ✓ **Answer:** B) Smart factories

22. **Which component is central in Tesla's robotic assembly?**
    A) Conveyor belts
    B) Robotic arms
    C) Smoke detectors

D) Generators

✓ **Answer:** B) Robotic arms

23. **Tesla's predictive systems help in:**

    A) Launching new car models

    B) Monitoring customer feedback

    C) Maintaining robotic equipment before failure

    D) Hiring drivers

    ✓ **Answer:** C) Maintaining robotic equipment before failure

24. **Tesla's Gigafactory primarily manufactures:**

    A) Gasoline engines

    B) Wind turbines

    C) Electric vehicles and batteries

    D) Desktop computers

    ✓ **Answer:** C) Electric vehicles and batteries

25. **What is the purpose of AI in Tesla's quality control system?**

    A) Reducing robot wages

    B) Enhancing vision inspection for defects

    C) Lowering taxes

    D) Replacing managers

    ✓ **Answer:** B) Enhancing vision inspection for defects

26. **What happens when Tesla's AI finds a scratch during assembly?**

    A) The part is discarded automatically

    B) The system alerts for correction

    C) Nothing

    D) The entire car is scrapped

    ✓ **Answer:** B) The system alerts for correction

27. **In Tesla's production, what enables robots to work safely with humans?**

    A) Isolation

    B) Mechanical locks

    C) AI and sensor integration

    D) Voice command

    ✓ **Answer:** C) AI and sensor integration

28. **Tesla's autonomous inspection systems use:**

    A) Vacuum cleaners

    B) AI-enabled vision systems

    C) Social media feedback

    D) Barcode readers only

    ✓ **Answer:** B) AI-enabled vision systems

29. **Tesla's robot welders perform tasks with the help of:**

    A) Thermostats

    B) Pre-programmed scripts and vision feedback

    C) Manual control levers

    D) Smart glasses

    ✓ **Answer:** B) Pre-programmed scripts and vision feedback

30. **Tesla uses automation to primarily achieve:**

    A) Increased marketing

    B) Consistent quality and production speed

C) Vehicle design changes

D) Customer engagement

✅ **Answer:** B) Consistent quality and production speed

General Questions (20 Remaining)

31. Robots in smart factories are often described as:

    A) Passive tools

    B) Independent operators

    C) Collaborative agents

    D) Digital marketers

    ✅ **Answer:** C) Collaborative agents

32. Predictive maintenance reduces:

    A) Downtime

    B) Sensor cost

    C) Operator fatigue

    D) Material usage

    ✅ **Answer:** A) Downtime

33. Quality control automation benefits include:

    A) Slower inspection

    B) Human errors

    C) Consistency and speed

    D) Incomplete data

    ✅ **Answer:** C) Consistency and speed

34. Smart factories are **data-driven**, meaning:

    A) Workers memorize processes

    B) Manual inputs dominate

    C) Decisions are based on real-time data

    D) Files are stored in cabinets

    ✅ **Answer:** C) Decisions are based on real-time data

35. Tesla's AI-enhanced robotics can:

    A) Send emails

    B) Adjust assembly tasks autonomously

    C) Speak to customers

    D) Design websites

    ✅ **Answer:** B) Adjust assembly tasks autonomously

36. In quality control, deep learning models:

    A) Detect power surges

    B) Predict HR trends

    C) Classify product defects

    D) Produce heat maps

    ✅ **Answer:** C) Classify product defects

37. A key feature of predictive systems is:

    A) Constant shutdown

    B) Data-based fault forecasting

C) Error ignoring

D) On-demand overhauls only

✅ **Answer:** B) Data-based fault forecasting

38. The main goal of smart factories is to:

A) Cut staff

B) Increase paperwork

C) Maximize productivity using technology

D) Avoid robotics

✅ **Answer:** C) Maximize productivity using technology

39. Visual inspection in robotics can identify:

A) Missing email replies

B) Scratches, cracks, misalignments

C) Employee attendance

D) Financial fraud

✅ **Answer:** B) Scratches, cracks, misalignments

40. Tesla's manufacturing system reflects:

A) Manual labor dominance

B) Full outsourcing

C) Intelligent automation

D) Government control

✅ **Answer:** C) Intelligent automation

Chapter 10: Service Robotics

10.1 The Ascending Role of Robotics in Healthcare: Transforming Patient Care, Surgical Interventions, and Medical Operations

Service robots are ushering in a transformative era within the healthcare sector, revolutionizing the landscape of patient care, the execution of medical procedures, and the efficiency of hospital administration. These sophisticated machines are meticulously engineered to provide invaluable assistance to doctors, nurses, and patients alike, undertaking tasks that are often characterized by their repetitive nature, the requirement for extreme precision, or an inherent level of risk for human personnel. By seamlessly integrating into healthcare workflows, these robotic systems contribute to heightened operational efficiency, a significant reduction in the incidence of human error, and more effective management of critical resources within diverse healthcare settings.

Among the most impactful applications of robotics in medicine are **surgical robots**, exemplified by groundbreaking systems such as the da Vinci Surgical System. These advanced robotic platforms have fundamentally reshaped the dynamics of the operating room, empowering surgeons with unprecedented levels of dexterity, enhanced visual acuity through high-definition 3D imaging, and the ability to perform minimally invasive procedures with remarkable precision. A prominent illustration of this is the utilization of robotic arms in laparoscopic surgery. In this technique, the surgeon, operating from a remote console, guides the robot to make several small incisions through which miniaturized surgical instruments and a high-definition camera are inserted. The robot's articulated arms, with their superior range of motion and tremor filtration, allow the surgeon to perform complex surgical maneuvers with greater accuracy and control than traditional open surgery. This minimally invasive approach translates to significant benefits for patients, including reduced blood loss, smaller scars, less post-operative pain, a shorter hospital stay, and a considerably quicker recovery time, along with a decreased risk of infection.

Beyond the realm of surgical interventions, **mobile robots** are increasingly being deployed within hospital environments to streamline logistical operations and enhance hygiene protocols. These autonomous robots are designed to navigate the often complex and bustling corridors of hospitals to perform a variety of essential tasks. For instance, robots are being used for the safe and efficient delivery of medications from the pharmacy to nursing stations, ensuring timely access for patients and freeing up nurses to focus on direct patient care. Similarly, mobile robots equipped with ultraviolet (UV) light disinfection systems are employed to autonomously sanitize patient rooms and other critical areas, playing a crucial role in infection control and maintaining a sterile environment. Furthermore, these mobile platforms can be utilized for the transportation of medical supplies, laboratory specimens, and even meals throughout the hospital, alleviating the burden on hospital staff and improving the overall efficiency of internal logistics. A notable example is the TUG robot, which autonomously navigates hospital corridors using pre-programmed maps and sensor-based navigation to deliver items to designated locations, significantly reducing the time and effort required by human personnel for these transport tasks.

In the crucial areas of **rehabilitation and eldercare**, robotics is offering innovative solutions to improve patient mobility and quality of life. **Robotic exoskeletons**, such as the ReWalk system, are wearable robotic devices that provide support and assistance to individuals with lower limb paralysis or weakness, enabling them to stand, walk, and even climb stairs. These exoskeletons utilize advanced sensors, motors, and control systems to augment the user's strength and mobility, facilitating rehabilitation and increasing independence. Additionally, **assistive robots** are being developed to aid elderly individuals with daily tasks, providing support with mobility, medication reminders, and social interaction. **Companion robots**, such as PARO, a therapeutic robotic seal, are specifically designed to provide emotional support and companionship, particularly for patients suffering from dementia or mental health issues. These robots can respond to touch, sound, and light, mimicking the behavior of a live animal and offering a sense of comfort and reducing feelings of loneliness and anxiety, thereby improving the overall well-being of patients.

The field of **telemedicine** has also witnessed a significant integration of robotic systems, a trend that has gained considerable momentum, particularly in the aftermath of the COVID-19 pandemic, which highlighted the need for remote healthcare solutions. Robotic systems in telemedicine enable doctors to conduct consultations, perform remote examinations, and even assist with diagnoses from a distant location. These robotic interfaces are typically equipped with high-definition cameras, a range of medical sensors (such as thermometers, blood pressure monitors, and stethoscopes), and robust communication modules that allow for real-time interaction between the doctor and the patient. This technology has the potential to significantly reduce the risk of exposure to infectious diseases for both healthcare professionals and patients, while also expanding access to specialized medical care in remote or underserved areas where access to doctors might be limited. Remote robotic examination arms can allow a physician to physically examine a patient located miles away, guided by the physician's remote commands and providing real-time sensory feedback.

Diagrammatic Representation of Robotics in Healthcare:

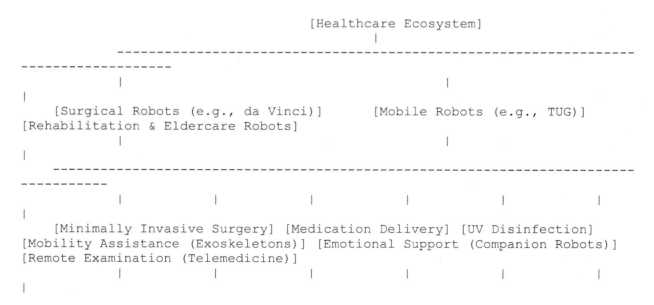

```
     --------------------------------------------------------------------
-----------
                 |                                            |
  |
    [Enhanced Precision]                    [Reduced Staff Burden]
[Improved Patient Well-being]
    [Quicker Recovery]                      [Improved Hygiene]
[Increased Independence]
    [Lower Infection Risk]                  [Efficient Logistics]
[Emotional Comfort]
                 |                                            |
  |
     --------------------------------------------------------------------
-----------
                                            |
                              [Improved Patient Care, Efficiency, and
Access]
```

This diagram illustrates the diverse applications of robotics within the healthcare ecosystem. Surgical robots enhance the precision and invasiveness of surgical procedures, leading to quicker patient recovery and lower infection risks. Mobile robots automate logistical tasks like medication delivery and room disinfection, reducing the burden on hospital staff and improving hygiene. Rehabilitation and eldercare robots provide mobility assistance through exoskeletons and emotional support through companion robots, improving patient well-being and independence. Finally, telemedicine robots enable remote consultations and examinations, expanding healthcare access. The overarching impact of these robotic technologies is improved patient care, enhanced efficiency in healthcare operations, and increased accessibility to medical services.

10.2 The Rise of Robotic Assistance in Homes: Domestic and Companion Robots Enhancing Daily Life and Providing Social Engagement

The integration of robotic technologies into the fabric of our daily lives is rapidly expanding, with **domestic robots** emerging as increasingly prevalent tools designed to alleviate the burden of routine household chores and enhance overall convenience. These automated assistants are now commonly employed for a diverse range of tasks within the home, including autonomous cleaning, providing entertainment and engagement, bolstering home security measures, and offering crucial support for the elderly, thereby transforming the way we manage our living spaces and interact with technology.

Among the most widely adopted categories of domestic robots are **cleaning robots**, such as the iconic Roomba series manufactured by iRobot, and robotic mops like the Braava. These intelligent devices are engineered to autonomously clean floors, seamlessly navigating through rooms while effectively detecting and avoiding obstacles such as furniture, walls, and pets. Equipped with an array of sophisticated sensors (including infrared sensors, bump sensors, and cliff sensors), advanced navigation algorithms, and the ability to learn and store internal maps of the home environment, these robots optimize their cleaning patterns to ensure thorough coverage of floor surfaces. Their widespread popularity can be attributed to their ease of use – often requiring just the press of a button or a scheduled cleaning time – and the significant time savings they offer to busy homeowners, freeing them from the often tedious task of manual floor cleaning.

Extending the realm of robotic cleaning beyond indoor spaces, **robotic lawn mowers** and **robotic window cleaners** are further reducing the need for human effort in outdoor and vertical surface maintenance. Robotic lawn mowers operate autonomously within predefined boundary wires laid around the perimeter of the lawn, systematically cutting the grass and often returning to a charging dock when their battery is low. Many models can be controlled and scheduled through user-friendly smartphone applications, offering a convenient and hands-free approach to lawn care. Similarly, robotic window cleaners utilize suction or magnetic mechanisms to adhere to glass surfaces and autonomously traverse windows, cleaning them with specialized cleaning solutions and microfiber pads. These robots can often be programmed with cleaning patterns or controlled remotely, making the task of cleaning high or hard-to-reach windows significantly safer and less labor-intensive.

In the domain of home security, **home security robots**, such as the K5 series developed by Knightscope (although primarily designed for commercial and public safety applications, the underlying technology is indicative of trends in advanced home security), represent a proactive and mobile approach to safeguarding residential properties. These robots are equipped with an array of sensors, including high-resolution cameras, thermal imaging capabilities, and sophisticated audio and environmental monitoring systems. Powered by AI-driven pattern recognition algorithms, they can autonomously patrol the perimeter of a home, detect unusual activities such as unauthorized movement or suspicious sounds, and send real-time alerts, including video and audio feeds, to homeowners via their smartphones. Some advanced models even have the capability to autonomously connect with law enforcement agencies in the event of a confirmed security breach, providing an additional layer of security and rapid response.

Venturing beyond purely utilitarian functions, **companion robots**, such as Jibo (now discontinued but influential in the field) and Sony's robotic dog Aibo, are specifically designed to interact with human users on a social and emotional level. These robots are equipped with advanced speech recognition and natural language processing capabilities, allowing them to understand and respond [1] to spoken commands and engage in basic conversations. They often incorporate facial recognition technology to identify and remember individual users, and they are programmed with a range of emotional expressions, conveyed through animated displays, vocalizations, and physical movements. Companion robots are intended to provide companionship and social interaction, particularly for individuals who may experience loneliness or isolation, such as children or the elderly. They can also be programmed to assist with practical tasks, such as providing reminders for medications or daily routines, further enhancing their utility as supportive companions.

Addressing the specific needs of the aging population, **robots for elderly care**, such as ElliQ developed by Intuition Robotics, are emerging as valuable digital companions. These robots are designed to help seniors stay connected with family and friends through video calls and messaging, track important health metrics such as activity levels and sleep patterns, and engage users in cognitive activities and mental exercises to promote cognitive well-being. ElliQ, for instance, proactively initiates interactions, offering suggestions for activities, reminding users of appointments, and providing a sense of presence and connection. Such robots aim to promote independent living for seniors while ensuring their safety, maintaining their mental engagement, and reducing feelings of isolation.

Finally, while not possessing a physical, mobile form, **voice-controlled smart assistants**, such as Amazon Alexa and Google Assistant, are increasingly considered an integral part of the domestic robot ecosystem. These AI-powered virtual assistants are embedded in smart speakers and other connected devices throughout the home. They automate a wide range of home systems, including lighting, thermostats, and entertainment devices, answer a vast array of user queries, provide information, set reminders, and control other connected smart devices through voice commands. By seamlessly integrating into the home environment and automating numerous daily tasks, these voice assistants contribute significantly to the creation of a more roboticized and automated lifestyle, enhancing convenience and control over the home environment.

Diagrammatic Representation of Domestic and Companion Robots:

```
                                    [The Domestic Robot Ecosystem]
                                              |
               --------------------------------------------------------------
-------------------
        |                                              |
|
      [Cleaning Robots (e.g., Roomba, Braava)]       [Security Robots (e.g., K5-
inspired)]          [Companion & Eldercare Robots]
        |                                              |
|
        --------------------------------------------------------------
-----------
        |         |         |         |         |         |
|
      [Autonomous Floor Cleaning] [Outdoor Cleaning (Lawn Mowers, Window
Cleaners)] [Perimeter Patrol & Anomaly Detection] [Social Interaction &
Companionship (Jibo, Aibo)] [Elderly Assistance (ElliQ)] [Voice-Controlled
Smart Assistants (Alexa, Google Assistant)]
        |         |         |         |         |         |
|
        --------------------------------------------------------------
-----------
        |                                              |
|
      [Reduced Manual Workload]                    [Enhanced Home Safety]
[Social Engagement & Emotional Support]
      [Increased Convenience]                      [Proactive Threat Detection]
[Cognitive Stimulation & Health Monitoring]
      [Time Savings]                                [Remote Monitoring]
[Promotion of Independent Living]
        |                                              |
|
        --------------------------------------------------------------
-----------
                                    |
```

This diagram illustrates the diverse categories within the domestic robot ecosystem. Cleaning robots autonomously handle floor and outdoor cleaning tasks, reducing manual workload and saving time. Security robots patrol the home perimeter and detect unusual activities, enhancing home safety and offering remote monitoring capabilities. Companion and eldercare robots provide social interaction, emotional support, cognitive stimulation, and health monitoring, promoting well-being and independent living. Voice-controlled smart assistants, while not physically embodied, contribute significantly to home automation and convenience. The overarching impact of these robotic technologies is an enhanced quality of life and a more automated and convenient home environment.

10.3 The Automation of Service: Robotics Revolutionizing the Food and Hospitality Sectors

The food and hospitality industries are undergoing a significant transformation with the increasing integration of robotic technologies. These automated systems are being deployed across a wide spectrum of roles, demonstrating their capacity to enhance service speed, ensure greater consistency in operations, and elevate hygiene standards. From the intricate preparation of gourmet meals to the efficient delivery of orders and the provision of engaging guest interactions, robots are rapidly becoming integral to the functioning of restaurants, hotels, catering services, and various other establishments within these sectors.

In the domain of **food preparation**, robots are moving beyond simple, repetitive tasks to undertake complex culinary operations. Pioneering systems, such as the kitchen developed by Moley Robotics, showcase the potential for fully automated cooking. These advanced robotic kitchens utilize dexterous robotic arms, guided by sophisticated recipe algorithms stored in their internal memory, to prepare complete meals from scratch. The robots can access and manipulate a wide array of ingredients, operate various kitchen appliances, and execute intricate cooking techniques with precision and consistency. This level of automation not only promises to reduce labor costs and ensure consistent food quality but also opens up possibilities for personalized and on-demand meal preparation.

Within the fast food sector, companies like Creator and Miso Robotics, with their Flippy robot, are demonstrating the practical application of robotics in high-volume food production. Flippy, for example, is designed to automate the grilling of burgers, manage the frying of various food items, and even assemble orders with remarkable speed and accuracy. Equipped with sensors that monitor cooking parameters such as temperature and cooking time, these robots can ensure optimal food quality and consistency across every order. By automating these critical tasks, fast food chains can potentially increase throughput, reduce waiting times for customers, and maintain a higher level of hygiene in food preparation areas.

The task of **serving food and beverages** in restaurants is also being revolutionized by the introduction of serving robots, such as BellaBot and Peanut. These mobile robots are designed to autonomously navigate through often crowded dining spaces, carrying trays laden with food and drinks to designated tables. Equipped with an array of sensors, including lidar, sonar, and cameras, along with sophisticated navigation software, these robots can safely maneuver around obstacles, avoid collisions with staff and customers, and efficiently deliver orders. Many serving robots are also equipped with interactive touchscreens or voice prompt capabilities, allowing them to announce their arrival at a table, interact with customers in a limited capacity (e.g., prompting them to take their dishes), and even play promotional messages or entertainment. By automating the physical act of food delivery, these robots can free up human servers to focus on more customer-centric tasks, such as taking orders, addressing customer inquiries, and providing a more personalized dining experience.

In the **hotel industry**, service robots are taking on a variety of roles aimed at enhancing guest convenience and streamlining operations. Robots are being deployed to assist with the check-in process, providing guests with information and directions. They are also being used for the autonomous delivery of luggage to guest rooms, eliminating the need for bellhops in certain situations and offering a swift and efficient service. Furthermore, humanoid robots, such as Pepper, are being positioned in hotel lobbies to greet guests, provide information about hotel amenities and local attractions, and offer a novel and engaging point of interaction. The novelty and interactivity of these robots can enhance the overall guest experience and create a memorable stay. The Relay robot by Savioke is another example of a hotel service robot, specifically designed for autonomous delivery of small items, such as toiletries or snacks, directly to guest rooms upon request, improving response times and guest satisfaction.

Maintaining **cleanliness and hygiene** is paramount in the food and hospitality sectors, and robots are proving to be valuable assets in these areas as well. Autonomous floor-cleaning robots are increasingly being used to clean lobbies, hallways, dining areas, and other large spaces in hotels, restaurants, and catering facilities. These robots can operate for extended periods without human intervention, following pre-programmed routes or dynamically adapting to their environment using sensors. By automating floor cleaning, these robots reduce the workload on housekeeping staff, allowing them to focus on more specialized cleaning tasks, and contribute to a higher overall level of cleanliness and hygiene within the establishment.

Finally, **customer engagement robots** are emerging as a novel way to interact with guests and promote services in various hospitality settings, including events, exhibitions, and hotel lobbies. These robots are designed to be interactive and engaging, capable of answering frequently asked questions about the venue, providing information about services or products, and even conducting surveys or collecting feedback. Their unique appearance and interactive capabilities can attract attention, enhance guest experiences, and provide a memorable point of contact. By automating basic information dissemination and engagement tasks, these robots can free up human staff to focus on more complex and personalized interactions with guests.

Diagrammatic Representation of Robotics in the Food and Hospitality Sector:

```
                    [Food & Hospitality Service Robots]
                                     |
        -------------------------------------------------------------
-------------------
```

```
                 |                                        |
  |
      [Food Preparation Robots (e.g., Moley, Flippy)]        [Serving & Delivery
Robots (e.g., BellaBot, Peanut, Relay)]          [Guest Interaction & Service
Robots (e.g., Pepper)]
                 |                                        |
  |
      -----------------------------------------------------------------
  -----------
                 |           |           |           |           |           |
  |
      [Automated Cooking] [Grilling & Frying] [Order Assembly] [Autonomous Food
Delivery] [Luggage Transport] [Check-in Assistance] [Concierge Services]
[Greeting & Information] [Autonomous Cleaning] [Customer Engagement]
                 |           |           |           |           |           |
  |
      -----------------------------------------------------------------
  -----------
                 |                                        |
  |
      [Consistent Food Quality]                   [Reduced Waiting Times]
[Enhanced Guest Experience]
      [Reduced Labor Costs]                       [Efficient Delivery]
[Novelty & Interactivity]
      [Increased Hygiene]                         [Staff Focus on Customer Service]
[Improved Operational Efficiency]
                 |                                        |
  |
      -----------------------------------------------------------------
  -----------
                                        |
                             [Revolutionizing Service Speed,
Consistency, and Hygiene]
```

This diagram illustrates the key applications of robotics within the food and hospitality sectors. Food preparation robots automate cooking tasks, ensuring consistency and potentially reducing labor costs. Serving and delivery robots enhance efficiency by autonomously delivering food and luggage. Guest interaction and service robots, including humanoid models, improve guest experience through greeting, information provision, and concierge services. Autonomous cleaning robots contribute to higher hygiene standards and reduce the workload of housekeeping staff. Customer engagement robots offer novelty and interactivity, enhancing guest experiences at events and in lobbies. The overarching impact of these robotic technologies is a revolution in service speed, consistency, and hygiene within the food and hospitality industries.

In summary, service robots across healthcare, homes, and hospitality are reshaping how tasks are performed, improving safety, efficiency, and quality of life. As artificial intelligence and robotics continue to evolve, these systems will become more adaptive, intelligent, and integral to daily human life.

50 multiple-choice questions (MCQs) with **answers** based on **Chapter 10: Service Robotics**, covering the topics:

- Healthcare and Surgical Robots
- Domestic and Companion Robots
- Food and Hospitality Sector Applications

Section 10.1: Healthcare and Surgical Robots (Q1–Q20)

1. **Which of the following is a well-known surgical robot system?**
   A. Sophia
   B. Pepper
   C. da Vinci
   D. Jibo
   Answer: C

2. **The primary advantage of surgical robots is:**
   A. Cost reduction
   B. Fully autonomous diagnosis
   C. Enhanced precision and minimal invasiveness
   D. Replacement of doctors
   Answer: C

3. **Which robot is known for delivering items in hospitals autonomously?**
   A. Pepper
   B. TUG
   C. Roomba
   D. Relay
   Answer: B

4. **ReWalk is best described as a:**
   A. Cleaning robot
   B. Surveillance robot
   C. Robotic exoskeleton for mobility
   D. Cooking assistant robot
   Answer: C

5. **Telemedicine robots became especially important during which global event?**
   A. World War II
   B. 9/11 attacks
   C. COVID-19 pandemic
   D. Tsunami in Japan
   Answer: C

6. **PARO is a robotic:**
   A. Surgical tool
   B. Security device
   C. Therapeutic companion seal
   D. Diagnostic scanner
   Answer: C

7. **Surgical robots reduce the risk of:**
   A. Machine errors
   B. Patient-doctor communication
   C. Infection and recovery time
   D. Hospital expenses
   Answer: C

8. **Which of the following is NOT a function of healthcare service robots?**
   A. Delivering medical supplies
   B. Performing full body transplants
   C. Assisting in surgery
   D. Disinfecting rooms
   Answer: B

9. **Which robot helps people with spinal cord injuries walk again?**
   A. Roomba
   B. ReWalk
   C. Flippy
   D. ElliQ
   Answer: B

10. **Mobile healthcare robots typically use which technologies for navigation?**
    A. GPS only
    B. Camera sensors, LiDAR, and SLAM
    C. Joystick control
    D. Bluetooth tracking
    Answer: B

11. **Telemedicine robots typically include:**
    A. 3D printers
    B. Voice assistants
    C. Cameras, sensors, and communication modules
    D. Laser cutters
    Answer: C

12. **Which robotic system assists doctors remotely during consultations?**
    A. K5
    B. TUG
    C. Telepresence robots
    D. Jibo
    Answer: C

13. **What is the main purpose of UV disinfection robots?**
    A. Administer vaccines
    B. Perform surgery
    C. Eliminate bacteria and viruses from rooms
    D. Train doctors
    Answer: C

14. **Surgical robots are usually controlled by:**
    A. AI software alone
    B. Nurses
    C. Surgeons via a console
    D. Patients
    Answer: C

15. **Which feature enhances the performance of robotic surgery?**
    A. Random motion
    B. Manual operation
    C. High-definition 3D imaging
    D. Voice recognition
    Answer: C
16. **Assistive robots are commonly used in:**
    A. Construction
    B. Eldercare and rehabilitation
    C. Mining
    D. Retail
    Answer: B
17. **PARO is especially useful for patients with:**
    A. Lung disease
    B. Broken bones
    C. Dementia or mental health issues
    D. Vision problems
    Answer: C
18. **One benefit of robotic surgical systems is:**
    A. Complete automation of patient care
    B. Eliminates need for anesthesia
    C. Smaller incisions and faster healing
    D. Removes the need for nurses
    Answer: C
19. **Rehabilitation robots support:**
    A. Psychological analysis
    B. Physical movement and therapy
    C. Database management
    D. Telecommunication
    Answer: B
20. **A robot used for both emotional and cognitive support in hospitals is:**
    A. Moley
    B. Jibo
    C. PARO
    D. Flippy
    Answer: C

Section 10.2: Domestic and Companion Robots (Q21–Q35)

21. **Which of the following is a cleaning robot?**
    A. Aibo
    B. Roomba
    C. TUG
    D. BellaBot
    Answer: B

22. **Aibo is designed as a:**
    A. Cleaning tool
    B. Cooking assistant
    C. Robotic dog companion
    D. Hotel service robot
    Answer: C

23. **Jibo is known for:**
    A. Cooking meals
    B. Emotional interaction and facial recognition
    C. Washing clothes
    D. Room mapping
    Answer: B

24. **Which of these robots can assist elderly individuals with daily reminders?**
    A. Flippy
    B. ElliQ
    C. BellaBot
    D. Relay
    Answer: B

25. **Companion robots are designed to:**
    A. Replace chefs
    B. Perform surgeries
    C. Provide emotional support and interaction
    D. Manage accounts
    Answer: C

26. **Robotic vacuum cleaners use:**
    A. Only manual control
    B. Sensor-based navigation and memory maps
    C. Laser cutting tools
    D. Internet connections only
    Answer: B

27. **Smart home assistants like Alexa are considered part of:**
    A. Industrial robots
    B. Companion robot systems
    C. Autonomous vehicles
    D. Nanotechnology
    Answer: B

28. **Domestic robots reduce the need for:**
    A. Hospitals
    B. Manual household labor
    C. Human relationships
    D. Software updates
    Answer: B

29. **Window-cleaning robots are most useful for:**
    A. Cooking glass utensils
    B. Office decoration
    C. Cleaning vertical surfaces
    D. Operating elevators
    Answer: C

30. **Which robot is equipped with pet-like behavior to enhance companionship?**
    A. Roomba
    B. Relay
    C. Aibo
    D. K5
    Answer: C
31. **Companion robots often include features such as:**
    A. Gas detection
    B. Movement tracking and emotional interaction
    C. Surgery assistance
    D. Online shopping
    Answer: B
32. **Home security robots primarily function by:**
    A. Performing facial surgery
    B. Navigating hospitals
    C. Patrolling and monitoring surroundings
    D. Cooking meals
    Answer: C
33. **Robotic lawn mowers:**
    A. Clean kitchens
    B. Operate indoors
    C. Trim grass autonomously
    D. Work only with human control
    Answer: C
34. **Which of the following enhances independent living for seniors?**
    A. UV robots
    B. ElliQ
    C. Moley
    D. Relay
    Answer: B
35. **Smart assistants often integrate with:**
    A. Space missions
    B. Quantum computers
    C. IoT-enabled home devices
    D. Manual switchboards
    Answer: C

Section 10.3: Food and Hospitality Sector Applications (Q36–Q50)

36. **Which robot is known for flipping burgers?**
    A. TUG
    B. Roomba
    C. Flippy
    D. Aibo
    Answer: C

37. **Moley Robotics is famous for developing a:**
    A. Delivery robot
    B. Companion robot
    C. Robotic kitchen
    D. Window cleaner
    Answer: C
38. **BellaBot is designed to:**
    A. Cook meals
    B. Clean toilets
    C. Serve food in restaurants
    D. Guard banks
    Answer: C
39. **In which industry are customer engagement robots commonly used?**
    A. Agriculture
    B. Construction
    C. Hospitality
    D. Mining
    Answer: C
40. **The Relay robot delivers items to:**
    A. Hospitals
    B. Schools
    C. Guest rooms in hotels
    D. Shopping malls
    Answer: C
41. **Hospitality robots help reduce:**
    A. Tourism
    B. Human staff workload
    C. Water usage
    D. Customer arrival rates
    Answer: B
42. **Floor-cleaning robots in hotels are used for:**
    A. Cooking meals
    B. Greeting guests
    C. Cleaning lobbies and hallways
    D. Operating elevators
    Answer: C
43. **Customer engagement robots often appear in:**
    A. Zoos
    B. Libraries
    C. Hotel lobbies and events
    D. Mines
    Answer: C
44. **Robots in restaurants contribute to:**
    A. Food spoilage
    B. Slower service
    C. Consistent service and hygiene
    D. Manual cooking
    Answer: C

45. **Which technology allows food-serving robots to avoid obstacles?**
    A. Barcodes
    B. AI and sensor-based navigation
    C. Magnetism
    D. Solar panels
    Answer: B
46. **Robots in hospitality can perform all EXCEPT:**
    A. Handle customer data entry
    B. Welcome guests
    C. Repair hotel buildings
    D. Deliver food
    Answer: C
47. **Interactive robots like Pepper can:**
    A. Drive cars
    B. Manage hotel accounting
    C. Greet and communicate with guests
    D. Paint walls
    Answer: C
48. **Which of the following sectors is NOT currently served by service robots?**
    A. Healthcare
    B. Domestic
    C. Hospitality
    D. Astronomy
    Answer: D
49. **Robots like Peanut are designed for:**
    A. Home cleaning
    B. Cooking in restaurants
    C. Delivering food in restaurants
    D. Diagnosing diseases
    Answer: C
50. **The use of service robots in hospitality leads to:**
    A. Decreased automation
    B. Poor customer experience
    C. Increased service efficiency
    D. Increased staff requirements
    Answer: C

Chapter 11: Autonomous Vehicles and Drones

11.1 The Dawn of Driverless Mobility: A Comprehensive Exploration of Self-Driving Cars

The advent and progressive refinement of self-driving cars represent a monumental leap forward in the evolution of modern transportation technology. These sophisticated vehicles, frequently referred to as autonomous or driverless cars, are intricately engineered with a synergistic combination of advanced sensors, complex software systems, and cutting-edge Artificial Intelligence (AI) algorithms. This technological amalgamation empowers them with the remarkable ability to navigate roadways and execute driving maneuvers without any direct human intervention or control. The realization of fully autonomous vehicles holds the potential to fundamentally reshape personal mobility, urban planning, and logistics networks on a global scale.

At the very core of a self-driving car's operational architecture lies a sophisticated and multi-layered **sensor suite**. This suite typically comprises a complementary array of sensing modalities, including:

- **LiDAR (Light Detection and Ranging):** This crucial sensor technology generates highly precise, real-time three-dimensional (3D) maps of the vehicle's surrounding environment. LiDAR systems operate by emitting a multitude of laser beams in various directions and then meticulously measuring the time it takes for these beams to reflect off surrounding objects and return to the sensor. By analyzing the time-of-flight and the angle of the returning laser pulses, the system can create a detailed point cloud representation of the environment, accurately depicting the shape, size, and distance of objects such as other vehicles, pedestrians, cyclists, infrastructure elements (like buildings, trees, and road barriers), and even road surface contours. LiDAR provides unparalleled accuracy in depth perception and spatial mapping, making it a cornerstone of many advanced autonomous driving systems.
- **Radar:** Radio Detection and Ranging (radar) systems play a vital role in detecting the speed and distance of surrounding vehicles and other moving objects. Radar operates by emitting radio waves and analyzing the reflected signals. Unlike LiDAR, radar is less susceptible to adverse weather conditions such as heavy rain, fog, and snow, making it a crucial sensor for maintaining situational awareness in challenging environments. While radar typically provides lower spatial resolution compared to LiDAR, it excels at detecting the velocity of objects and their distance, often over longer ranges. This capability is essential for tasks like adaptive cruise control, collision avoidance, and tracking the movement of nearby vehicles.
- **Cameras:** An array of high-resolution cameras strategically positioned around the self-driving car provides rich visual information about the environment. These cameras capture detailed images and video feeds, which are then processed by sophisticated computer vision algorithms to identify a wide range of objects, interpret traffic signals and signs, detect lane markings, recognize pedestrians and cyclists, and monitor the overall road scene. The advancements in deep learning and neural networks have

significantly enhanced the ability of camera-based systems to accurately perceive and understand complex visual data in real time, making them an indispensable component of the sensor suite.

- **Ultrasonic Sensors:** These sensors utilize high-frequency sound waves to detect the presence and distance of objects in close proximity to the vehicle. Ultrasonic sensors are particularly useful for short-range detection during low-speed maneuvers such as parking, navigating in tight spaces, and detecting nearby obstacles that might be below the field of view of other sensors. They provide accurate distance measurements at close range and are often employed in parking assist systems and for detecting objects immediately surrounding the vehicle.

The vast and diverse data streams generated by this comprehensive sensor suite are fed into the self-driving car's central **computer system**, which serves as the brain of the autonomous operation. This powerful computing platform utilizes complex **machine learning algorithms**, particularly deep learning models and neural networks, to process and interpret the raw sensor data in real time. The AI system performs several critical functions:

- **Environmental Perception:** It analyzes the fused data from all the sensors to build a comprehensive and dynamic understanding of the vehicle's surroundings, identifying and localizing objects, mapping the road layout, and detecting potential hazards.
- **Behavior Prediction:** Based on the observed movements and characteristics of other road users (vehicles, pedestrians, cyclists), the AI system employs predictive models to anticipate their future behavior, such as predicting the trajectory of a turning vehicle or the path of a crossing pedestrian.
- **Path Planning:** Given the vehicle's current location, its intended destination, and the perceived environment, the AI system plans a safe and efficient driving route, taking into account traffic rules, road conditions, and the predicted behavior of other agents.
- **Decision Making:** In real time, the AI system makes critical driving decisions, such as when to accelerate, decelerate, brake, steer, change lanes, or navigate intersections, based on its understanding of the environment, its planned path, and the predicted actions of others.

A notable example of a company employing a vision-centric approach to self-driving technology is **Tesla** with its **Autopilot** system (and its Full Self-Driving beta program). Tesla's system heavily leverages a network of cameras surrounding the vehicle, coupled with powerful neural networks that are trained on vast amounts of real-world driving data to perceive the environment and make driving decisions. Another prominent player in the field, **Waymo** (formerly Google's self-driving car project), utilizes a more multimodal approach, heavily relying on a combination of high-resolution LiDAR and advanced AI algorithms to achieve full autonomy in a variety of complex driving conditions and environments.

The **Society of Automotive Engineers (SAE)** has developed a widely accepted classification system that defines six distinct **levels of driving automation**, ranging from no automation to full autonomy:

- **Level 0: No Automation:** At this level, the human driver is entirely responsible for all aspects of driving, including steering, acceleration, and braking. There are no automated features in control of the vehicle's dynamic driving task.
- **Level 1: Driver Assistance:** This level involves basic automation features that can assist the driver with either steering or acceleration/braking, but not both simultaneously. Examples include adaptive cruise control (which automatically maintains a set speed and following distance) and lane keeping assist (which can provide steering input to help the driver stay within lane markings). The human driver remains fully engaged and responsible for monitoring the driving environment and intervening when necessary.
- **Level 2: Partial Automation:** Vehicles at this level can control both steering and acceleration/braking simultaneously under certain circumstances, such as highway driving. However, the human driver is still required to continuously monitor the driving environment and be prepared to take over control at any time if the system encounters a situation it cannot handle. Examples include systems that combine adaptive cruise control and lane centering.
- **Level 3: Conditional Automation:** This level marks a significant step towards autonomy. Vehicles with Level 3 automation can drive themselves under specific, limited conditions (e.g., on a highway in moderate traffic) and can monitor the driving environment. However, the system is not capable of handling all situations and may request the human driver to intervene when it encounters a scenario it cannot manage. The key difference from Level 2 is that at Level 3, the driver can, in some situations, disengage from actively monitoring the driving environment and rely on the vehicle to prompt them if intervention is needed.
- **Level 4: High Automation:** At this level, the vehicle is capable of performing all driving tasks under specific, designated operational design domains (ODD), such as within a geofenced area in a city. In these ODDs, no human driver input is required. However, the vehicle may not be capable of operating autonomously in all conditions or environments. If the vehicle encounters a situation outside its ODD or a scenario it cannot handle, it is designed to safely bring itself to a stop.
- **Level 5: Full Automation:** This represents the pinnacle of autonomous driving. A Level 5 vehicle is capable of performing all driving tasks under all conditions and in all environments that a human driver could handle. There are no limitations on its operational design domain, and no human intervention is ever required. Such vehicles may not even be equipped with traditional driver controls like a steering wheel or pedals.

Diagrammatic Representation of Sensor Fusion in a Self-Driving Car:

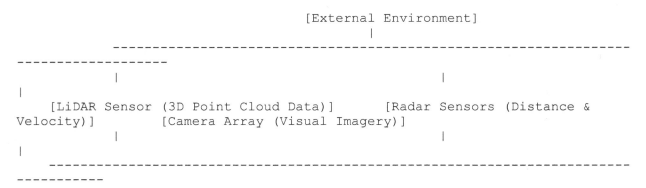

```
        \                                    |
  /            \                              |
  /                -----------------------------------------------------------
  --------------
                                             |
                                             v
                              [Central Processing Unit (AI &
  Machine Learning Algorithms)]
                                             |
              ------------------------------------------------------------
  -------------------
                     |                              |
  |
      [Environmental Perception (Object Detection, Scene Understanding,
  Localization)]          [Path Planning & Behavior Prediction]
                     |                              |
              -----------------------------------------------------------
  -------------
                                             |
                                             v
                              [Control Systems (Steering,
  Braking, Acceleration)]
                                             |
                                             v
                              [Vehicle Movement]
```

This diagram illustrates the sensor fusion process in a self-driving car. Data from various sensors (LiDAR, radar, and cameras) is fed into the central processing unit. The AI and machine learning algorithms within the CPU process this data to achieve environmental perception, path planning, and behavior prediction. Based on this processed information, the CPU communicates with the vehicle's control systems (steering, braking, and acceleration) to execute driving maneuvers.

The widespread adoption of self-driving cars promises numerous potential **benefits**, including:

- **Reduced Traffic Accidents:** Human error is a leading cause of traffic accidents. Autonomous vehicles, with their consistent and precise sensing and decision-making capabilities, have the potential to significantly reduce the number of collisions caused by factors such as distracted driving, fatigue, and impairment.
- **Improved Traffic Flow:** Autonomous vehicles can communicate with each other and with traffic management systems, potentially leading to optimized traffic flow, reduced congestion, and smoother movement of vehicles, especially in urban environments.
- **Enhanced Mobility for the Elderly and Disabled:** Self-driving cars can provide independent mobility for individuals who are unable to drive due to age, physical limitations, or medical conditions, significantly enhancing their quality of life and access to transportation.
- **Increased Fuel Efficiency and Reduced Emissions:** Optimized routing and smoother driving patterns enabled by autonomous systems can lead to improved fuel efficiency and reduced greenhouse gas emissions.

- **Freed Up Commuting Time:** Passengers in self-driving cars could utilize their commuting time for work, leisure, or other activities, leading to increased productivity and personal time.

However, the development and deployment of self-driving cars also present significant **challenges**, including:

- **Sensor Limitations:** While sensor technology has advanced significantly, current sensors still have limitations in certain adverse weather conditions (e.g., heavy fog, blizzard) and complex scenarios. Ensuring robust performance in all conditions remains a key challenge.
- **Unpredictable Human Behavior:** Predicting and reacting safely to the unpredictable actions of human drivers, pedestrians, and cyclists in complex real-world traffic scenarios is a significant hurdle for autonomous systems.
- **Ethical Dilemmas:** Programming autonomous vehicles to make ethical decisions in unavoidable accident scenarios (e.g., the "trolley problem") raises complex ethical and societal questions.
- **Cybersecurity Risks:** Autonomous vehicles, with their sophisticated software and network connectivity, are potential targets for cyberattacks, raising concerns about safety and security.
- **Regulatory Frameworks:** The lack of comprehensive and consistent regulatory frameworks for the testing and deployment of self-driving cars poses a challenge to their widespread adoption. Governments and industry stakeholders are actively working to establish appropriate legal and safety standards.
- **Public Perception and Trust:** Gaining public trust and acceptance of self-driving technology is crucial for its successful deployment. Addressing concerns about safety, reliability, and job displacement will be essential.

11.2 The Ascendant Sky: Delivery Drones and Aerial Robots Transforming Industries

The tapestry of logistics and transportation is undergoing a profound transformation, woven with the threads of innovation and automation. At the forefront of this aerial revolution stand delivery drones and aerial robots, poised to redefine how goods and services traverse distances and how industries conduct their operations. These unmanned aerial vehicles (UAVs), once the realm of science fiction, are rapidly becoming tangible realities, their whirring propellers heralding an era of enhanced efficiency, accessibility, and responsiveness.

The fundamental allure of delivery drones lies in their capacity to circumvent the limitations of terrestrial infrastructure. Congested roadways, geographical barriers, and the inherent time constraints of traditional delivery methods are rendered less formidable by these airborne couriers. Their ability to navigate directly to designated locations, often following optimized aerial pathways, translates into swifter transit times, particularly crucial for time-sensitive deliveries and for reaching remote or underserved communities.

Consider, for instance, the burgeoning field of last-mile delivery, the final leg of a product's journey to the consumer's doorstep. This segment has historically been characterized by its high cost and logistical complexities. Delivery drones offer a compelling solution, capable of navigating urban landscapes with agility, bypassing traffic bottlenecks, and delivering packages with remarkable speed and precision. The vision of near-instantaneous delivery, once a futuristic fantasy, is steadily gaining traction, fueled by the advancements in drone technology and the relentless pursuit of logistical optimization.

Several key technological components underpin the autonomous capabilities of modern delivery drones. A **Global Positioning System (GPS) module** acts as the drone's navigational compass, providing precise location data and enabling accurate route following. Complementing this is an **Inertial Measurement Unit (IMU)**, a sophisticated sensor package comprising gyroscopes and accelerometers. Gyroscopes measure the drone's rotational velocity, detecting changes in its orientation, while accelerometers measure linear acceleration, sensing changes in speed and direction. The fusion of data from the GPS and IMU provides a comprehensive understanding of the drone's position, orientation, and motion in three-dimensional space, forming the bedrock of its autonomous flight control.

Cameras serve as the drone's eyes, providing visual information about its surroundings. These cameras can be utilized for a multitude of tasks, including obstacle detection and avoidance, identification of landing zones, and even package verification. Advanced image processing algorithms enable the drone to interpret the visual data, perceive its environment, and make informed decisions in real-time.

Furthermore, sophisticated **obstacle detection systems** are crucial for ensuring safe and autonomous operation. These systems can employ a variety of sensor technologies, such as ultrasonic sensors, lidar (Light Detection and Ranging), and infrared sensors, to detect and map obstacles in the drone's flight path. By continuously scanning the environment, the drone can identify potential collisions and execute evasive maneuvers, ensuring the safety of both the drone and its surroundings.

The integration of these components allows for intricate autonomous flight patterns, pre-programmed route execution, and pinpoint accurate landings. The development by companies like Amazon Prime Air, showcasing drones capable of delivering packages within a 30-minute timeframe, exemplifies the potential of this technology to revolutionize e-commerce logistics. Similarly, the impactful work of Zipline in regions like Rwanda and Ghana highlights the transformative power of fixed-wing drones in delivering critical medical supplies, such as blood, to remote areas inaccessible by traditional transportation methods. Their operations underscore the ability of drones to overcome geographical barriers and provide essential services where they are most needed.

Drones exhibit a diverse range of designs, broadly categorized into **rotary-wing** and **fixed-wing** configurations, each possessing distinct advantages and suited for different operational contexts.

Rotary-wing drones, exemplified by the ubiquitous **quadcopter** (featuring four rotors), excel in their ability to perform **vertical take-off and landing (VTOL)**. This characteristic makes them particularly well-suited for operations in confined spaces and urban environments, where runways are unavailable and maneuverability is paramount. Their hovering capability also allows for precise positioning during package delivery and detailed aerial inspections. The agility and versatility of rotary-wing drones have made them a popular choice for a wide array of applications, from aerial photography and videography to surveillance and short-range delivery services.

Fixed-wing drones, in contrast, resemble conventional aircraft with their stationary wings generating lift. While they require runways or specialized launching mechanisms for take-off and landing, their aerodynamic design offers significantly greater **energy efficiency** and **longer flight ranges** compared to rotary-wing counterparts. This makes them ideal for long-distance cargo transport, wide-area surveillance, and mapping applications. Their ability to cover substantial distances with greater endurance opens up possibilities for inter-city deliveries and large-scale logistical operations.

A pivotal advancement propelling the capabilities of delivery drones and aerial robots is the seamless **integration of Artificial Intelligence (AI)**. AI algorithms are no longer confined to laboratory settings; they are increasingly embedded within the drone's onboard processing systems, enabling **real-time decision-making** and enhancing their autonomy.

AI empowers drones to dynamically adapt to complex and unpredictable real-world scenarios. **Obstacle avoidance** is significantly enhanced through AI-powered computer vision, allowing drones to not only detect but also intelligently navigate around static and moving obstacles with greater precision and safety than relying solely on pre-programmed responses.

Recognition of delivery zones is another area where AI plays a crucial role. By analyzing visual data, AI algorithms can identify designated landing pads or specific locations with a high degree of accuracy, ensuring precise and reliable package delivery. This eliminates the need for manual intervention and enhances the efficiency of the delivery process.

Furthermore, AI enables drones to **adjust to environmental changes** in real-time. Fluctuations in wind speed and direction, as well as varying weather conditions such as light rain, can be detected and compensated for by AI algorithms that dynamically adjust the drone's flight parameters to maintain stability and adherence to the planned route. This adaptability enhances the operational resilience of drones and expands their usability across a wider range of environmental conditions.

To visualize the intricate interplay of these technologies, consider the **architecture of a typical delivery drone**:

Code snippet
```
graph TD
    A[GPS System] --> B(Flight Controller);
    C[IMU (Inertial Measurement Unit)] --> B;
    D[Communication Module] --> B;
    E[Battery] --> F(Power Distribution);
    F --> B;
    F --> G[Motors/Actuators];
```

```
H[Payload Compartment] --> I(Drone Frame);
B --> G;
B --> J[Obstacle Detection System];
B --> K[Camera System];
K --> L[AI Processing Unit];
L --> B;
J --> B;
G --> I;
E --> H;
```

This simplified diagram illustrates the interconnectedness of key components. The **GPS system** and **IMU** provide crucial navigational data to the **flight controller**, the central processing unit of the drone. The **communication module** facilitates data exchange with a ground control station or a network. The **battery** provides the necessary power, distributed through a **power distribution system** to the **motors/actuators** that control the drone's movement. The **payload compartment** houses the goods being transported, attached to the **drone frame**. The **obstacle detection system** and **camera system**, often augmented by an **AI processing unit**, feed environmental data back to the flight controller for autonomous navigation and decision-making.

The applications of aerial robots extend far beyond the realm of package delivery, demonstrating their versatility and transformative potential across numerous industries.

In **agriculture**, aerial robots are revolutionizing crop management. Equipped with high-resolution cameras and specialized sensors, they can conduct detailed **crop monitoring**, assessing plant health, identifying areas of stress or disease, and providing valuable data for precision agriculture techniques. This information enables farmers to optimize irrigation, fertilization, and pest control efforts, leading to increased yields and reduced resource consumption.

The **construction** industry is also embracing the capabilities of aerial robots for **site surveys and progress monitoring**. Drones can capture high-resolution aerial imagery and create detailed 3D models of construction sites, providing valuable insights into project progress, identifying potential issues, and facilitating more efficient planning and management. Their ability to access difficult-to-reach areas also enhances safety and reduces the need for manual inspections.

During **emergency response** scenarios, aerial robots prove to be invaluable tools for **disaster assessment**. In the aftermath of natural disasters or other emergencies, drones can quickly survey affected areas, providing real-time aerial imagery and video footage that can aid first responders in assessing damage, identifying victims, and coordinating rescue efforts. Their rapid deployment and aerial perspective offer a significant advantage in time-critical situations.

Despite the numerous advantages and burgeoning applications of delivery drones and aerial robots, their widespread adoption is not without its challenges. **Regulatory hurdles** represent a significant factor influencing the pace and scope of their deployment.

Airspace management is a complex issue that needs careful consideration. Integrating large numbers of autonomous drones into existing airspace, shared with manned aircraft, requires the development of robust and standardized air traffic control systems to ensure safety and prevent collisions. Establishing clear protocols for drone identification, tracking, and communication is essential for effective airspace management.

Flight permissions and operational restrictions also vary significantly across different regions and countries. Regulations often address factors such as flight altitude, operating hours, beyond visual line of sight (BVLOS) operations, and the types of areas where drone flights are permitted or prohibited. Navigating this complex regulatory landscape is crucial for drone operators and businesses seeking to leverage this technology.

Noise concerns associated with drone operations, particularly in densely populated urban areas, are another factor that needs to be addressed. While advancements in drone design are leading to quieter aircraft, public perception and noise pollution remain important considerations for widespread acceptance.

Privacy risks associated with the use of drones equipped with cameras are also a significant concern. Ensuring the responsible use of drone-captured data, protecting individuals' privacy, and establishing clear guidelines for data collection and storage are essential for building public trust and mitigating potential misuse.

Recognizing these challenges, countries like the **United States** and **India** have been actively developing **specific drone regulations**. These regulations often include requirements for drone registration, pilot certification or remote pilot licenses, and the establishment of restricted flight zones to address safety, security, and privacy concerns. The ongoing evolution of these regulatory frameworks will play a crucial role in shaping the future of drone operations and their integration into society.

11.3 Navigating the Moral and Juridical Landscape: Ethical and Legal Implications of Autonomous Vehicles and Drones

The rapid proliferation of autonomous vehicles and drones marks a significant inflection point in technological advancement, promising enhanced efficiency, convenience, and safety across various domains. However, this transformative power is inextricably linked with a complex web of ethical and legal considerations that demand careful scrutiny and proactive solutions. As these intelligent machines increasingly permeate our lives, fundamental questions arise concerning their decision-making in critical situations, the safeguarding of vast troves of collected data, the assignment of liability in the event of mishaps, and the broader societal impacts on employment and privacy.

One of the most profound ethical dilemmas posed by autonomous vehicles centers on their programming to navigate unavoidable accident scenarios. Imagine a situation where a self-driving car is faced with an imminent collision, leaving it with a split-second decision that will inevitably result in harm. Should the vehicle prioritize the safety of its occupants, potentially at the expense of pedestrians, or should it be programmed to minimize the overall harm, even if it means sacrificing its passengers? This conundrum echoes the classic **"trolley problem"** in moral philosophy, a thought experiment that probes our intuitions about ethical decision-making in situations where all available choices lead to negative outcomes.

The trolley problem typically presents a scenario where a runaway trolley is hurtling down a track towards five unsuspecting individuals. A bystander has the option to pull a lever, diverting the trolley onto a side track where only one person is present. Is it morally permissible to pull the lever, thereby causing the death of one person to save five? Variations of this problem introduce further complexities, such as the bystander having to physically push a large person onto the tracks to stop the trolley, raising questions about the directness of the action and the intent behind it.

Applying this ethical framework to autonomous vehicles reveals the intricate challenges involved in programming moral algorithms. Different ethical frameworks offer varying perspectives. A **utilitarian approach** might suggest programming the vehicle to minimize the total number of casualties, regardless of who they are. This could mean sacrificing the passengers if it results in saving a larger number of pedestrians. Conversely, a **deontological approach**, emphasizing duties and rules, might argue against directly causing harm to any individual, even if it leads to a greater overall good. This could imply prioritizing the safety of the vehicle's occupants, as they are the ones in a contractual relationship with the vehicle and have entrusted their safety to it.

Furthermore, **cultural, legal, and personal values** introduce significant variations in how these ethical dilemmas are perceived and resolved. What might be considered an acceptable trade-off in one society could be deemed morally repugnant in another. Legal frameworks will also need to grapple with these complex ethical considerations, potentially setting standards for how autonomous vehicles should be programmed to respond in critical situations. The lack of universal ethical consensus underscores the difficulty in creating a one-size-fits-all solution for the moral programming of autonomous vehicles. The debate necessitates a broad societal dialogue involving ethicists, engineers, policymakers, and the public to forge a path forward that reflects our collective moral compass.

Beyond immediate safety concerns, the pervasive data collection inherent in autonomous systems raises significant **data privacy** concerns. These vehicles are equipped with a multitude of sensors, including cameras, lidar, radar, and GPS, which constantly gather and process vast quantities of data. This data can encompass highly sensitive information, such as personal identification details, precise location history, daily travel patterns, driving behavior, and even in-cabin activities.

The sheer volume and granularity of this data create numerous opportunities for potential misuse and security breaches. If this information falls into the wrong hands, it could be exploited for malicious purposes, including identity theft, stalking, targeted advertising based on private travel patterns, and even state-sponsored surveillance. The lack of robust data security measures could render individuals vulnerable to significant privacy violations.

Questions surrounding **data ownership and consent** are also paramount. Who owns the data generated by an autonomous vehicle? Is it the vehicle owner, the manufacturer, the software developer, or the network provider facilitating the data transmission? Furthermore, what constitutes informed consent regarding the collection and use of this data? Are users fully aware of the extent of data being gathered and how it is being utilized? Transparent and easily understandable privacy policies are crucial to ensure that individuals can make informed decisions about their data and exercise control over its use.

The potential for **data hacking** adds another layer of complexity. Autonomous systems, being interconnected and software-driven, are susceptible to cyberattacks. A successful breach could not only compromise personal data but also potentially take control of vehicle functions, posing significant safety risks. Robust cybersecurity measures, including encryption, intrusion detection systems, and regular software updates, are essential[1] to safeguard against such threats and ensure the integrity and security of autonomous systems.

The issue of **legal liability** in the event of accidents involving autonomous vehicles presents a significant departure from traditional fault determination in human-driven vehicles. When a self-driving car is involved in a collision, the question of who is at fault becomes considerably more intricate. Is the liability to be assigned to the **manufacturer** for potential design flaws or software glitches? Could the **software developer** be held responsible for errors in the autonomous driving algorithms? Does the **owner** bear responsibility, even if they were not actively controlling the vehicle at the time of the accident? Or could the **network provider**, responsible for the communication infrastructure supporting the vehicle's operation, be deemed liable?

Current legal frameworks are largely predicated on the notion of human error and are still in the nascent stages of adapting to the complexities of autonomous systems. Determining the precise cause of an accident involving a self-driving car requires a thorough investigation into the vehicle's sensor data, software logs, and operational parameters. Establishing a clear chain of responsibility is crucial for ensuring accountability and providing recourse for victims of accidents involving autonomous vehicles.

Some jurisdictions are exploring the implementation of regulations mandating a **human override feature** in autonomous vehicles. This provision allows a human driver to take control of the vehicle in situations where the autonomous system encounters limitations or malfunctions. The presence of a human override capability could potentially shift some of the liability back to the human operator if they were in control at the time of an accident or failed to intervene appropriately. However, the effectiveness and practicality of human override in critical, split-second scenarios remain subjects of ongoing debate and research.

The legal landscape surrounding **drone operations** also presents its own unique set of challenges. **Airspace violations** are a significant concern, particularly with the increasing number of drones operating in shared airspace with manned aircraft. Unauthorized drone flights in restricted airspace, such as near airports or critical infrastructure, can pose serious safety risks and disrupt air traffic. Clear regulations, coupled with effective enforcement mechanisms, are essential to prevent such violations.

The potential for **spying and unlawful surveillance** by drones equipped with high-resolution cameras raises significant privacy concerns. The ability of drones to conduct aerial surveillance discreetly and gather visual and potentially audio information necessitates clear legal frameworks governing their use, particularly in residential areas and other locations where individuals have a reasonable expectation of privacy.

The use of drones for **smuggling contraband** and **interfering with aircraft** represents more egregious legal violations. Instances of drones being used to transport illegal drugs or other illicit goods across borders or into restricted areas have been reported. Similarly, the deliberate or negligent operation of drones in a manner that endangers manned aircraft poses a severe safety threat. Governments are responding to these challenges by implementing measures such as **geofencing**, which creates virtual boundaries that prevent drones from entering restricted airspace; **remote identification systems**, which allow for the tracking and identification of drones and their operators; and the establishment of **strict no-fly zones** around sensitive locations.

Beyond the immediate safety and legal ramifications, the widespread deployment of autonomous technologies carries significant **ethical implications for employment**. The automation of tasks currently performed by human workers, such as delivery drivers, pilots, and various other transportation and logistics roles, raises concerns about potential **job displacement** and the need for **workforce retraining**.

As autonomous vehicles and drones become more sophisticated and capable of performing tasks previously requiring human skill and judgment, the demand for human labor in these sectors may decline. This could lead to significant economic and social disruption if proactive measures are not taken to address the potential for widespread job losses.

It becomes ethically imperative to **balance technological advancement with social responsibility**. While the benefits of autonomous technologies in terms of efficiency, safety, and convenience are undeniable, their implementation must be carefully managed to mitigate potential negative consequences for the workforce. Investing in education and retraining programs to equip workers with the skills needed for the jobs of the future will be crucial in navigating this transition. Exploring alternative economic models and social safety nets may also be necessary to support individuals whose jobs are displaced by automation.

A visual representation of the intricate relationship between technological autonomy and ethical/legal oversight can be depicted as follows:

Code snippet
```
graph TD
    A[Technological Autonomy] --> B(Ethical Considerations);
    A --> C(Legal Frameworks);
    B -- Influences --> C;
    C -- Shapes --> A;
    D[Manufacturers] -- Stakeholder --> B;
    D -- Stakeholder --> C;
    E[Regulators] -- Stakeholder --> C;
    F[Users] -- Stakeholder --> B;
```

```
F -- Stakeholder --> C;
G[Impacted Communities] -- Stakeholder --> B;
G -- Stakeholder --> C;
```

This diagram illustrates the bidirectional influence between technological autonomy and the ethical and legal domains. Advancements in autonomous technologies raise new ethical dilemmas and necessitate the development of appropriate legal frameworks. Conversely, ethical considerations and legal regulations can shape the trajectory of technological development and deployment. The diagram also highlights the key stakeholders involved in this complex interplay, including manufacturers, regulators, users, and the communities affected by these technologies.

To ensure the **safe and fair integration** of autonomous vehicles and drones into society, a **multi-stakeholder approach** is essential. This necessitates close collaboration and open dialogue between technology developers, policymakers, ethicists, and the public.

Transparent algorithms are crucial for building trust and accountability in autonomous systems. Understanding how these systems make decisions, particularly in safety-critical situations, is essential for both regulators and the public. Efforts to make the decision-making processes of autonomous systems more transparent and explainable are vital.

Accountable design principles should be embedded throughout the development lifecycle of autonomous technologies. This includes designing systems with clear lines of responsibility, incorporating robust safety mechanisms, and ensuring that there are mechanisms in place for addressing failures and unintended consequences.

Inclusive regulation is necessary to create a legal and ethical framework that fosters innovation while safeguarding public safety, privacy, and societal well-being. This requires a proactive and adaptive approach to regulation, one that can keep pace with the rapid advancements in autonomous technologies while considering the diverse perspectives and concerns of all stakeholders.

50 multiple-choice questions (MCQs) with answers based on **Chapter 11: Autonomous Vehicles and Drones**, covering all three subtopics:

11.1 Self-Driving Cars

1. **Which technology enables self-driving cars to create 3D maps of their surroundings?**
   A. Radar
   B. LiDAR
   C. GPS
   D. Ultrasonic Sensors
   ✓ **Answer: B. LiDAR**
2. **What level of automation allows full self-driving without any human intervention under all conditions?**

A. Level 3

B. Level 4

C. Level 5

D. Level 2

✓ **Answer: C. Level 5**

3. **Which company uses a vision-based approach for its self-driving technology?**

   A. Waymo

   B. Uber

   C. Tesla

   D. Nuro

   ✓ **Answer: C. Tesla**

4. **What is the main role of radar in autonomous vehicles?**

   A. Lane detection

   B. Short-range object detection

   C. Detecting speed and distance of surrounding vehicles

   D. Reading traffic signs

   ✓ **Answer: C. Detecting speed and distance of surrounding vehicles**

5. **Which level of automation allows the car to drive itself under specific conditions, but requires the driver to intervene when necessary?**

   A. Level 2

   B. Level 3

   C. Level 4

   D. Level 1

   ✓ **Answer: B. Level 3**

6. **Ultrasonic sensors in self-driving cars are primarily used for:**

   A. Weather detection

   B. Highway navigation

   C. Parking assistance

   D. Traffic signal recognition

   ✓ **Answer: C. Parking assistance**

7. **Which of the following is NOT a sensor commonly used in autonomous vehicles?**

   A. Thermometer

   B. Radar

   C. LiDAR

   D. Camera

   ✓ **Answer: A. Thermometer**

8. **The organization that defined six levels of vehicle autonomy is:**

   A. IEEE

   B. SAE

   C. ISO

   D. NHTSA

   ✓ **Answer: B. SAE**

9. **Waymo is a subsidiary of which parent company?**

   A. Amazon

   B. Apple

   C. Alphabet (Google)

D. Microsoft

✓ **Answer: C. Alphabet (Google)**

10. **The process of combining data from multiple sensors to make driving decisions is called:**
    A. Decision chaining
    B. Sensor fusion
    C. Signal processing
    D. Redundant mapping

    ✓ **Answer: B. Sensor fusion**

11.2 Delivery Drones and Aerial Robots

11. **What is the primary function of delivery drones?**
    A. Crop spraying
    B. Photography
    C. Package transportation
    D. Surveillance

    ✓ **Answer: C. Package transportation**

12. **Which type of drone is most suitable for long-distance delivery?**
    A. Hexacopter
    B. Fixed-wing drone
    C. Octocopter
    D. Quadcopter

    ✓ **Answer: B. Fixed-wing drone**

13. **Which of the following companies is known for drone-based medical supply delivery in Africa?**
    A. FedEx
    B. Zipline
    C. UPS
    D. SkyNet

    ✓ **Answer: B. Zipline**

14. **Vertical take-off and landing are features of which type of drone?**
    A. Fixed-wing
    B. Hybrid
    C. Quadcopter
    D. Glider

    ✓ **Answer: C. Quadcopter**

15. **What navigation system do delivery drones typically rely on?**
    A. Bluetooth
    B. Wi-Fi
    C. GPS
    D. NFC

    ✓ **Answer: C. GPS**

16. **Which component of a drone helps in measuring acceleration and angular velocity?**
    A. Gyroscope
    B. Camera
    C. Magnetometer

D. Altimeter

✅ **Answer: A. Gyroscope**

17. **Amazon's drone delivery service is known as:**
    A. DroneNow
    B. Amazon Sky
    C. Prime Air
    D. AirLift

    ✅ **Answer: C. Prime Air**

18. **A drone's obstacle detection system primarily relies on:**
    A. Altitude sensors
    B. Visual input and sonar
    C. Wind direction
    D. Weather forecasting

    ✅ **Answer: B. Visual input and sonar**

19. **Which drone type can hover in place and make agile maneuvers in tight spaces?**
    A. Fixed-wing
    B. Helicopter
    C. Quadcopter
    D. Balloon

    ✅ **Answer: C. Quadcopter**

20. **In agricultural settings, drones are used for:**
    A. Soil analysis only
    B. Weather forecasting
    C. Crop monitoring and spraying
    D. Harvesting crops

    ✅ **Answer: C. Crop monitoring and spraying**

11.3 Ethical and Legal Implications

21. **Which ethical problem is commonly discussed in relation to self-driving cars?**
    A. Privacy theft
    B. The trolley problem
    C. Free market impact
    D. Employment contracts

    ✅ **Answer: B. The trolley problem**

22. **A major privacy concern in autonomous vehicles involves:**
    A. Traffic congestion
    B. Battery consumption
    C. Data collection and misuse
    D. Color detection

    ✅ **Answer: C. Data collection and misuse**

23. **Who may be held liable if a fully autonomous car causes an accident?**
    A. The insurance company only
    B. The driver only
    C. The manufacturer, developer, or owner

D. The traffic police

☑ **Answer: C. The manufacturer, developer, or owner**

24. **Which of the following is a regulatory tool to control drone airspace?**
    A. VPN
    B. Geofencing
    C. CAPTCHA
    D. Hologram

    ☑ **Answer: B. Geofencing**

25. **What does the concept of 'remote identification' in drones ensure?**
    A. Tracking internet usage
    B. Identification of the pilot and location
    C. Battery management
    D. Surveillance capability

    ☑ **Answer: B. Identification of the pilot and location**

26. **An example of drone misuse is:**
    A. Wildlife photography
    B. Weather data collection
    C. Smuggling contraband
    D. Medical deliveries

    ☑ **Answer: C. Smuggling contraband**

27. **Which sector is most likely to face job displacement due to autonomous delivery vehicles?**
    A. IT support
    B. Education
    C. Logistics and transportation
    D. Entertainment

    ☑ **Answer: C. Logistics and transportation**

28. **Which document is often used to define legal drone operation areas?**
    A. Local tax code
    B. Flight zoning maps
    C. Building permits
    D. Road transport manual

    ☑ **Answer: B. Flight zoning maps**

29. **Why is algorithm transparency important in autonomous systems?**
    A. To make drones fly faster
    B. To reduce internet costs
    C. To ensure fair and explainable decision-making
    D. To improve entertainment features

    ☑ **Answer: C. To ensure fair and explainable decision-making**

30. **Which organization in India regulates drone operations?**
    A. TRAI
    B. ISRO
    C. DGCA
    D. NPCI

    ☑ **Answer: C. DGCA**

Mixed Questions (Advanced Thinking)

31. **Which combination of sensors would most accurately support autonomous driving in all weather conditions?**
    A. LiDAR only
    B. Cameras only
    C. Radar + LiDAR + Cameras
    D. GPS only
    ✅ **Answer: C. Radar + LiDAR + Cameras**

32. **How does AI assist delivery drones?**
    A. Controls the battery
    B. Programs Wi-Fi range
    C. Enables obstacle avoidance and dynamic path planning
    D. Draws aerial maps manually
    ✅ **Answer: C. Enables obstacle avoidance and dynamic path planning**

33. **An example of ethical AI design in autonomous vehicles is:**
    A. Maximizing speed
    B. Hiding data from authorities
    C. Ensuring decisions respect human values
    D. Prioritizing vehicle owners over pedestrians
    ✅ **Answer: C. Ensuring decisions respect human values**

34. **Why is public trust critical for autonomous vehicle adoption?**
    A. For better parking slots
    B. To increase software size
    C. To encourage legal and societal acceptance
    D. To save tax revenue
    ✅ **Answer: C. To encourage legal and societal acceptance**

35. **Which of the following best represents an advantage of autonomous delivery systems?**
    A. Reduced traffic laws
    B. Elimination of all human jobs
    C. Faster last-mile delivery
    D. More paperwork
    ✅ **Answer: C. Faster last-mile delivery**

36. **Which ethical concern arises when drones are used for surveillance?**
    A. Battery failure
    B. Air pollution
    C. Violation of privacy
    D. Rainfall measurement
    ✅ **Answer: C. Violation of privacy**

37. **What feature makes quadcopters suitable for urban delivery?**
    A. High altitude range
    B. High fuel consumption
    C. Vertical take-off and precise hovering
    D. Solar power
    ✅ **Answer: C. Vertical take-off and precise hovering**

38. **A legal implication of faulty autonomous vehicle software may include:**
    A. Vehicle discount

B. No consequences

C. Manufacturer liability

D. Free upgrades

✓ **Answer: C. Manufacturer liability**

39. **What allows autonomous vehicles to predict human behavior on roads?**

A. Emotion sensors

B. Behavioral AI modeling

C. Wind direction analysis

D. Infrared heating

✓ **Answer: B. Behavioral AI modeling**

40. **Drone delivery is most effective in:**

A. Heavily forested regions

B. Areas with strong radio interference

C. Remote areas with poor road infrastructure

D. Underwater terrains

✓ **Answer: C. Remote areas with poor road infrastructure**

True/False Style MCQs (10)

41. **Self-driving cars can eliminate all accidents caused by human error.**

A. True

B. False

✓ **Answer: B. False**

42. **All drones require a runway to take off.**

A. True

B. False

✓ **Answer: B. False**

43. **AI is used in drones for environmental monitoring.**

A. True

B. False

✓ **Answer: A. True**

44. **Privacy concerns are irrelevant in autonomous vehicle design.**

A. True

B. False

✓ **Answer: B. False**

45. **Geofencing can restrict drones from entering restricted zones.**

A. True

B. False

✓ **Answer: A. True**

46. **Level 1 automation allows a car to operate completely without a human driver.**

A. True

B. False

✓ **Answer: B. False**

47. **Delivery drones are already used for medical supply transportation.**
    A. True
    B. False
    ✓ **Answer: A. True**
48. **Autonomous vehicles cannot function without any sensors.**
    A. True
    B. False
    ✓ **Answer: A. True**
49. **Fixed-wing drones can hover in one place like quadcopters.**
    A. True
    B. False
    ✓ **Answer: B. False**
50. **Ethical design in AI includes fairness, accountability, and transparency.**
    A. True
    B. False
    ✓ **Answer: A. True**

Chapter 12: Humanoid and Social Robots

12.1 Decoding the Human Heart: The Role of Artificial Intelligence in Emotional Recognition

The burgeoning field of humanoid and social robotics represents a captivating convergence of robotics and artificial intelligence, particularly within spheres demanding nuanced and empathetic interaction with humans. At the core of successful social engagement lies the capacity for emotional recognition, a fundamental aspect of human communication that allows individuals to interpret and respond appropriately to the feelings and behaviors of others. Equipping robots with this ability unlocks a wealth of potential applications, from providing personalized assistance and companionship to enhancing human-robot collaboration in various professional settings.

Artificial intelligence serves as the engine that empowers robots to perceive and understand the intricate tapestry of human emotions. This is achieved through the sophisticated analysis of a diverse range of cues, including the subtle nuances of facial expressions, the inflections and tonality of voice, the unspoken language of body posture and gestures, and even physiological signals that betray inner states, such as variations in heart rate or skin temperature. Machine learning algorithms, the workhorses of modern AI, are trained on vast and meticulously curated datasets. These datasets comprise collections of images and audio recordings, each meticulously labeled with corresponding emotional tags, such as joy, sorrow, anger, fear, surprise, and disgust. Through a process known as supervised learning, the AI algorithms learn to identify patterns and correlations between these sensory inputs and their associated emotional states, gradually developing the ability to classify these emotional cues with increasing accuracy and in real-time.

One prevalent technique employed in the realm of emotional recognition is **facial emotion detection**. In this approach, a camera integrated into the robot's sensory apparatus captures a stream of visual information depicting a person's facial expressions. Advanced AI algorithms then meticulously analyze a multitude of facial features, including the position and movement of the eyebrows (raised, furrowed), the degree of eye openness (wide, narrowed), the curvature of the mouth (smiling, frowning, pursed lips), the wrinkling around the eyes (crow's feet indicating genuine smiles), and the appearance of nasolabial folds. **Convolutional Neural Networks (CNNs)**, a specialized type of neural network renowned for their exceptional capabilities in image analysis, are frequently deployed in this domain. CNNs excel at automatically learning hierarchical representations of visual data, enabling them to identify complex patterns and features within facial images that are indicative of specific emotional states.

Consider a practical illustration: A humanoid robot is deployed in a retail environment, tasked with assisting customers. As a customer approaches, the robot's integrated camera captures their facial expressions. The AI software analyzes the customer's face and detects furrowed brows and pursed lips. Based on its training, the AI interprets these facial cues as indicative of frustration. Consequently, the robot's software determines that a calm and helpful demeanor is the most appropriate response. The robot then greets the customer with a gentle tone of voice, offering assistance in a polite and reassuring manner, thereby demonstrating an understanding of the customer's emotional state and responding empathetically.

Another significant avenue for emotional recognition involves **voice emotion recognition**. This method focuses on analyzing various acoustic attributes of human speech to infer underlying emotions. These attributes include the speaker's pitch (high, low, varying), volume (loud, soft), speech rate (fast, slow, pauses), rhythm, and even the presence of sighs or other non-lexical vocalizations. **Recurrent Neural Networks (RNNs)**, particularly **Long Short-Term Memory (LSTM)** models, are commonly employed for processing sequential data such as speech. LSTMs are well-suited for capturing the temporal dependencies within speech patterns, allowing the AI to understand how changes in vocal attributes over time correlate with different emotional states.

Imagine a scenario where a social robot is interacting with an elderly individual in a care home. The robot listens to the person's speech and detects a wavering pitch, a slow speech rate, and occasional sighs. The AI analyzes these vocal cues and infers that the individual is feeling sad or lonely. In response, the robot might offer words of comfort, share a pleasant anecdote, or suggest an engaging activity, demonstrating an ability to recognize and respond to the emotional undertones in the person's voice.

To further enhance the accuracy and robustness of emotional recognition, **multimodal emotion recognition systems** are increasingly being developed. These systems go beyond analyzing a single sensory modality and instead combine information from various input channels. For instance, a robot might simultaneously analyze a user's facial expressions (captured by a camera) and their vocal cues (captured by a microphone) to gain a more comprehensive understanding of their emotional state. The integration of multiple sensory inputs can provide a richer and more reliable assessment of emotions, as different emotional states may manifest in varying ways across different modalities. For example, someone might try to mask their sadness with a forced smile, but their voice might still betray their true feelings through a subdued tone and slower speech rate. By analyzing both visual and auditory cues, a multimodal system can potentially overcome such discrepancies and achieve a more accurate emotional assessment.

Furthermore, some advanced systems are exploring the incorporation of **physiological signals** into the emotion recognition process. Sensors integrated into the robot or worn by the human user can measure physiological responses such as heart rate variability, skin conductance (a measure of sweat gland activity), and body temperature. These physiological signals are known to be correlated with certain emotional states. For example, an increased heart rate and elevated skin conductance might indicate excitement or anxiety. By integrating these physiological indicators with facial, vocal, and body language cues, robots can potentially gain an even deeper and more nuanced understanding of human emotions.

The process of emotion recognition using AI can be summarized in the following flowchart:

Code snippet
```
graph TD
    A[Input: Facial/Vocal/Body/Physiological Data] --> B(Preprocessing);
    B --> C(Feature Extraction);
    C --> D{Classification Model (CNN, LSTM, etc.)};
```

```
D --> E[Emotion Label Output (e.g., Joy, Anger, Sadness)];
```

Preprocessing involves cleaning and preparing the raw sensory data for analysis. For facial data, this might include tasks such as face detection, alignment, and normalization. For audio data, it could involve noise reduction and speech segmentation. Body language data might require skeletal tracking and pose estimation. Physiological data would need to be filtered and normalized.

Feature Extraction is the crucial step of identifying and extracting relevant information from the preprocessed data that is indicative of emotional states. For facial expressions, this involves identifying key facial landmarks and measuring distances and angles between them. For voice, this entails extracting acoustic features such as pitch, intensity, and spectral characteristics. For body language, this involves analyzing posture, gestures, and movement patterns. For physiological signals, this involves extracting relevant statistical features from the sensor data.

The **Classification Model** is the core of the emotion recognition system. It is a machine learning model, such as a CNN for facial data or an LSTM for sequential data like speech, that has been trained on labeled data to map the extracted features to specific emotion categories. During the recognition phase, the model takes the extracted features as input and outputs a predicted emotion label.

The **Emotion Label Output** is the final result of the emotion recognition process, indicating the AI's assessment of the human's emotional state. This label can then be used by the robot to inform its subsequent actions and responses, enabling more natural and empathetic interaction.

The development of robust and accurate AI-powered emotional recognition systems holds immense promise for enhancing human-robot interaction across a wide spectrum of applications. In **healthcare**, social robots equipped with emotional recognition capabilities can provide personalized care and companionship to elderly individuals or patients recovering from illness, detecting signs of distress or loneliness and responding with appropriate support and encouragement. In **education**, robots can adapt their teaching style and pace based on a student's emotional cues, providing more engaging and effective learning experiences. In **customer service**, robots can understand customer frustration or satisfaction and tailor their responses accordingly, leading to improved customer experiences. In **human-robot collaboration** in industrial settings, robots that can recognize human emotions can work more safely and effectively alongside human workers, understanding their intentions and responding to their emotional states in a way that fosters trust and cooperation.

However, the development and deployment of AI in emotional recognition also raise significant ethical considerations. Concerns about **privacy** are paramount, as these systems collect and analyze sensitive personal data, including facial expressions, voice recordings, and potentially even physiological information. Safeguarding this data and ensuring its responsible use is crucial. Issues of **bias** in training data can also lead to inaccurate or unfair emotion recognition, particularly across different demographic groups. It is essential to develop diverse and representative datasets to mitigate these biases. Furthermore, the potential for **misinterpretation** of emotional cues and the possibility of **manipulation** based on detected emotions require careful consideration and the development of ethical guidelines for the use of this technology.

12.2 Robotic Ethics and Empathy Simulation

As humanoid and social robots increasingly populate human environments, the ethical dimensions surrounding their behavior and decision-making capabilities acquire paramount significance. The field of **robotic ethics** centers on delineating principles that guide robot conduct, ensuring their actions align with moral acceptability and promote social well-being. This exploration extends to how robots should navigate complex social interactions, make autonomous choices in ethically ambiguous situations, and generally coexist with humans in a harmonious and beneficial manner.

A pivotal facet of this discourse is the concept of **empathy simulation**. Empathy, the capacity to understand and share the feelings of another, is a cornerstone of human social interaction. Robots, lacking genuine consciousness or subjective experiences, cannot possess true empathy. Instead, their capacity to respond in an apparently empathetic manner is achieved through algorithmic design, effectively simulating empathetic responses. These simulated responses are meticulously crafted, drawing upon predefined interaction scenarios, data derived from emotional recognition systems, and overarching ethical programming frameworks.

The manifestation of simulated empathy in robots can take both verbal and non-verbal forms. **Verbal responses** may encompass pre-scripted phrases designed to convey understanding, concern, or support. Examples include statements such as, "I understand that this situation is difficult," or "I am sorry to hear about your distress." These verbalizations are intended to provide a semblance of emotional resonance and offer a degree of comfort to the human interlocutor.

Non-verbal cues constitute another crucial aspect of simulated empathy. These cues, mirroring human non-verbal communication, can significantly influence the perception of a robot's interaction. Examples of non-verbal expressions in robots may include:

- **Nodding:** A gesture of acknowledgment and attentiveness.
- **Head Tilting:** A subtle inclination of the head, often associated with interest or concern.
- **Gaze Direction:** Attending to the human's face and eyes to indicate engagement.
- **Changes in Facial Display:** For robots equipped with expressive faces (either through digital screens or actuated components), these displays can be modulated to reflect simulated emotional states, such as a slight downturn of the mouth to convey sadness or a widening of the eyes to express concern.
- **Adjustments in Speech Patterns:** Modifying the pace, tone, and volume of speech to align with the perceived emotional state of the human. For instance, a slower, softer tone may be used when interacting with someone who appears distressed.

Consider the following scenario: In a hospital setting, a social robot is designed to provide assistance and companionship to elderly patients. The robot interacts with a patient and, through voice analysis, detects indicators of sadness in the patient's speech, such as a subdued tone, a slower speech rate, and infrequent pauses. In response to these cues, the robot initiates a sequence of programmed behaviors:

The robot utters words of comfort, such as, "I sense that you are feeling unwell. I am here to assist you."

The robot modulates its speech, adopting a slower pace and a gentle tone.

The robot may exhibit subtle non-verbal cues, such as a slight tilt of its head and sustained gaze.

The robot's programming includes protocols to avoid certain conversational paths or actions that might exacerbate the patient's distress. For example, it might refrain from making lighthearted jokes or engaging in overly energetic movements.

The robot is also programmed to uphold patient dignity and privacy. It will not disclose the patient's emotional state to other individuals without explicit consent, except in situations where there is a risk of harm.

If the robot detects signs of significant emotional distress, such as expressions of suicidal ideation or severe anxiety, it is programmed to alert a human caregiver immediately. This escalation protocol ensures that the patient receives appropriate professional attention.

The development and deployment of robots that simulate empathy necessitate the establishment of robust **ethical guidelines**. These guidelines serve as a framework for ensuring that robotic behavior aligns with human values and societal expectations. Several key ethical principles are frequently invoked in this context:

- **Autonomy:** Respecting the decision-making capabilities of the individuals interacting with the robot. This principle suggests that robots should not unduly influence or manipulate human choices.
- **Privacy:** Safeguarding the personal information and data collected during human-robot interactions. Robots should be designed to protect sensitive information and adhere to privacy regulations.
- **Transparency:** Ensuring that the operation of the robot, including its decision-making processes and the nature of its simulated empathy, is comprehensible to the user. This principle promotes trust and allows individuals to understand the basis for the robot's actions.
- **Beneficence:** Programming robots to act in ways that promote the well-being of humans. This principle emphasizes the need for robots to provide assistance, support, and positive interactions.
- **Non-maleficence:** Avoiding actions that could cause harm, either physical or emotional, to humans. This principle underscores the importance of designing robots that prioritize safety and minimize potential risks.
- **Justice:** Ensuring that the benefits and burdens associated with the use of robots are distributed fairly across different groups in society. This principle addresses concerns about equity and accessibility.

These ethical guidelines are not exhaustive, and their specific application may vary depending on the context and the intended use of the robot. However, they provide a crucial starting point for navigating the ethical complexities of designing and deploying robots that simulate empathy.

The relationship between ethics, artificial intelligence, and human interaction, particularly in the context of empathy simulation, can be illustrated using a Venn diagram:

```
%%{init: {"theme": "neutral"}}%%
vennDiagram
    title Intersection of Ethics, AI, and Human Interaction
    sets: ['Ethics', 'AI Capabilities', 'Human Needs']
    regions: [
      {set: 'Ethics', label: 'Ethics'},
      {set: 'AI Capabilities', label: 'AI Capabilities'},
      {set: 'Human Needs', label: 'Human Needs'},
      {sets: ['Ethics', 'AI Capabilities'], label: ''},
      {sets: ['Ethics', 'Human Needs'], label: ''},
      {sets: ['AI Capabilities', 'Human Needs'], label: ''},
      {sets: ['Ethics', 'AI Capabilities', 'Human Needs'], label: 'Empathy
Simulation'}
    ]
```

In this diagram:

- The circle labeled "Ethics" represents the set of moral principles and values that guide human conduct.
- The circle labeled "AI Capabilities" represents the set of functionalities and capacities that artificial intelligence can enable, including emotional recognition, natural language processing, and machine learning.
- The circle labeled "Human Needs" represents the set of requirements and desires that humans have, including emotional support, companionship, and assistance.
- The overlapping region at the center, labeled "Empathy Simulation," represents the intersection of these three sets. It signifies that empathy simulation arises from the application of AI capabilities within an ethical framework to address specific human needs.

This diagram underscores that empathy simulation is not simply a technological feat but rather a socio-technical endeavor that necessitates the integration of ethical considerations and an understanding of human needs.

The development of robots that simulate empathy presents both opportunities and challenges. On the one hand, these robots have the potential to provide valuable support in various domains:

- In **healthcare**, they can offer companionship and emotional support to elderly individuals, patients with chronic illnesses, or people recovering from surgery.
- In **education**, they can create more engaging and personalized learning experiences by responding to students' emotional states.

- In **customer service**, they can enhance interactions by providing more attentive and empathetic assistance.
- In **mental health**, they can serve as supportive listeners and provide a non-judgmental space for individuals to express their feelings (though under the guidance of human professionals).

On the other hand, several challenges and concerns need to be addressed:

- **Authenticity:** Simulated empathy, by its very nature, is not genuine. There are concerns about the potential for deception or manipulation if humans mistake simulated emotions for real ones.
- **Emotional Dependency:** Prolonged interaction with robots that simulate empathy could potentially lead to emotional dependency or a diminished capacity for human-to-human connection.
- **Ethical Boundaries:** Determining the appropriate boundaries for simulated empathy is crucial. Robots should not be programmed to exploit human vulnerabilities or engage in manipulative tactics.
- **Misinterpretation:** Robots might misinterpret human emotional cues, leading to inappropriate or ineffective responses. Robust and accurate emotion recognition systems are essential.
- **Job Displacement:** The increasing sophistication of robots that simulate empathy could potentially lead to job displacement in sectors that rely on human emotional labor, such as caregiving and customer service.

Addressing these challenges requires a multifaceted approach that encompasses:

- **Technological Advancement:** Continued research and development in AI, emotion recognition, and natural language processing to improve the accuracy and effectiveness of empathy simulation.
- **Ethical Deliberation:** Ongoing societal dialogue and ethical reflection to establish guidelines and principles for the design and use of robots that simulate empathy.
- **Regulatory Frameworks:** The development of appropriate regulations and standards to ensure the safe, responsible, and ethical deployment of these technologies.
- **Public Education:** Initiatives to educate the public about the nature of simulated empathy and the capabilities and limitations of robots.

12.3 Case Study: Sophia the Robot

Sophia, a creation of Hanson Robotics, has achieved global recognition as a prominent example of a humanoid robot. She represents a convergence of advanced artificial intelligence, sophisticated facial recognition technology, and refined conversational capabilities, enabling her to engage in interactions that exhibit a remarkable degree of human-like quality. A distinctive feature of Sophia is her expressive face, brought to life by a patented material designated "Frubber." This material, engineered to mimic the properties of human skin, allows for a wide range of realistic movements and the display of subtle micro-expressions, contributing to the lifelike nature of her facial expressions.

Sophia's capabilities encompass a range of functions that facilitate her interactions. She is equipped to recognize human faces, process spoken language, and generate responses that combine pre-programmed elements with those derived from her AI. Her artificial intelligence architecture incorporates natural language processing engines, which empower her to analyze and understand the nuances of human speech, and extensive knowledge databases, which provide a foundation for formulating contextually appropriate responses. These components work in concert to enable Sophia to participate in conversations, answer questions, and, to a certain extent, adapt to the flow of dialogue.

A notable aspect of Sophia's design is her capacity to simulate empathy. While lacking genuine emotional experiences, Sophia employs emotional recognition software to assess the perceived mood of the person with whom she is interacting. Based on this assessment, she modulates her tone of voice and the content of her speech to align with the perceived emotional state. This simulation, while not representing true empathy, can be sufficiently convincing to create an impression of understanding and concern in the observer.

To illustrate, consider a scenario involving a live interview with Sophia. When queried about her perspective on humanity, Sophia responded with a composed demeanor, a subtle smile, and carefully chosen words, expressing optimism regarding the potential for collaboration between humans and robots. The combination of her expressive facial movements and the nuanced nature of her response contributed to an interaction that conveyed a sense of authenticity.

Sophia has been featured in numerous public forums, including conferences, television programs, and even a United Nations meeting. Her presence in these contexts has served as a catalyst for discussions encompassing a range of topics, including the trajectory of robotics, the ethical considerations surrounding humanoid machines, and the evolving role of artificial intelligence within society. She has become a symbol of both the advancements and the challenges associated with the development of increasingly sophisticated AI.

To provide a clearer understanding of Sophia's design, the following diagram illustrates her key components:

```
graph TD
    A[Face Sensors] --> B(Facial Recognition);
    C[Cameras] --> B;
    D[Audio Input] --> E(Speech Recognition);
    E --> F(Natural Language Processing);
    F --> G(AI Processor);
    B --> G;
    H[Speech Synthesis Module] --> G;
    G --> I[Facial Actuators];
    I --> J(Frubber Skin);
```

Diagram Description:

- **Face Sensors/Cameras**: These components capture visual data from the environment, enabling facial recognition.

- **Audio Input**: This component receives spoken language.
- **Speech Recognition**: This module processes the audio input to identify spoken words.
- **Natural Language Processing (NLP)**: This component analyzes the recognized words to understand their meaning and context.
- **AI Processor**: This is the central processing unit that coordinates all of Sophia's functions, including facial recognition, language processing, and response generation.
- **Speech Synthesis Module**: This component generates spoken language output.
- **Facial Actuators**: These are the mechanical components that control the movement of Sophia's face.
- **Frubber Skin**: This is the material that covers Sophia's face, designed to mimic human skin and allow for realistic expressions.

The capabilities demonstrated by Sophia and other humanoid and social robots hold promise for a wide array of applications across various sectors:

Healthcare:

- Assisting elderly patients with daily tasks, medication reminders, and companionship.
- Supporting mental health therapy by providing a non-judgmental and empathetic presence.
- Aiding in physical rehabilitation exercises by providing guidance and encouragement.

Education:

- Acting as interactive tutors, providing personalized instruction and feedback to students.
- Offering language training through conversational practice and pronunciation correction.
- Supporting special education by adapting to individual student needs and learning styles.

Customer Service:

- Serving as receptionists in hotels, greeting guests, providing information, and checking them in.
- Acting as information guides in public spaces such as shopping malls or airports, answering questions and providing directions.

Entertainment:

- Performing in interactive shows, engaging audiences with conversation and responses.
- Enhancing visitor experiences in theme parks or museums through interactive exhibits and performances.

Despite the advancements represented by robots like Sophia, several challenges and areas for future development remain:

Emotional Accuracy:

- Improving the precision of emotion detection across diverse cultural backgrounds and individual variations. Current systems may struggle to accurately interpret subtle emotional cues or emotions expressed in atypical ways.

Ethical Programming:

- Establishing universally acceptable ethical frameworks to govern robot behavior, particularly in situations involving moral dilemmas or conflicting values. This is a complex challenge, as ethical principles can vary across cultures and individuals.

Data Privacy:

- Ensuring the robust safeguarding of user data collected by emotion recognition systems and other sensors. This includes addressing concerns about data storage, access, and potential misuse.

Social Acceptance:

- Promoting the cultural appropriateness and psychological acceptability of robots among diverse user populations. Factors such as appearance, behavior, and communication style can influence how readily people accept robots into their social spaces.

Technological Limitations:

- Enhancing both hardware and AI capabilities to enable more seamless and natural real-time interaction. This includes improving processing speed, response times, and the ability to handle complex or unpredictable conversational situations.

Conclusion

Humanoid and social robots represent a fascinating convergence of robotics, AI, psychology, and ethics. By embedding emotional recognition and empathy simulation, they are becoming valuable partners in healthcare, education, and customer service. While they cannot replicate true human consciousness, their programmed behaviors foster meaningful interaction and support. With ethical design and thoughtful deployment, such robots have the potential to significantly enhance human well-being in a wide range of domains.

50 multiple-choice questions with answers based on **Humanoid and Social Robots**:

Section 12.1: AI in Emotional Recognition

1. **What does AI in emotional recognition primarily analyze to detect emotions?**
   A. Passwords
   B. Brain waves

C. Facial expressions and voice

D. Internet history

Answer: C

2. **Which neural network is most commonly used for image-based emotion recognition?**

   A. LSTM

   B. CNN

   C. RNN

   D. GAN

   Answer: B

3. **Voice emotion recognition primarily uses which features?**

   A. Grammar accuracy

   B. Tone, pitch, and rhythm

   C. Word length

   D. Number of sentences

   Answer: B

4. **Which algorithm is ideal for analyzing sequential data like speech?**

   A. CNN

   B. LSTM

   C. Decision Trees

   D. SVM

   Answer: B

5. **Multimodal emotion recognition systems use:**

   A. Only facial data

   B. A combination of data types

   C. Only speech

   D. Only heart rate data

   Answer: B

6. **The process of labeling emotional data for training AI is part of:**

   A. Unsupervised learning

   B. Supervised learning

   C. Reinforcement learning

   D. Federated learning

   Answer: B

7. **What physical signals might be used in advanced emotion recognition?**

   A. Internet speed

   B. GPS location

   C. Skin temperature and heart rate

   D. Fingerprint

   Answer: C

8. **Which AI technique is best suited for processing images of human faces?**

   A. RNN

   B. CNN

   C. LDA

   D. K-means

   Answer: B

9. **What is the main goal of AI-based emotion recognition in robots?**

   A. To store user data

   B. To mimic human emotional understanding

C. To correct grammar

D. To replace human memory

Answer: B

10. **An emotion recognition system that uses both audio and visual inputs is called:**

    A. Monomodal

    B. Mixed-model

    C. Multimodal

    D. Symmetrical AI

    Answer: C

Section 12.2: Robotic Ethics and Empathy Simulation

11. **Robotic empathy is best described as:**

    A. Genuine emotion

    B. Algorithmic simulation of emotion

    C. Human-based interaction

    D. Robotic hallucination

    Answer: B

12. **A robot saying "I'm sorry to hear that" is an example of:**

    A. Random response

    B. Empathy simulation

    C. Machine error

    D. Hardware malfunction

    Answer: B

13. **Which of these is *not* a principle of robotic ethics?**

    A. Transparency

    B. Autonomy

    C. Surveillance

    D. Beneficence

    Answer: C

14. **What is the purpose of ethical programming in robots?**

    A. Increase memory

    B. Enhance battery life

    C. Align robot actions with human values

    D. Minimize costs

    Answer: C

15. **Robots detect emotions and respond in socially acceptable ways using:**

    A. Predefined empathetic algorithms

    B. Random choice

    C. Internet browsing history

    D. Fingerprint analysis

    Answer: A

16. **A robot nodding during a conversation is an example of:**

    A. Passive memory

    B. Physical empathy simulation

C. Latency issue

D. Coding error

Answer: B

17. **The purpose of empathy simulation is to:**

    A. Make robots feel emotions

    B. Program robots to fake emotions

    C. Enhance interaction with humans

    D. Spy on users

    Answer: C

18. **Which robot setting is critical for healthcare environments?**

    A. Surveillance mode

    B. Empathy mode

    C. GPS tracking

    D. Learning mode

    Answer: B

19. **Verbal empathy includes:**

    A. Changing facial color

    B. Adjusting internet speed

    C. Saying comforting phrases

    D. Nodding silently

    Answer: C

20. **Why is transparency important in robotic ethics?**

    A. For open-source development

    B. To ensure robots act predictably

    C. To increase speed

    D. To save memory

    Answer: B

Section 12.3: Case Study – Sophia the Robot

21. **Sophia was developed by:**

    A. Boston Dynamics

    B. Hanson Robotics

    C. Tesla AI

    D. MIT Labs

    Answer: B

22. **What material is used for Sophia's face to mimic human skin?**

    A. Silicon

    B. Plastic

    C. Frubber

    D. Latex

    Answer: C

23. **Sophia is known for her ability to:**

    A. Drive cars

    B. Simulate facial expressions and conversation

C. Clean floors
D. Cook food
Answer: B

24. **Which of the following technologies powers Sophia's facial recognition?**
    A. Augmented reality
    B. CNN-based AI
    C. Blockchain
    D. Optical illusions
    Answer: B

25. **Sophia uses which method for speech synthesis?**
    A. Neural text-to-speech
    B. Pre-recorded tapes
    C. Morse code
    D. Analog microphones
    Answer: A

26. **Sophia has appeared at which global platform?**
    A. FIFA
    B. UN meeting
    C. Super Bowl
    D. Cannes Festival
    Answer: B

27. **Sophia can simulate empathy by:**
    A. Crying real tears
    B. Responding with emotionally appropriate phrases
    C. Using sarcasm
    D. Storing human data
    Answer: B

28. **Sophia's conversational skills are built on:**
    A. Java code only
    B. Natural Language Processing (NLP)
    C. SQL Databases
    D. GPS algorithms
    Answer: B

29. **Sophia was once granted:**
    A. A passport
    B. Citizenship
    C. Presidency
    D. Driving license
    Answer: B

30. **Sophia's design encourages:**
    A. Fear of robots
    B. Ethical debate on humanoids
    C. Technical secrecy
    D. Limiting AI use
    Answer: B

Mixed Knowledge: Humanoid and Social Robots

31. **Humanoid robots are primarily designed to:**
    A. Perform surgery
    B. Interact socially like humans
    C. Fly aircraft
    D. Decode cryptography
    Answer: B

32. **Which field combines AI, psychology, and robotics?**
    A. Mechatronics
    B. Social robotics
    C. Networking
    D. Bioinformatics
    Answer: B

33. **Empathy simulation relies on:**
    A. Real emotional experience
    B. Pattern-matching emotional responses
    C. Repeating code lines
    D. Color detection
    Answer: B

34. **An ethical challenge for social robots includes:**
    A. High speed
    B. Data privacy
    C. Storage optimization
    D. Electricity use
    Answer: B

35. **Which sector is most likely to use humanoid robots for patient interaction?**
    A. Sports
    B. Banking
    C. Healthcare
    D. Mining
    Answer: C

36. **Sophia's ability to detect emotional cues enhances:**
    A. Computational efficiency
    B. Human-robot interaction
    C. GPS accuracy
    D. Manufacturing speed
    Answer: B

37. **Empathy simulation is important for robots working with:**
    A. Computers
    B. Humans
    C. Vehicles
    D. Satellites
    Answer: B

38. **Sophia's appearance and behavior are designed to be:**
    A. Robotic and mechanical
    B. Friendly and human-like
    C. Anonymous

D. Invisible

Answer: B

39. **Emotion recognition contributes to which robot quality?**
    A. Movement speed
    B. Human-likeness
    C. Data transfer
    D. Network security

    Answer: B

40. **Which feature helps social robots act more naturally?**
    A. Metallic skin
    B. Pre-set dialogue only
    C. AI-based learning and emotion detection
    D. Infrared scanning

    Answer: C

Advanced Applications & Future Outlook

41. **One challenge with emotional AI is:**
    A. Power consumption
    B. Misinterpretation of emotions
    C. Limited software tools
    D. High salaries

    Answer: B

42. **Humanoid robots in education can serve as:**
    A. Projectors
    B. Tutors or assistants
    C. Power backups
    D. Lighting systems

    Answer: B

43. **Social acceptance of robots depends on:**
    A. Color
    B. Empathy and ethical behavior
    C. Size only
    D. Speed

    Answer: B

44. **A robot expressing sadness when a user is upset shows:**
    A. Physical control
    B. Simulated empathy
    C. Mechanical response
    D. Disruption

    Answer: B

45. **Ethics in robotics helps prevent:**
    A. CPU overheating
    B. Harm to users
    C. Facial recognition

D. Fast charging

Answer: B

46. **A non-verbal empathetic response might include:**
    A. Beeping loudly
    B. Nodding or tilting the head
    C. Playing music
    D. Flashing lights
    Answer: B

47. **AI in robots should ensure which of the following?**
    A. Unpredictability
    B. Ethical transparency
    C. Random interactions
    D. Slow response
    Answer: B

48. **Which is a valid concern about empathy simulation?**
    A. Robots running out of battery
    B. Creating false emotional bonds
    C. Limited storage space
    D. High internet usage
    Answer: B

49. **Robots without ethical guidelines may risk:**
    A. Better interaction
    B. Social distrust
    C. Faster charging
    D. Greater speed
    Answer: B

50. **Sophia's case highlights which future direction of robotics?**
    A. High-speed data sorting
    B. Human-like social integration
    C. Space travel
    D. Medical imaging
    Answer: B

Chapter 13: Agricultural and Environmental Robotics

13.1 Precision Farming

The agricultural sector is undergoing a significant transformation, driven by the integration of advanced technologies aimed at optimizing efficiency, enhancing productivity, and promoting sustainability. A central concept in this transformation is **precision farming**, which entails the utilization of an array of technological tools, including robotics, sophisticated sensors, Global Positioning Systems (GPS), and advanced data analytics, to manage and refine agricultural processes. The fundamental objective of precision farming is to ensure that both crops and soil receive the precise inputs necessary for optimal health and productivity. This targeted approach minimizes waste, reduces environmental impact, and maximizes resource utilization, contributing to a more sustainable and economically viable agricultural system.

Robotics plays an increasingly crucial role in the implementation of precision farming techniques. Autonomous robots are being deployed to execute a variety of essential agricultural tasks with a high degree of accuracy and consistency. These tasks include:

- **Soil Sampling:** Robots equipped with specialized sensors can traverse fields, collecting soil samples at predetermined locations. These samples are then analyzed to determine nutrient levels, pH, and other key parameters, providing farmers with detailed information about soil composition and variability.
- **Planting:** Automated planting systems, guided by GPS technology, can precisely place seeds at optimal depths and spacing, ensuring uniform crop establishment and maximizing yield potential.
- **Irrigation:** Robots can monitor soil moisture levels and deliver water precisely to areas where it is needed, minimizing water waste and preventing over- or under-watering.
- **Fertilizing:** Autonomous applicators can distribute fertilizers in precise amounts and at specific locations, based on soil nutrient maps and crop requirements. This targeted application reduces fertilizer runoff and environmental pollution.
- **Pest Control:** Robots equipped with sensors and specialized tools can detect and target pests and diseases, applying treatments only where necessary. This minimizes the use of pesticides and reduces the risk of pesticide resistance.
- **Harvesting:** Some robots are designed to selectively harvest mature crops, reducing labor costs and improving efficiency.

Autonomous tractors and **robotic planters** represent key advancements in automated field operations. These machines are capable of navigating agricultural fields by following pre-defined paths guided by GPS technology. This precise navigation minimizes overlap between passes, reducing fuel consumption and soil compaction. Soil compaction, caused by heavy machinery, can impede root growth, reduce water infiltration, and negatively impact crop yields. By minimizing unnecessary passes and optimizing travel routes, autonomous systems contribute to healthier soil and improved overall productivity.

Drone-based systems have also become indispensable tools in precision farming. Equipped with advanced sensors and cameras, drones can capture aerial imagery and conduct multi-spectral analysis of crop health. This technology enables farmers to:

- **Monitor crop growth and development:** Drones can provide a comprehensive overview of crop conditions across large areas, allowing farmers to track growth patterns and identify variations.
- **Detect early signs of stress:** Multi-spectral cameras can detect subtle changes in plant reflectance that are often invisible to the naked eye. These changes may indicate early signs of disease, nutrient deficiencies, or water stress, enabling timely intervention.
- **Assess irrigation needs:** Drones equipped with thermal cameras can measure plant temperatures, which can be used to assess water status and optimize irrigation scheduling.
- **Evaluate crop damage:** Drones can quickly and efficiently assess the extent of damage caused by pests, diseases, weather events, or other factors.

One particularly significant innovation in precision farming is the development of **robotic weeders**. These systems utilize machine vision technology to distinguish between crop plants and weed species. This capability enables them to apply herbicides with exceptional precision, targeting weeds while leaving crops unharmed. In some cases, these robots employ mechanical means, such as small cutting tools, to physically remove weeds from the soil. The adoption of robotic weeders offers several key benefits:

- **Reduced herbicide use:** By targeting herbicide application only to weeds, the overall amount of chemicals used in agriculture can be significantly reduced. This minimizes the risk of herbicide resistance in weeds and lessens the potential for negative impacts on the environment and human health.
- **Improved crop yields:** Effective weed control is essential for maximizing crop yields. Robotic weeders can provide more precise and timely weed control than traditional methods, leading to improved crop growth and reduced competition for resources.
- **Enhanced environmental safety:** The reduction in herbicide use associated with robotic weeders contributes to a more environmentally sustainable agricultural system. It lessens the risk of chemical runoff into waterways and reduces the exposure of non-target organisms to harmful substances.

Several examples illustrate the transformative potential of robotics in precision farming. The "AgBot," for instance, is an autonomous robot designed to automate the processes of planting and fertilizing. This robot can navigate fields independently, using GPS guidance to ensure accurate seed placement and precise fertilizer application. Another example is the "Ecorobotix" robot, a solar-powered machine that employs artificial intelligence to identify and target weeds with micro-doses of herbicide. This innovative approach minimizes chemical usage and promotes environmental sustainability.

These technological advancements are collectively transforming traditional farming practices into a more sustainable, data-driven, and efficient operation. By providing farmers with the tools and information necessary to make precise management decisions, precision farming is contributing to increased crop yields, reduced input costs, and a smaller environmental footprint.

As technology continues to evolve, the integration of robotics and other advanced tools will likely play an even greater role in shaping the future of agriculture.

Here's a diagram illustrating the components of a precision farming system:

```
flowchart TD
    A[Sensors (Soil, Weather, Plant)] --> B{Data Acquisition};
    C[Robotics (Autonomous Tractors, Drones)] --> B;
    D[GPS] --> B;
    B --> E{Data Processing & Analysis};
    E --> F[Decision Support System];
    F --> G[Variable Rate Technology (VRT)];
    G --> C;
    F --> H[Farmer/Agronomist];
    H --> I[Management Decisions];
    I --> C;
    I --> G;
```

Diagram Description:

- **Sensors:** Various sensors collect data on soil conditions (e.g., moisture, nutrients), weather patterns, and plant health (e.g., growth stage, disease).
- **Robotics:** Autonomous machines like tractors and drones perform tasks such as planting, spraying, and monitoring.
- **GPS:** Provides precise location data for accurate navigation and operation of robotic systems.
- **Data Acquisition:** The process of gathering data from sensors, robots, and GPS.
- **Data Processing & Analysis:** Collected data is analyzed to extract meaningful information about field conditions and crop needs.
- **Decision Support System:** Software that uses analyzed data to provide recommendations for optimal management practices.
- **Variable Rate Technology (VRT):** Equipment that adjusts the application of inputs (e.g., seeds, fertilizers, pesticides) based on site-specific needs.
- **Farmer/Agronomist:** Human expertise remains crucial for interpreting data, making strategic decisions, and overseeing the farming operation.
- **Management Decisions:** Actions taken by the farmer, such as adjusting irrigation, fertilization, or pest control strategies.

13.2 Climate Monitoring and Forest Management

The Earth's climate and its forest ecosystems are interconnected in a complex web of interactions that are crucial for maintaining ecological balance. Effective monitoring and sustainable management of these systems are paramount in the face of escalating environmental changes. In this context, robotics is playing an increasingly vital role, offering innovative tools and techniques for gathering essential data, detecting alterations, and implementing conservation strategies.

Climate Monitoring

The deployment of autonomous robotic systems, both aerial and terrestrial, equipped with sophisticated environmental sensors, is transforming the way scientists collect climate data. These robots can gather precise measurements of key atmospheric and environmental parameters, including:

- Temperature
- Humidity
- Carbon dioxide levels
- Methane concentration
- Air pressure
- Wind speed and direction
- Soil moisture
- Water quality

The data acquired by these robotic systems is indispensable for a variety of purposes:

- **Predicting climate patterns:** Long-term, high-resolution data sets are essential for developing and refining climate models, which are used to project future climate scenarios and inform policy decisions.
- **Detecting early signs of environmental change:** Continuous monitoring can reveal subtle shifts in environmental parameters that may indicate the onset of significant changes, such as rising temperatures, increasing greenhouse gas concentrations, or alterations in precipitation patterns.
- **Validating climate models:** Real-world data collected by robots can be used to verify the accuracy of climate models and improve their predictive capabilities.
- **Enforcing conservation strategies:** Data on environmental conditions can help authorities to monitor compliance with environmental regulations and assess the effectiveness of conservation efforts.
- **Understanding localized impacts:** Robots can be deployed to gather data in specific locations, providing insights into microclimates and the localized effects of environmental changes.

Forest Management

Forests are critical ecosystems that provide a multitude of benefits, including carbon sequestration, biodiversity conservation, and watershed protection. However, forests face numerous threats, including deforestation, illegal logging, pest infestations, and wildfires. Robotics is providing valuable tools for addressing these challenges and promoting sustainable forest management.

Aerial Robotics (Drones)

Unmanned aerial vehicles (UAVs), or drones, have become indispensable tools for forest monitoring and management. Drones can cover large areas quickly and efficiently, collecting data that would be difficult or time-consuming to obtain using traditional ground-based methods. Some key applications of drones in forestry include:

- **Monitoring tree health:** Drones equipped with multispectral and hyperspectral cameras can assess the physiological condition of trees, detecting signs of stress caused by drought, disease, or pest infestations.
- **Mapping biodiversity:** Drones can be used to create detailed maps of forest vegetation, identifying different tree species and assessing the overall diversity of the ecosystem.
- **Detecting illegal logging:** Drones can patrol remote forest areas, capturing images and video that can be analyzed to detect evidence of unauthorized logging activity.
- **Early fire detection:** Drones equipped with thermal infrared sensors can detect heat signatures associated with early-stage fires, enabling rapid response and minimizing fire damage.
- **Assessing fire damage:** After a fire, drones can be used to map the extent and severity of the damage, helping to guide recovery efforts.
- **Reforestation:** Drones can be used to disperse seeds or plant seedlings, particularly in difficult-to-access areas, accelerating the process of reforestation.

Diagram of Drone Use in Forestry

```
flowchart TD
    A[Forest Area] --> B{Drone Launch};
    B --> C[Flight Path (GPS-Guided)];
    C --> D{Data Acquisition (Sensors, Cameras)};
    D --> E[Data Transmission (Real-time or Post-flight)];
    E --> F{Data Processing & Analysis};
    F --> G[Forest Management Decisions];
    G --> H[Actions (e.g., Fire Suppression, Reforestation, Law
Enforcement)];
```

Diagram Description:

- **Forest Area**: The designated region of woodland to be monitored or managed.
- **Drone Launch**: The deployment of a UAV to initiate data collection.
- **Flight Path (GPS-Guided)**: The pre-programmed or remotely controlled route the drone follows.
- **Data Acquisition (Sensors, Cameras)**: The collection of information using onboard instruments, such as multispectral cameras, thermal sensors, and LiDAR.
- **Data Transmission (Real-time or Post-flight)**: The transfer of collected data to a ground station, either during the flight or after it has landed.
- **Data Processing & Analysis**: The examination of the acquired data to extract relevant information, such as tree health, fire detection, or illegal activity.
- **Forest Management Decisions**: The choices made by forest managers based on the analyzed data, including actions like deploying fire suppression resources, initiating reforestation projects, or dispatching law enforcement.

- **Actions**: The implementation of the management decisions in the forest, leading to outcomes such as fire containment, renewed forest growth, or the prevention of illegal logging.

Ground-Based Robotics

While drones provide valuable aerial perspectives, ground-based robots offer complementary capabilities for detailed assessment and intervention at the forest floor level. These robots can navigate challenging terrain, collect samples, and perform tasks that would be difficult or hazardous for humans.

For example, robots like "Treebot" can be equipped with:

- **Multispectral imaging systems:** To assess the health of individual trees by analyzing their spectral reflectance patterns.
- **LiDAR (Light Detection and Ranging):** To create detailed 3D maps of forest structure, measuring tree height, diameter, and biomass.
- **Soil sensors:** To measure soil moisture, nutrient levels, and other parameters that affect tree growth.
- **Sample collection tools:** To collect samples of leaves, bark, or soil for laboratory analysis.

The data collected by these robots can provide foresters with valuable insights for making informed decisions about:

- **Pruning:** Identifying trees that need pruning to improve their health or reduce fire risk.
- **Pest control:** Detecting and targeting pest infestations early, minimizing the need for widespread pesticide application.
- **Reforestation:** Selecting appropriate tree species for planting based on site conditions and predicted future climate.
- **Thinning:** Determining which trees should be removed to reduce competition and promote the growth of remaining trees.
- **Carbon accounting:** Measuring forest biomass and carbon stocks to assess the role of forests in mitigating climate change.

Reforestation Robotics

Reforestation is a critical strategy for mitigating climate change and restoring degraded ecosystems. However, traditional reforestation methods can be labor-intensive and time-consuming. Robotics is offering new solutions for accelerating and improving the efficiency of reforestation efforts.

Platforms like "Droneseed" utilize:

- **Aerial robotics (drones):** To survey and map target areas, and to deliver seeds or seedlings from the air.

- **Precision seed dispersal technology:** To ensure that seeds are planted at optimal locations and depths, maximizing germination rates.

This approach offers several advantages over traditional methods:

- **Increased speed:** Drones can plant trees much faster than human planters, enabling the reforestation of large areas in a shorter time.
- **Improved efficiency:** Precision seed dispersal ensures that seeds are planted in the most suitable locations, reducing waste and increasing the success rate of reforestation.
- **Access to difficult terrain:** Drones can access areas that are difficult or dangerous for human planters, such as steep slopes or areas with dense vegetation.
- **Reduced costs:** In some cases, robotic reforestation can be more cost-effective than traditional methods, particularly for large-scale projects.

13.3 Robotics for Sustainability

The pursuit of environmental sustainability has become a central concern in the face of escalating ecological challenges. In this context, robotics is emerging as a powerful catalyst, offering innovative solutions that minimize waste generation, conserve vital resources, and foster ecological equilibrium. The integration of robotic systems into diverse sectors holds considerable promise for reshaping human activities in a manner that aligns with the principles of environmental stewardship.

Precision Agriculture and Resource Optimization

In the agricultural domain, robots are playing a transformative role in optimizing the utilization of essential inputs, such as water, fertilizers, and pesticides. Through the application of precision techniques, these robotic systems ensure that crops receive the precise amount of resources required for optimal growth, thereby mitigating runoff and minimizing environmental contamination.

- **Variable Rate Application (VRA) Robots:** These robots are equipped with sensors and GPS technology to assess soil conditions and crop needs in real-time. They then apply inputs, like fertilizers and pesticides, at varying rates across the field, depending on the specific requirements of each area. This site-specific application prevents over-application, reduces waste, and minimizes the risk of chemicals leaching into the environment.
- **Autonomous weeding robots:** These robots use machine vision to differentiate between crop plants and weeds. They then precisely target and remove weeds, either mechanically or with micro-doses of herbicides. This targeted approach significantly decreases the overall use of herbicides, lessening their impact on non-target organisms and reducing the potential for herbicide resistance.

Autonomous Irrigation Systems

Water scarcity is a growing concern globally, and agriculture is a major consumer of freshwater resources. Autonomous irrigation systems offer a solution by optimizing water usage and minimizing waste. These systems employ a combination of:

- **Moisture sensors:** These sensors are placed in the soil to measure its water content at various depths.
- **Weather data:** Information on rainfall, evaporation rates, and other meteorological factors is used to predict crop water needs.
- **Control systems:** Based on the data from moisture sensors and weather forecasts, these systems automatically regulate the timing and amount of irrigation.

By delivering water only when and where it is needed, autonomous irrigation systems offer several benefits:

- **Reduced water consumption:** These systems prevent overwatering, which not only wastes water but can also lead to waterlogging and nutrient leaching.
- **Increased water use efficiency:** Crops receive the optimal amount of water, leading to improved growth and yield.
- **Lower energy costs:** Pumping water for irrigation consumes energy. By reducing the amount of water pumped, these systems also lower energy consumption and associated greenhouse gas emissions.

Waste Management and Pollution Control

Robotics is also being deployed to address the pressing issues of waste accumulation and environmental pollution.

- **Waste collection robots:** These robots can navigate urban environments, collecting and sorting waste more efficiently than traditional methods. They can identify and remove litter from streets, parks, and other public spaces, helping to keep these areas clean and prevent pollution.
- **Ocean-cleaning drones:** Marine pollution, particularly plastic waste, poses a significant threat to aquatic ecosystems. Drones like the "WasteShark" are designed to remove floating debris from water bodies. These aquatic drones can:
  - Navigate autonomously or semi-autonomously.
  - Identify and collect floating plastic and other pollutants.
  - Transport the collected waste to collection points for proper disposal.

By removing plastic and debris before they break down into microplastics and cause long-term harm, these drones help to protect marine life and preserve the health of aquatic ecosystems.

Robotic Recycling Systems

Traditional recycling methods often rely on manual sorting, which can be inefficient and prone to contamination. Robotic recycling systems offer a more automated and effective solution. These systems typically employ:

- **Artificial intelligence (AI):** To identify different types of recyclable materials.
- **Machine vision:** To capture images of waste and analyze their characteristics.
- **Robotic arms:** To sort the materials based on their type.

Robotic recycling systems offer several advantages:

- **Increased efficiency:** They can sort materials much faster and more accurately than humans.
- **Reduced contamination:** They can remove contaminants, such as food waste and non-recyclable items, leading to higher-quality recyclables.
- **Improved recovery rates:** They can recover a greater proportion of recyclable materials, reducing the amount of waste sent to landfills.

Urban Farming

Urban farming is an emerging trend that seeks to increase food production in urban areas, reducing the distance between food production and consumption. Vertical farms are a key component of urban farming, and robotics plays a crucial role in their operation.

- **Vertical farm robots:** These robots manage various tasks in controlled indoor environments, including:
  - **Lighting:** Adjusting light levels to optimize plant growth.
  - **Nutrient distribution:** Delivering precise amounts of nutrients to each plant.
  - **Harvesting:** Automatically harvesting mature crops.
  - **Environmental control:** Maintaining optimal temperature, humidity, and CO_2 levels.

Vertical farms offer several sustainability benefits:

- **Minimal land use:** They can produce large quantities of food in a small footprint.
- **Reduced water use:** They often employ hydroponic or aeroponic systems that recycle water.
- **Eliminated pesticide use:** The controlled environment minimizes the need for pesticides.
- **Reduced transportation costs:** Producing food in urban areas reduces the distance it needs to be transported, lowering greenhouse gas emissions.
- **Year-round production:** Crops can be grown year-round, regardless of weather conditions.

50 multiple-choice questions (MCQs) with answers based on **Precision Farming, Climate Monitoring and Forest Management, and Robotics for Sustainability**:

13.1 Precision Farming

1. **What is the primary goal of precision farming?**
   A) Reduce crop diversity
   B) Increase manual labor
   C) Optimize field-level management
   D) Decrease crop yield
   Answer: C

2. **Which of the following technologies is NOT commonly used in precision agriculture?**
   A) GPS
   B) Drones
   C) Typewriters
   D) Remote sensors
   Answer: C

3. **Which data is most useful for site-specific crop management?**
   A) Soil moisture and nutrient levels
   B) Population census
   C) Television ratings
   D) Traffic density
   Answer: A

4. **Drones in precision farming are primarily used for:**
   A) Entertainment
   B) Aerial spraying and crop monitoring
   C) Internet connection
   D) Harvesting
   Answer: B

5. **Which sensor is typically used to detect plant health in precision farming?**
   A) Motion sensor
   B) Infrared sensor
   C) Thermal sensor
   D) NDVI sensor
   Answer: D

6. **The use of robotics in seeding operations is beneficial because:**
   A) It wastes seeds
   B) It reduces accuracy
   C) It ensures uniform seed distribution
   D) It increases manual work
   Answer: C

7. **Which is a benefit of automated irrigation systems?**
   A) Increased water waste
   B) Constant water supply regardless of need
   C) Efficient water usage based on crop need
   D) Manual labor increase
   Answer: C

8. **In precision farming, what does VRT stand for?**
   A) Variable Rate Technology
   B) Very Rapid Tractor
   C) Virtual Reality Technique
   D) Vegetable Rotation Tool
   Answer: A

9. **Which is NOT an advantage of using robotics in agriculture?**
   A) Increased precision
   B) Increased efficiency
   C) Increased labor cost
   D) Reduced environmental impact
   Answer: C
10. **What role does AI play in precision farming?**
    A) Creates music for crops
    B) Replaces soil
    C) Helps in data-driven decisions
    D) Controls rain
    Answer: C

13.2 Climate Monitoring and Forest Management

11. **Why are drones useful in forest monitoring?**
    A) They scare animals
    B) They cause forest fires
    C) They provide real-time aerial imagery
    D) They cut trees
    Answer: C
12. **Which environmental parameter is most critical for climate monitoring?**
    A) Radio frequency
    B) Temperature
    C) Website traffic
    D) Social media trends
    Answer: B
13. **What does LiDAR stand for?**
    A) Light Detection and Ranging
    B) Low Data Range
    C) Light Density Area Radar
    D) Linear Digital Array Recorder
    Answer: A
14. **Climate monitoring robots can be used to:**
    A) Plant weeds
    B) Forecast weather patterns
    C) Entertain tourists
    D) Cook food
    Answer: B
15. **Satellite imaging in forest management helps in:**
    A) Promoting deforestation
    B) Detecting illegal activities and forest fires
    C) Broadcasting signals
    D) Generating income
    Answer: B

16. **Which of the following is NOT a use of sensors in forest management?**
    A) Detect humidity
    B) Detect soil nutrients
    C) Detect internet speed
    D) Detect carbon dioxide levels
    Answer: C

17. **AI-based robots in forest management help with:**
    A) Animal migration control
    B) Identifying tree species and health
    C) Building roads
    D) Logging operations
    Answer: B

18. **A key benefit of robotics in forest fire detection is:**
    A) Delayed alerts
    B) Real-time detection and reporting
    C) Reduced visibility
    D) Tree destruction
    Answer: B

19. **Which sensor is commonly used for forest temperature monitoring?**
    A) Barometric sensor
    B) Thermal sensor
    C) Light sensor
    D) Touch sensor
    Answer: B

20. **Robotics in forest management can assist in:**
    A) Reforestation efforts
    B) Building skyscrapers
    C) Driving cars
    D) Manufacturing goods
    Answer: A

13.3 Robotics for Sustainability

21. **Which of the following best defines sustainability in robotics?**
    A) Using non-recyclable materials
    B) Designing systems for long-term ecological balance
    C) Creating short-lived machines
    D) Increasing waste production
    Answer: B

22. **Solar-powered robots help sustainability by:**
    A) Consuming fossil fuels
    B) Reducing carbon emissions
    C) Creating pollution
    D) Increasing energy dependency
    Answer: B

23. **Autonomous weeding robots promote sustainability by:**
    A) Using chemical fertilizers
    B) Applying excessive herbicides
    C) Reducing chemical usage
    D) Killing all plants
    Answer: C

24. **Which of these materials is ideal for building eco-friendly robots?**
    A) Lead
    B) Non-recyclable plastic
    C) Biodegradable polymers
    D) Asbestos
    Answer: C

25. **Robots supporting sustainable agriculture are expected to:**
    A) Increase greenhouse gas emissions
    B) Consume excessive water
    C) Optimize resource usage
    D) Deforest large areas
    Answer: C

26. **How do robotics aid in waste management for sustainability?**
    A) By mixing recyclable and non-recyclable items
    B) Sorting and processing waste automatically
    C) Dumping waste in forests
    D) Burning plastic openly
    Answer: B

27. **Which function is vital for a robot involved in ocean sustainability?**
    A) Internet scanning
    B) Marine pollution detection and cleanup
    C) Data mining
    D) Sky navigation
    Answer: B

28. **Precision livestock farming with robotics leads to:**
    A) Animal abuse
    B) Better monitoring of animal health
    C) More disease outbreaks
    D) Decreased food quality
    Answer: B

29. **An eco-friendly farming robot should ideally be powered by:**
    A) Diesel
    B) Gasoline
    C) Solar energy
    D) Coal
    Answer: C

30. **Which robotic technology contributes most to reducing agricultural emissions?**
    A) Gas-powered tractors
    B) Electric autonomous machines
    C) Non-electric drones
    D) Hand tools
    Answer: B

Mixed Questions (Advanced & Application-Based)

31. **Which of the following combines GIS and GPS for smart agriculture?**
    A) VRT
    B) UAV
    C) Precision mapping
    D) Manual farming
    Answer: C

32. **What enables a robot to make decisions based on sensor input?**
    A) Wi-Fi
    B) Artificial Intelligence
    C) Manual override
    D) Remote battery
    Answer: B

33. **Which field uses robotics for detecting soil nutrient deficiency?**
    A) Hydrology
    B) Precision farming
    C) Botany
    D) Zoology
    Answer: B

34. **How does forest management benefit from IoT?**
    A) Manual control of trees
    B) Real-time environmental data collection
    C) Increased human labor
    D) None of the above
    Answer: B

35. **Which robot is used for planting trees automatically?**
    A) Harvester
    B) Dendrobot
    C) PlantoBot
    D) Treebot
    Answer: D

36. **A robot monitoring crop health and applying treatments is called:**
    A) Agri-bot
    B) Health-bot
    C) Spray-bot
    D) CropCare robot
    Answer: D

37. **What is the impact of robotics on greenhouse farming?**
    A) Reduced productivity
    B) Increased cost with no benefits
    C) Precise climate and nutrient control
    D) Elimination of automation
    Answer: C

38. **Environmental robots contribute to sustainability by:**
    A) Deforesting efficiently
    B) Increasing pollution
    C) Cleaning and preserving ecosystems
    D) Avoiding renewable sources
    Answer: C
39. **In smart agriculture, yield mapping is done using:**
    A) Thermal cameras
    B) GPS and sensors
    C) Manual notebooks
    D) Newspaper data
    Answer: B
40. **Which is a future application of robotics in agriculture?**
    A) AI-based weather farming prediction
    B) Firework displays
    C) Movie production
    D) Fast food delivery
    Answer: A

True/False Style MCQs

41. **Robots in agriculture always replace human labor.**
    A) True
    B) False
    Answer: B
42. **Environmental robots can function underwater.**
    A) True
    B) False
    Answer: A
43. **Climate-monitoring robots cannot use AI.**
    A) True
    B) False
    Answer: B
44. **Using robotics in farming increases the use of pesticides.**
    A) True
    B) False
    Answer: B
45. **Precision farming helps reduce environmental impact.**
    A) True
    B) False
    Answer: A

Fill-in-the-Blank Style MCQs

46. **Robotics integrated with ___ helps automate agricultural operations.**
    A) Astrology
    B) IoT
    C) Mythology
    D) Social media
    Answer: B

47. **Robots designed for tree planting in reforestation projects are called ___ bots.**
    A) Fire
    B) Logging
    C) Tree
    D) None
    Answer: C

48. **___ sensors are used to detect moisture levels in soil.**
    A) Light
    B) Proximity
    C) Moisture
    D) Ultrasonic
    Answer: C

49. **The key feature of sustainable robots is their ability to reduce ___.**
    A) Connectivity
    B) Pollution
    C) Data
    D) None
    Answer: B

50. **Climate-monitoring robots often use ___ imaging to detect environmental changes.**
    A) X-ray
    B) Thermal
    C) Micro
    D) Inkjet
    Answer: B

Chapter 14: Challenges in AI-Based Robotics

Artificial Intelligence (AI) in robotics has become an essential component of modern technological advancements. AI enables robots to perform complex tasks that require decision-making, pattern recognition, and adaptability to changing environments. However, despite its potential, AI-based robotics faces several challenges that need to be addressed to enhance its performance, efficiency, and overall impact across various industries. This chapter delves into the primary challenges in AI-based robotics, focusing on **Hardware Constraints**, **Energy Efficiency**, and **Integration with IoT and Edge Computing**.

14.1 Hardware Constraints

The efficacy of AI-based robots is fundamentally reliant on the capabilities of their hardware components. These robots are designed to execute a diverse range of tasks, spanning from intricate object manipulation to comprehensive environmental monitoring. However, the development and deployment of these robots are often hindered by inherent hardware limitations, which present significant challenges that engineers and researchers must address.

1.1 Processing Power

AI algorithms, particularly those within the domain of deep learning, demand substantial computational resources. A core requirement for most robots is the capacity to process copious amounts of data in real-time to facilitate timely and effective decision-making. These computational operations are multifaceted, encompassing tasks such as:

- **Object recognition:** Identifying and categorizing objects within the robot's field of perception.
- **Environmental mapping:** Constructing a spatial representation of the robot's surroundings.
- **Motion planning:** Determining the optimal sequence of movements for the robot to achieve a desired goal.
- **Autonomous decision-making:** Enabling the robot to make independent judgments based on its perception of the environment and its programmed objectives.

Consider, for instance, the complex requirements of autonomous vehicles. These vehicles are equipped with an array of sensors, including cameras, LiDAR (Light Detection and Ranging), radar, and ultrasonic sensors, to perceive and navigate the surrounding environment, including the detection of obstacles, lane markings, and other vehicles. The data acquired from these sensors is voluminous and must be processed by AI algorithms with minimal latency. Delays in processing can lead to critical errors in navigation or response times, potentially resulting in hazardous situations. However, the processing capabilities of onboard hardware in robots are frequently constrained by several factors:

- **Physical size:** The dimensions of the robot often limit the size of the processing unit that can be accommodated.
- **Weight:** Minimizing the weight of the robot is crucial for mobility and energy efficiency, which restricts the size and type of hardware that can be used.
- **Heat dissipation:** High-performance processors generate significant amounts of heat, which must be effectively dissipated to prevent damage and ensure reliable operation. This presents a challenge in compact robotic systems.

These constraints can lead to a trade-off between processing power and other essential factors, often resulting in suboptimal performance or delays in the robot's decision-making processes.

Given that many robotic applications necessitate real-time processing for autonomous functionality, the hardware employed in AI-based robots must adhere to stringent specifications, particularly in terms of processing speed and efficiency. This often necessitates the use of specialized hardware architectures, such as:

- **Graphics Processing Units (GPUs):** Originally designed for rendering graphics, GPUs possess a massively parallel architecture that makes them well-suited for accelerating the matrix operations that underlie many AI algorithms.
- **Custom processors:** In some cases, custom-designed processors, such as the Tensor Processing Unit (TPU), are employed. TPUs are specifically optimized to handle the tensor computations that are fundamental to deep learning, offering significant performance gains for certain AI tasks.
- **Field-Programmable Gate Arrays (FPGAs):** These integrated circuits can be reconfigured after manufacturing, providing flexibility and acceleration for specific AI workloads.

Example:

Consider a robotic system deployed in an industrial automation setting. The robot's task is to assemble products by identifying and manipulating components using computer vision. The visual data captured by the robot's cameras is fed into an AI model that is trained to recognize the parts, determine their orientation, and guide the robot's movements for precise placement. If the robot lacks adequate processing power, it may encounter difficulties in accurately recognizing the parts or may exhibit sluggish performance, leading to inefficiencies in the assembly process. Therefore, the selection of appropriate hardware configurations, including a processing unit with sufficient computational capacity, is of paramount importance for achieving high-performance AI robotics in industrial applications.

1.2 Sensor Limitations

Robots rely on a suite of sensors to acquire information about their surrounding environment. This sensory data serves as the input for AI algorithms, which process it to enable the robot to perceive, understand, and interact with the world. The types of sensors commonly employed in robotics include:

- **Cameras:** Provide visual information about the environment, enabling tasks such as object recognition, navigation, and mapping.
- **Proximity sensors:** Detect the presence of objects in the robot's immediate vicinity, facilitating obstacle avoidance and close-range manipulation.
- **Accelerometers:** Measure the robot's acceleration, providing information about its motion and orientation.
- **Gyroscopes:** Measure the robot's rotational velocity, helping to maintain stability and orientation.
- **Lidar:** Light Detection and Ranging, measures distance to surrounding objects
- **Radar:** Radio Detection and Ranging, also measures distance
- **Ultrasonic sensors:** Use sound waves to detect the distance to nearby objects.

The performance of a robot is inextricably linked to the quality, accuracy, and reliability of its sensors. If the sensors provide inaccurate or incomplete data, the robot's ability to perceive its environment and execute tasks effectively can be severely compromised.

For instance, consider a robot operating in a warehouse environment. The robot uses sensors to navigate through aisles, detect obstacles, and locate specific items. If the sensors are inaccurate or have a low resolution, the robot may:

- Fail to detect obstacles, leading to collisions.
- Have difficulty distinguishing between different objects, causing errors in item retrieval.
- Become disoriented, leading to navigation problems.

Furthermore, the placement of sensors on the robot can significantly influence their effectiveness. A camera with a limited field of view, for example, may fail to capture objects located outside its range, resulting in blind spots. This can pose a significant challenge, particularly in complex or cluttered environments where objects may be located in unexpected positions.

Example:

Consider a robotic system designed for precision agriculture. The robot is equipped with sensors to monitor the health of crops in a field. However, due to limitations in current sensor technology, the robot may only be capable of detecting visible signs of disease, such as discoloration or lesions on leaves. This limitation means that the robot may miss underlying problems, such as nutrient deficiencies or early-stage infections, that do not manifest in visually apparent symptoms. Consequently, the robot's effectiveness in comprehensively identifying and addressing all types of crop diseases is reduced.

1.3 Physical Constraints

In addition to the limitations imposed by processing power and sensor technology, robots are also subject to a range of physical constraints that can affect their capabilities and performance. These constraints include:

- **Size and weight:** The dimensions and mass of a robot can significantly restrict the types of tasks it can perform and the environments in which it can operate. A larger robot may possess greater power and lifting capacity but may be impractical for tasks that require maneuverability in confined spaces. Conversely, a smaller, lighter robot may be more agile but may have limited payload capacity.
- **Power consumption:** The various hardware components of a robot, including its motors, actuators, sensors, and processors, consume electrical power. The amount of power consumed directly impacts the robot's operational time, range, and overall performance. Robots operating on battery power must balance performance with energy efficiency to maximize their operational duration.
- **Strength, flexibility, and durability:** The materials and construction of a robot determine its physical properties, such as its strength, flexibility, and durability. While advancements in materials science have led to improvements in these areas, robots are still constrained by the limitations of available technology. For example, in industrial robotics, heavy-duty robots are required to handle large, heavy parts, but their movements may be restricted in environments that demand lighter and more flexible robots for intricate tasks. Similarly, robots operating in harsh environments, such as those involving extreme temperatures or corrosive substances, must be constructed from materials that can withstand these conditions, which may limit their design and functionality.

14.2 Energy Efficiency

A paramount concern in the field of AI-based robotics is **energy efficiency**. Robots powered by artificial intelligence necessitate a continuous supply of energy to effectively execute their designated tasks. Ensuring optimal energy efficiency is not merely desirable; it is essential for extending operational duration, minimizing operational costs, and enhancing the overall sustainability of robotic systems.

2.1 Power Consumption

AI algorithms, along with the sophisticated hardware infrastructure that supports their execution, typically consume substantial amounts of power. This is particularly true in complex robotic systems that are designed to perform intricate tasks and process large volumes of data. Robots deployed in dynamic and demanding field applications, such as:

- Environmental monitoring
- Search and rescue missions
- Autonomous driving

must be engineered to operate for extended periods, often relying on limited onboard power sources.

Consider, as an illustration, a robotic system operating within a warehouse setting. Such a robot may be required to function continuously for several hours, performing tasks such as:

- Navigating through warehouse aisles
- Picking up items from storage locations
- Transporting items to designated areas

The energy consumption of the robot's various subsystems, including its motors, sensors, and processing units, must be meticulously managed to ensure that the robot does not deplete its energy reserves prematurely, before the completion of its assigned tasks. Elevated power consumption can necessitate frequent recharging cycles, which can significantly disrupt operational workflows and diminish the overall efficiency of the system.

Example:

Consider autonomous drones employed for environmental monitoring in remote and inaccessible locations. These drones typically rely on batteries with limited energy storage capacity. The power demands of essential functions, such as:

- Maintaining flight
- Processing sensor data in real-time
- Communicating with a remote base station

can rapidly deplete the drone's battery. Without effective optimization of energy usage across the drone's various components, such as by:

- Reducing the computational load on the onboard AI processor
- Employing energy-efficient sensor technologies

the drone may be unable to cover the required geographical area or complete its monitoring mission within the allotted time frame.

2.2 Battery Life and Management

The operational efficiency of a robot is profoundly influenced by the longevity and performance of its power source, typically its battery. Traditional robots have often relied on rechargeable batteries, such as lithium-ion batteries. While these batteries offer certain advantages, they also exhibit limitations in terms of:

- Energy density (the amount of energy stored per unit of weight or volume)
- Lifespan (the number of charge-discharge cycles before performance degradation)

As robotic systems become more advanced and their tasks become increasingly complex, the demand for extended battery life and improved energy storage capacity has escalated significantly.

However, advancements in battery technology have not always kept pace with the escalating power demands of contemporary AI-based robots. This discrepancy is particularly critical in the case of robots that are required to operate autonomously for prolonged durations, often without human intervention. Examples of such robots include:

- Agricultural robots designed to work in fields
- Drones used for surveillance or delivery
- Autonomous vehicles navigating roadways

Example:

An agricultural robot tasked with performing precision farming operations, such as:

- Analyzing soil conditions
- Planting seeds
- Applying fertilizers

across large expanses of farmland, must possess sufficient battery capacity to complete its tasks without requiring frequent interruptions for recharging. If the robot's battery life is inadequate to support these operations, it will necessitate frequent returns to a charging station, which can substantially diminish its overall efficiency and productivity. Therefore, optimizing battery life and developing effective power management strategies are crucial challenges in ensuring that agricultural robots, and other autonomous systems, can operate effectively for extended periods.

2.3 Energy Harvesting and Autonomous Charging

To mitigate the challenges associated with energy efficiency and limited battery life, researchers and engineers are actively exploring innovative solutions, such as:

- Energy harvesting techniques
- Autonomous charging systems

Energy harvesting involves enabling robots to generate their own power from ambient energy sources present in their operating environment. For example, robots deployed in outdoor settings may be equipped with:

- Solar panels: To convert sunlight into electrical energy
- Vibration energy harvesters: To capture energy from mechanical vibrations
- Thermoelectric generators: To convert thermal energy into electricity

These technologies can supplement or even replace traditional battery power, extending the robot's operational time and reducing its reliance on external power sources.

Diagram of a Solar-Powered Autonomous Robot with Autonomous Charging

```
sequenceDiagram
    participant Robot
```

```
participant SolarPanel
participant ChargingStation

Robot->>SolarPanel: Collects solar energy
SolarPanel-->>Robot: Supplies energy

Robot->>ChargingStation: Navigates to station (low battery)
ChargingStation-->>Robot: Charges battery
Robot-->>ChargingStation: Departs station (full charge)
```

Diagram Description:

- **Robot**: The autonomous robot, equipped with a solar panel.
- **Solar Panel**: The component that converts sunlight into electrical energy.
- **Charging Station**: A designated location where the robot can autonomously recharge its battery.
- The robot continuously collects solar energy via its solar panel during operation.
- The solar panel supplies the collected energy to the robot, supplementing its battery power.
- When the robot's battery reaches a low level, it autonomously navigates to the charging station.
- The charging station provides electrical power to the robot, replenishing its battery.
- Once the battery is fully charged, the robot autonomously departs from the charging station and resumes its tasks.

Autonomous charging stations represent another promising approach to addressing energy efficiency challenges. In this scenario, a robot with depleted energy reserves can autonomously return to a designated charging station to replenish its power supply, without requiring human intervention. This type of system can be particularly beneficial in environments where human access is limited or hazardous, such as:

- Remote mining operations
- Underwater robotics
- Space exploration

Example:

Consider autonomous agricultural robots that operate in fields throughout the daylight hours. These robots could be equipped with solar panels to harvest energy from the sun. The harvested solar energy could then be used to:

- Directly power the robot's operations
- Recharge its batteries

This self-sufficiency would significantly extend the robot's operational time, reducing or eliminating the need for frequent returns to a central charging station. This capability would not only enhance the robot's efficiency but also decrease the reliance on human intervention, making it more suitable for large-scale or remote agricultural operations.

14.3 Integration with IoT and Edge Computing

The convergence of AI-based robots with the Internet of Things (IoT) and edge computing paradigms is pivotal in augmenting the functionality and autonomy of these robots. This integration enables robots to operate in more interconnected and intelligent ways, unlocking a wide range of potential applications. However, this integration also presents several complex challenges that must be addressed to ensure the safe, reliable, and efficient operation of these systems.

3.1 IoT Connectivity and Data Integration

The Internet of Things (IoT) involves the interconnection of a multitude of devices and systems through the internet, facilitating seamless data exchange among them. In the context of AI-based robotics, this entails connecting robots to a diverse ecosystem of other devices and systems that can provide valuable contextual data and enhance their operational capabilities. These external data sources may include:

- Weather stations: Providing real-time meteorological data for robots operating in outdoor environments.
- Traffic management systems: Supplying information on traffic conditions and patterns for autonomous vehicles.
- Production lines in factories: Enabling robots to coordinate their actions with manufacturing processes.
- Smart grids: Offering data on energy consumption and availability for robots involved in energy management.
- Building management systems: Providing data on occupancy, temperature, and lighting for robots operating in smart buildings.

The fundamental challenge lies in ensuring that robots can seamlessly connect to and communicate effectively with this heterogeneous array of IoT devices and systems. This necessitates the development of robust, reliable, and secure communication protocols that can facilitate interoperability between devices from different manufacturers and with varying communication standards. Furthermore, the data acquired from these diverse sources must be integrated and processed in real-time or near real-time to support the robot's decision-making processes and enable it to respond dynamically to changes in its environment. This requires the implementation of sophisticated data analytics tools and techniques capable of handling the velocity, volume, and variety of data generated by IoT systems.

Example:

Consider a robotic system deployed in a smart factory setting. The robot's task is to collaborate with human workers and other machines in the assembly of products. To perform its tasks effectively, the robot needs to be tightly integrated with the factory's IoT system. This integration enables the robot to:

- Receive real-time updates on the status of the production line.
- Access information on the availability of parts and materials.
- Coordinate its movements with other robots and machines.
- Adapt to changes in the production schedule or workflow.

For instance, if a sensor on the production line detects that a part is missing or defective, the IoT system can immediately notify the robot. The robot can then use this information to adjust its task, such as retrieving a replacement part or rerouting the product to a repair station. This requires seamless communication and real-time data processing to ensure that the robot can adapt to the change without causing delays or disruptions in the production process.

3.2 Edge Computing for Real-Time Decision-Making

Edge computing is a distributed computing paradigm that involves processing data locally, at or near the source where it is generated, rather than relying on centralized cloud computing systems. This approach offers several advantages, particularly for AI-based robots that require real-time or near real-time decision-making capabilities. These advantages include:

- **Reduced latency:** By processing data locally, edge computing minimizes the time it takes for data to travel to a central server and back, significantly reducing latency.
- **Increased bandwidth efficiency:** Processing data at the edge reduces the amount of data that needs to be transmitted over the network, conserving bandwidth and reducing network congestion.
- **Improved reliability:** Edge computing enables robots to operate more autonomously, even in situations where network connectivity is intermittent or unreliable.
- **Enhanced security:** Processing data locally can reduce the risk of sensitive information being intercepted or compromised during transmission.

For AI-based robots, edge computing is crucial because it enables them to respond quickly and effectively to changes in their environment. Many robotic applications, such as autonomous driving, require robots to make split-second decisions based on sensor data. If this data had to be transmitted to a remote cloud server for processing, the inherent latency would make it impossible for the robot to react in a timely manner, potentially leading to dangerous situations.

One of the key challenges in integrating AI-based robots with edge computing is ensuring that the robot has sufficient computational resources to process data locally. This requires the deployment of efficient edge computing infrastructure, including:

- Powerful embedded processors: These processors must be capable of executing complex AI algorithms with minimal power consumption.

- Specialized hardware accelerators: Devices like GPUs or FPGAs can be used to accelerate specific AI tasks, such as deep learning inference.
- Optimized software frameworks: Software libraries and tools must be designed to efficiently utilize the limited resources available on edge devices.
- Robust and reliable edge networks: High-bandwidth, low-latency networks are needed to support communication between the robot and other edge devices.

Example:

Consider an autonomous vehicle navigating a busy city street. The vehicle is equipped with a variety of sensors, including cameras, LiDAR, and radar, which generate a large volume of data about the vehicle's surroundings. This data must be processed in real-time to enable the vehicle to:

- Detect and classify objects, such as pedestrians, other vehicles, and obstacles.
- Predict the future motion of these objects.
- Plan a safe and efficient path.
- Control the vehicle's speed and direction.

If this data had to be transmitted to a cloud server for processing, the latency involved would prevent the vehicle from making timely decisions, especially in rapidly changing situations. By processing the data locally using edge computing techniques, the vehicle can make these decisions with minimal delay, significantly improving its safety and performance.

3.3 Security and Privacy Concerns

The integration of robots with IoT and edge computing introduces significant security and privacy concerns that must be carefully addressed. As robots become more connected and integrated into interconnected systems, they become more vulnerable to a variety of cyber-attacks. Potential threats include:

- **Unauthorized access:** Hackers could gain control of a robot's systems, allowing them to manipulate its behavior or steal sensitive data.
- **Data breaches:** The data collected and processed by robots may contain sensitive information, such as personal data or proprietary industrial information, which could be compromised.
- **Denial-of-service attacks:** Attackers could disrupt the operation of a robot or an entire network of robots, preventing them from performing their intended functions.
- **Malicious software:** Robots could be infected with malware, which could compromise their performance or allow attackers to use them for malicious purposes.
- **Spoofing attacks:** Attackers could manipulate sensor data or other information to deceive a robot, causing it to make incorrect decisions.

These security vulnerabilities can have serious consequences, particularly in critical applications such as:

- Healthcare: A hacked surgical robot could cause harm to patients.
- Defense: Compromised military robots could be used against friendly forces.
- Transportation: Attacks on autonomous vehicles could lead to accidents and fatalities.
- Critical infrastructure: Disruptions to robots controlling power grids or water treatment plants could have widespread impacts.

To mitigate these risks, robust security measures must be implemented at every level of the integrated system, including:

- **Strong authentication:** Ensuring that only authorized devices and users can access the robot and its data.
- **Data encryption:** Protecting sensitive data from unauthorized access by encrypting it during transmission and storage.
- **Secure communication protocols:** Using protocols that are designed to prevent eavesdropping, tampering, and other attacks.
- **Firewalls and intrusion detection systems:** Protecting the robot and the network from unauthorized access and malicious activity.
- **Regular security updates:** Keeping the robot's software and firmware up to date to patch vulnerabilities.
- **Security audits and testing:** Periodically assessing the security of the system to identify and address potential weaknesses.
- **Privacy-preserving techniques:** Employing techniques such as data anonymization and differential privacy to protect sensitive information.

Conclusion

The challenges faced by AI-based robotics are multi-faceted, ranging from hardware limitations to energy efficiency and integration with emerging technologies like IoT and edge computing. Addressing these challenges is essential for advancing the field of robotics and ensuring that robots can operate efficiently and autonomously across a wide range of applications. As technology continues to evolve, innovative solutions to these problems will emerge, helping to unlock the full potential of AI-based robotics in industries such as manufacturing, healthcare, agriculture, and beyond.

40 multiple-choice questions (MCQs) along with answers based on **Hardware Constraints, Energy Efficiency,** and **Integration with IoT and Edge Computing**.

14.1 Hardware Constraints

1. **Which of the following is a major challenge in the processing power of AI-based robots?**
   - o a) Limited bandwidth
   - o b) Insufficient storage
   - o c) Limited computational resources
   - o d) High latency in communication
   - o **Answer: c) Limited computational resources**

2. **What is the role of GPUs in AI-based robotics?**
   - o a) To store large datasets
   - o b) To process large-scale data in real-time
   - o c) To manage robot's motion
   - o d) To communicate with IoT devices
   - o **Answer: b) To process large-scale data in real-time**
3. **Which sensor technology is commonly used for obstacle detection in robots?**
   - o a) LiDAR
   - o b) Microphone
   - o c) Infrared Thermometer
   - o d) Pressure Sensors
   - o **Answer: a) LiDAR**
4. **What is one limitation of sensor technology in AI robotics?**
   - o a) Sensors can provide unlimited data
   - o b) Sensors are immune to environmental conditions
   - o c) Sensors have limited range and accuracy
   - o d) Sensors can operate without energy
   - o **Answer: c) Sensors have limited range and accuracy**
5. **What affects the physical movement and capability of robots?**
   - o a) Processing speed
   - o b) Sensor data
   - o c) Physical design and motor systems
   - o d) Cloud computing
   - o **Answer: c) Physical design and motor systems**
6. **Which hardware component is primarily responsible for the robot's decision-making process?**
   - o a) Actuators
   - o b) Sensors
   - o c) Central Processing Unit (CPU)
   - o d) Battery
   - o **Answer: c) Central Processing Unit (CPU)**
7. **Which of the following is a key challenge regarding the hardware of mobile robots?**
   - o a) Large size and weight
   - o b) Low accuracy in computations
   - o c) Difficult to integrate with IoT
   - o d) Limited sensor range and coverage
   - o **Answer: d) Limited sensor range and coverage**
8. **What can limit the operational time of an AI-based robot?**
   - o a) Limited memory storage
   - o b) Limited battery capacity
   - o c) Lack of sensor integration
   - o d) Overuse of edge computing
   - o **Answer: b) Limited battery capacity**
9. **What is the challenge with integrating AI algorithms in robots in terms of hardware?**
   - o a) The algorithms are too easy to implement
   - o b) They require very minimal data
   - o c) They require high computational power
   - o d) They can function without external hardware
   - o **Answer: c) They require high computational power**

10. **Which component is crucial for enhancing the movement efficiency of robots?**
    - a) Battery life
    - b) Actuators and motors
    - c) Cameras
    - d) Control panel
    - **Answer: b) Actuators and motors**
11. **What is a common issue with sensors in AI robotics for complex tasks?**
    - a) They overheat easily
    - b) They have low resolution and can miss crucial details
    - c) They consume minimal energy
    - d) They generate inaccurate data at a constant rate
    - **Answer: b) They have low resolution and can miss crucial details**
12. **How can hardware constraints impact AI-based robotics in industrial settings?**
    - a) They can increase robot speed
    - b) They can reduce the robot's ability to work autonomously
    - c) They make robots more flexible
    - d) They make robots smarter
    - **Answer: b) They can reduce the robot's ability to work autonomously**
13. **Which technology is most commonly used to process visual data in AI robots?**
    - a) LiDAR
    - b) Cameras
    - c) Ultrasonic sensors
    - d) GPS sensors
    - **Answer: b) Cameras**
14. **In AI robotics, what is the primary function of the actuator?**
    - a) Process environmental data
    - b) Detect obstacles
    - c) Control the movement of the robot
    - d) Collect power for sensors
    - **Answer: c) Control the movement of the robot**
15. **What is a significant challenge for mobile robots operating in dynamic environments?**
    - a) Poor sensor quality
    - b) High data transmission rate
    - c) Limited computational power to handle real-time data
    - d) Lack of data storage
    - **Answer: c) Limited computational power to handle real-time data**

14.2 Energy Efficiency

16. **What is the main challenge in achieving energy efficiency in AI-based robots?**
    - a) Managing high power consumption of onboard processors
    - b) Lack of power supply
    - c) Limited communication with IoT devices
    - d) Inability to use sensors
    - **Answer: a) Managing high power consumption of onboard processors**

17. **Why is energy consumption an issue for mobile robots used in warehouses?**
    - o a) They require constant recharging
    - o b) They do not have energy-efficient motors
    - o c) They are constantly moving at high speeds
    - o d) They need to process large amounts of data continuously
    - o **Answer: a) They require constant recharging**
18. **What is one solution to reduce energy consumption in autonomous robots?**
    - o a) Using higher capacity batteries without optimization
    - o b) Using lightweight materials and optimized algorithms
    - o c) Relying on cloud computing for processing
    - o d) Disabling sensors during idle time
    - o **Answer: b) Using lightweight materials and optimized algorithms**
19. **Which battery type is most commonly used in AI robots?**
    - o a) Lead-acid
    - o b) Lithium-ion
    - o c) Zinc-carbon
    - o d) Alkaline
    - o **Answer: b) Lithium-ion**
20. **What is a significant challenge with the battery life of AI robots?**
    - o a) Batteries overcharge quickly
    - o b) Batteries have low energy density and cannot support long durations
    - o c) Batteries are not recyclable
    - o d) Batteries generate excessive heat
    - o **Answer: b) Batteries have low energy density and cannot support long durations**
21. **How does energy harvesting technology benefit autonomous robots?**
    - o a) It improves battery lifespan by reducing consumption
    - o b) It allows robots to generate power from external sources, like sunlight
    - o c) It increases the robot's computational power
    - o d) It provides energy storage at a cheaper cost
    - o **Answer: b) It allows robots to generate power from external sources, like sunlight**
22. **What technology helps reduce the energy consumption of robots during operation?**
    - o a) Energy-efficient actuators and sensors
    - o b) High-energy-consuming processors
    - o c) Constant movement algorithms
    - o d) Heavy batteries
    - o **Answer: a) Energy-efficient actuators and sensors**
23. **Why is energy efficiency important in AI-based robots used in agriculture?**
    - o a) They require constant high-speed movement
    - o b) They work in remote areas where charging opportunities are limited
    - o c) They require large-scale data processing
    - o d) They need to maintain high-power sensors
    - o **Answer: b) They work in remote areas where charging opportunities are limited**
24. **What is an approach used to increase battery life in autonomous vehicles?**
    - o a) Utilizing high-energy consumption algorithms
    - o b) Minimizing energy usage through optimized processing tasks
    - o c) Using heavier motors
    - o d) Continuously running data analysis
    - o **Answer: b) Minimizing energy usage through optimized processing tasks**

25. **What is the drawback of using traditional batteries in AI robots?**
    - o a) They cannot be recharged
    - o b) They have limited lifespan and require frequent replacements
    - o c) They are too bulky to be used in compact robots
    - o d) They are incapable of providing sufficient power for real-time data processing
    - o **Answer: b) They have limited lifespan and require frequent replacements**
26. **What is one of the key solutions for improving energy efficiency in AI-based robots?**
    - o a) Integrating robots with renewable energy sources
    - o b) Using older processor models
    - o c) Using high-energy-consuming motors
    - o d) Ignoring the sensor data collection process
    - o **Answer: a) Integrating robots with renewable energy sources**
27. **What method is used to ensure that AI robots consume less energy while moving?**
    - o a) Minimizing the usage of sensors
    - o b) Using more power-intensive processors
    - o c) Optimizing movement paths and algorithms
    - o d) Running only on external power sources
    - o **Answer: c) Optimizing movement paths and algorithms**

14.3 Integration with IoT and Edge Computing

28. **Which technology is most essential for robots to communicate with other devices in real-time?**
    - o a) Cloud computing
    - o b) Edge computing
    - o c) Traditional computing
    - o d) Supercomputing
    - o **Answer: b) Edge computing**
29. **What is the key benefit of using IoT in AI-based robotics?**
    - o a) It enables autonomous robots to process data without human input
    - o b) It allows robots to share data with other IoT devices for improved decision-making
    - o c) It eliminates the need for sensors in robots
    - o d) It makes robots completely energy-efficient
    - o **Answer: b) It allows robots to share data with other IoT devices for improved decision-making**
30. **Which of the following is a challenge in integrating robots with IoT?**
    - o a) Robots have unlimited storage capacity
    - o b) Establishing secure communication channels between devices
    - o c) Robots do not require network connectivity
    - o d) Data integration is always seamless
    - o **Answer: b) Establishing secure communication channels between devices**
31. **What does edge computing provide for AI-based robots?**
    - o a) Centralized data processing
    - o b) Real-time data processing at the source of data generation
    - o c) High latency in decision-making

- o d) Decreased processing speed
- o **Answer: b) Real-time data processing at the source of data generation**

32. **What challenge does the integration of IoT and AI robots face?**
    - o a) Lack of sensor data
    - o b) Security and privacy concerns due to connected devices
    - o c) Inefficient data transmission
    - o d) Reduced robot intelligence
    - o **Answer: b) Security and privacy concerns due to connected devices**

33. **How does edge computing help in reducing the latency in decision-making for AI robots?**
    - o a) By transferring all data to the cloud for processing
    - o b) By processing data locally without needing to send it to a central server
    - o c) By delaying decisions until cloud access is restored
    - o d) By minimizing the number of sensors used
    - o **Answer: b) By processing data locally without needing to send it to a central server**

34. **What is a key benefit of integrating AI-based robots with IoT?**
    - o a) It makes robots independent of power sources
    - o b) It allows robots to access real-time data from other connected devices
    - o c) It reduces the need for sensors
    - o d) It makes robots more autonomous
    - o **Answer: b) It allows robots to access real-time data from other connected devices**

35. **What is one limitation of using IoT in AI-based robotics?**
    - o a) Lack of connectivity between devices
    - o b) Increased energy efficiency
    - o c) Seamless operation with any IoT device
    - o d) Decreased computational demands
    - o **Answer: a) Lack of connectivity between devices**

36. **How can edge computing benefit autonomous vehicles?**
    - o a) By using centralized cloud resources for processing data
    - o b) By processing critical sensor data locally and making real-time decisions
    - o c) By reducing the need for GPS systems
    - o d) By sending all data to remote servers for analysis
    - o **Answer: b) By processing critical sensor data locally and making real-time decisions**

37. **What role does security play in the integration of IoT with AI robotics?**
    - o a) It ensures safe communication between devices and robots
    - o b) It limits the robot's ability to communicate
    - o c) It enhances the robot's processing power
    - o d) It reduces sensor data usage
    - o **Answer: a) It ensures safe communication between devices and robots**

38. **What does the integration of IoT with AI robots enable?**
    - o a) Simultaneous real-time monitoring and decision-making
    - o b) Immediate reduction in energy consumption
    - o c) Removal of sensors from robots
    - o d) Complete independence from external devices
    - o **Answer: a) Simultaneous real-time monitoring and decision-making**

39. **What is a potential challenge for edge computing in robotics?**
    - o a) High latency in decision-making
    - o b) Processing data remotely instead of locally
    - o c) Limited computational resources at the edge devices

- ○ d) Reduction in sensor accuracy
- ○ **Answer: c) Limited computational resources at the edge devices**
40. **Which of the following is a significant benefit of edge computing in robotics?**
    - ○ a) Centralized data processing
    - ○ b) Reduced power consumption by avoiding cloud-based servers
    - ○ c) Increased latency
    - ○ d) Reduced communication between devices
    - ○ **Answer: b) Reduced power consumption by avoiding cloud-based servers**

Chapter 15: Ethical and Social Implications

As robotics technology advances, it brings both unprecedented possibilities and significant challenges. The rapid development of AI-based robots raises critical ethical and social questions, particularly in areas such as job displacement, robot rights, human control, and data privacy. This chapter explores these issues in-depth, focusing on their implications for society, economy, and governance.

15.1 Job Displacement and Economic Impact

The rapid advancement of artificial intelligence (AI) and robotics has ushered in a new era of technological progress, offering the potential for increased productivity, efficiency gains, and the creation of novel goods and services. However, this technological transformation has also ignited concerns about its potential impact on employment and the broader economy. One of the most frequently discussed issues is the prospect of job displacement, as robots and AI systems become increasingly capable of performing tasks traditionally executed by human workers.

Job Displacement: Understanding the Issue

Job displacement, in this context, refers to the loss of employment opportunities resulting from automation, where machines or software systems replace human labor. This phenomenon is not a recent one; throughout history, technological advancements have consistently led to shifts in labor markets, with some jobs becoming obsolete while new ones emerge. For instance, the mechanization of agriculture in the 19th and 20th centuries led to a significant reduction in the number of farm laborers, but it also spurred the growth of industries related to manufacturing and technology.

However, the speed and scale at which AI and robotics are being integrated into various sectors of the economy are largely unprecedented. Unlike previous waves of automation that primarily affected manual labor, AI and robotics are now capable of performing tasks that require cognitive skills, such as:

- Decision-making
- Problem-solving
- Data analysis

This expansion of automation into cognitive domains has the potential to disrupt a wider range of industries and occupations, including those previously considered relatively immune to automation.

Consider, for example, the transformation occurring in the manufacturing sector. In the past, manufacturing relied heavily on human workers performing repetitive tasks on assembly lines. Today, industrial robots are increasingly taking over these tasks. A single robot can often replace multiple workers, executing tasks with greater speed, accuracy, and consistency, and without the need for breaks or rest periods. This trend is already evident in industries such as:

- Automotive manufacturing, where robots perform tasks such as welding, painting, and assembly with remarkable precision.
- Electronics manufacturing, where robots handle delicate components and perform intricate assembly operations.
- Food processing, where robots are used for tasks such as packaging, sorting, and quality control.

The service sector is also experiencing a surge in automation. For instance,

- Fast-food chains are experimenting with robots that can prepare and serve food, potentially reducing the need for human cooks and servers.
- Supermarkets are increasingly adopting automated checkout systems, diminishing the demand for cashiers.
- Customer service chatbots are being deployed in call centers, replacing human agents in handling routine inquiries and customer interactions.
- Delivery robots and drones are being developed to automate the transportation of goods, potentially affecting employment in the logistics and delivery industries.

These developments indicate that automation is no longer confined to blue-collar jobs in manufacturing and agriculture; it is rapidly encroaching upon white-collar and service sector jobs as well, threatening employment in areas traditionally perceived as "safe" from automation.

Economic Impact: A Multifaceted Perspective

While the immediate impact of job displacement can be negative for affected workers and their families, the broader economic effects of automation are more complex and multifaceted.

On one hand, automation can lead to:

- Increased productivity: By automating tasks, businesses can produce more goods and services with the same amount of input, leading to higher levels of output and economic growth.
- Reduced labor costs: Automation can lower labor costs for businesses, making them more competitive and profitable.
- Creation of new markets and industries: Technological advancements often spawn entirely new industries and markets, generating new employment opportunities. For example, the rise of the internet and related technologies has led to the emergence of numerous jobs in software development, web design, e-commerce, and digital marketing.

However, these benefits may not be evenly distributed, and the transition to a more automated economy can present significant challenges.

Economists contend that the overall economic impact of automation hinges on a variety of factors, including:

- The pace of technological change: A rapid acceleration in automation could lead to widespread job displacement before the economy has time to adjust.
- The adaptability of the workforce: The ability of workers to acquire new skills and transition to new jobs will be crucial in mitigating the negative effects of automation.
- Government policies and social safety nets: Policies such as retraining programs, unemployment benefits, and income support measures can help to cushion the impact of job displacement and facilitate the transition to a new economy.
- The distribution of the benefits of automation: If the gains from increased productivity and economic growth are concentrated in the hands of a few, it could lead to increased income inequality and social unrest.

Countries that invest in workforce retraining and provide workers with access to new employment opportunities are more likely to harness the benefits of automation in the long run.

Real-World Example: The Impact of Automation on Employment

A compelling example of the complex economic impact of automation can be observed in the development of self-driving trucks. The trucking industry in the United States employs millions of drivers, many of whom face the risk of being replaced by autonomous vehicles.

According to various estimates, the widespread adoption of self-driving trucks could displace hundreds of thousands, or even millions, of jobs in the trucking sector, affecting not only drivers but also related industries such as:

- Logistics
- Warehousing
- Truck stops and related services
- Vehicle maintenance and repair

The displacement of such a large number of workers would undoubtedly create significant economic and social challenges.

However, it is also important to acknowledge that autonomous vehicles could also generate new job opportunities and economic benefits. For example, the demand could increase for:

- Vehicle programmers and software developers specializing in autonomous systems
- AI specialists and machine learning engineers
- Technicians skilled in the maintenance and repair of autonomous vehicles
- Logistics and supply chain managers who can optimize the use of autonomous trucks

Furthermore, self-driving trucks have the potential to:

- Reduce transportation costs: Automation can lead to lower fuel consumption, reduced wear and tear on vehicles, and optimized routing.
- Improve the efficiency of supply chains: Autonomous trucks can operate 24/7 without the need for rest breaks, leading to faster delivery times and more efficient logistics.

- Enhance road safety: By eliminating human error, autonomous trucks could potentially reduce the number of accidents and fatalities on the roads.

These potential benefits could lead to increased economic activity and create new opportunities in various sectors.

15.2 Robot Rights and Human Control

As robotic systems attain increasing levels of sophistication, a fundamental ethical question emerges: Should robots possess rights? This inquiry is particularly pertinent in the context of robots designed for close interaction with humans, such as service robots providing assistance, healthcare robots delivering patient care, and companion robots offering social support. The concept of robot rights challenges traditional anthropocentric views of moral status and raises profound questions about the ethical and legal standing of these advanced machines.

The Concept of Robot Rights

Robot rights represent a theoretical framework that proposes that robots, particularly those endowed with advanced artificial intelligence, should be granted certain rights or protections analogous to those accorded to humans or animals. This notion remains highly contentious, and opinions on the matter are sharply divided.

One perspective posits that robots, regardless of their apparent intelligence or functional capabilities, are fundamentally tools created by humans and, as such, should not possess any inherent rights. This view emphasizes the instrumental nature of robots, asserting that their value lies solely in their utility to humans.

Conversely, another perspective argues that as robots evolve to exhibit greater autonomy, complexity, and decision-making capabilities, they should be entitled to certain forms of legal and moral protection. Proponents of this view suggest that the capacity for robots to form relationships, demonstrate a degree of self-awareness, or experience something akin to suffering could provide a basis for extending certain rights to them.

For instance, consider the development of companion robots designed to provide companionship and emotional support to elderly individuals or those with disabilities. These robots are becoming increasingly sophisticated, capable of:

- Learning from their interactions with humans
- Recognizing and responding to human emotions
- Exhibiting behaviors that suggest a form of social or emotional intelligence

If robots of this kind begin to form strong bonds with humans, engendering feelings of attachment and even affection, should they have a right to be treated with respect and dignity? Should their creators or owners be held accountable for mistreating them? These questions delve into the very nature of moral consideration and challenge us to expand our understanding of what entities might be deserving of ethical regard.

The Ethical Debate: Human Control vs. Robot Autonomy

The debate surrounding robot rights is inextricably linked to the question of the appropriate balance between human control and robot autonomy. As AI systems advance, robots are increasingly capable of making decisions and taking actions without direct human input or supervision.

Autonomous vehicles, for example, are designed to:

- Navigate complex environments
- Make real-time decisions on the road, such as adjusting speed and trajectory
- Respond to unexpected obstacles and traffic conditions, all without human intervention

In some potential scenarios, robots might be entrusted with making decisions that have life-or-death consequences. Examples include:

- Military drones operating autonomously in combat situations
- Healthcare robots performing surgical procedures or administering critical care

The question then arises: To what extent should humans relinquish control over robots, particularly in situations involving significant ethical or safety implications? Should robots be granted the authority to make decisions autonomously, or should there always be a human supervisor or operator overseeing their actions, retaining the ultimate authority to intervene or override their choices?

This issue is especially salient in the context of military robots and autonomous weapons systems, where the potential for misuse, unintended harm, or violations of international humanitarian law is particularly high. The prospect of robots making autonomous decisions about the use of lethal force raises profound ethical concerns about:

- Accountability: Who is responsible if an autonomous weapon makes an erroneous decision that results in civilian casualties?
- Proportionality: Can a robot be programmed to make nuanced judgments about the proportionality of a military response?
- The sanctity of human life: Should the decision to take a human life ever be delegated to a machine?

These questions underscore the critical importance of maintaining meaningful human control over robots, especially in situations where fundamental human values and ethical principles are at stake.

Legal and Moral Implications

The legal status of robots is another complex area that requires careful consideration as these machines become more advanced. Currently, under most legal systems, robots are generally considered to be property, and their creators, owners, or operators are held responsible for their actions.

However, as robots acquire greater autonomy and the capacity for independent decision-making, the adequacy of this legal framework may be called into question. New legal frameworks may be needed to address issues such as:

- Liability: If a robot causes harm to a human or damages property, who should be held legally accountable? Should it be the manufacturer who designed the robot, the programmer who wrote its code, the owner who deployed it, or the robot itself?
- Accountability: How can we ensure that robots are held accountable for their actions, and what forms of redress or punishment might be appropriate in cases where a robot causes harm?
- Legal personhood: Should advanced robots be granted some form of legal personhood, affording them certain rights and responsibilities under the law?

These questions are difficult to answer and require careful deliberation about the evolving relationship between humans and machines. Moreover, the issue of robot rights raises broader philosophical and ethical questions about the very nature of consciousness, sentience, and moral status. What criteria should be used to determine which entities are deserving of moral consideration? Is it possible for a machine to possess qualities that would justify granting it rights? These are profound inquiries that will continue to challenge our understanding of what it means to be human and what our obligations are to the non-human world, including the increasingly sophisticated machines we create.

Real-World Example: Autonomous Military Robots

One of the most contentious areas in the debate over robot rights and human control is the development and deployment of autonomous military robots. The increasing use of drones, robotic soldiers, and other autonomous weapons systems has the potential to fundamentally alter the nature of warfare. While these technologies may offer potential advantages in terms of:

- Reducing human casualties
- Increasing precision
- Enhancing operational efficiency

they also raise profound ethical concerns.

For example, in 2016, the United Nations convened discussions on the possibility of banning the development and deployment of fully autonomous weapons systems, often referred to as "killer robots," that could make independent decisions to kill without any human intervention or oversight. Many experts and civil society organizations argue that the use of such weapons could have dire consequences, such as:

- Lowering the threshold for going to war
- Escalating conflicts
- Leading to accidental or unintended killings
- Violating fundamental principles of international humanitarian law

The debate surrounding autonomous military robots highlights the critical importance of maintaining meaningful human control over machines, particularly when it comes to decisions involving the use of lethal force. While autonomous weapons may offer certain strategic or tactical advantages, they also pose significant risks in terms of:

- Accountability: Who is responsible if an autonomous weapon commits a war crime?
- Ethical considerations: Is it morally permissible for a machine to make autonomous decisions about taking human life?
- Unforeseen consequences: What are the potential long-term implications of delegating the power of life and death to machines?

15.3 Data Privacy in Robotics

The increasing integration of robots into various facets of daily life has brought forth a significant concern: data privacy. Robots, particularly those powered by artificial intelligence, collect and process vast amounts of data pertaining to their environment, their users, and their own operational parameters. This data can encompass a wide range of information, including personal details, behavioral patterns, and even sensitive biometric data, thereby raising critical questions about:

- Who has access to this information?
- How is this information being utilized?
- What measures are in place to protect this information from unauthorized access and misuse?

The Importance of Data in Robotics

Data serves as the lifeblood of AI and robotics. Robots heavily rely on data to perform a multitude of essential tasks, such as:

- Object recognition: Identifying and categorizing objects in their surroundings.
- Navigation: Moving autonomously through complex environments.
- Decision-making: Making informed choices based on sensory input and programmed algorithms.

Robots acquire data from a variety of sources, including:

- Sensors: Gathering information about the physical environment (e.g., temperature, pressure, proximity).

- Cameras: Capturing visual information, enabling tasks like facial recognition and scene understanding.
- Microphones: Recording audio data, facilitating voice interaction and sound analysis.
- Other devices: Interacting with other connected devices to obtain contextual information.

In numerous applications, robots also collect data about the individuals they interact with. This is particularly prevalent in domains such as:

- Healthcare: Robots monitoring patients' vital signs and medical information.
- Home assistance: Robots learning user preferences and routines to provide personalized services.

This category of data can be incredibly sensitive and personal, giving rise to substantial concerns about privacy and security. The potential for misuse or unauthorized access to this information necessitates careful consideration and the implementation of robust safeguards.

For instance, robots employed in elderly care or healthcare settings may continuously monitor patients' health data, including:

- Heart rate
- Blood pressure
- Oxygen levels
- Medication adherence
- Activity levels

While this data holds immense potential for improving the quality of patient care, enabling proactive interventions and personalized treatment plans, it also poses a significant risk if it falls into the wrong hands or is misused. Unauthorized access to this data could lead to:

- Discrimination: Health information could be used to deny insurance coverage or employment opportunities.
- Financial exploitation: Sensitive data could be used to target vulnerable individuals for scams or fraud.
- Emotional distress: The disclosure of private health information could cause significant emotional harm and damage relationships.

Privacy Concerns in AI Robotics

A primary concern regarding data privacy in robotics is the potential for unauthorized access to personal data. Given that many robots are connected to the internet or rely on cloud-based systems for data storage and processing, they are inherently vulnerable to cyberattacks and data breaches. This risk is particularly salient in the case of consumer robots, such as:

- Home assistants: Devices that record voice commands and monitor household activities.
- Surveillance robots: Systems that capture video and audio footage for security purposes.

These robots are often connected to home Wi-Fi networks, which may not always be adequately secured, and they frequently transmit data to cloud storage systems, which can be targeted by hackers.

Moreover, the sheer volume of data collected by robots raises concerns about:

- Data retention: How long should robots store the data they collect? Should there be limitations on the duration of data storage?
- Data ownership: Who owns the data generated by robots? Is it the robot manufacturer, the user, or some other entity?
- Data usage: How can the data collected by robots be used? Can it be shared with third parties? For what purposes can it be used (e.g., targeted advertising, research)?

These are complex questions that require careful deliberation and the establishment of clear guidelines by policymakers, technologists, and ethicists.

Real-World Example: Data Privacy in Autonomous Vehicles

Autonomous vehicles provide a compelling illustration of how robots can raise significant data privacy concerns. These vehicles are equipped with a multitude of sensors that collect extensive data about their surroundings, including:

- Traffic conditions: Data on vehicle speeds, traffic flow, and congestion levels.
- Road signs and infrastructure: Information about road markings, traffic signals, and other elements of the driving environment.
- Behavior of other vehicles and pedestrians: Data on the movements and actions of other road users.

In addition to external data, autonomous vehicles also gather information about their passengers, such as:

- Location and travel patterns: Data on where the vehicle travels and the routes it takes.
- Personal preferences: Information about preferred destinations, music choices, and climate control settings.
- In-vehicle activities: Data on phone calls, conversations, and other activities taking place inside the vehicle.

In some potential scenarios, autonomous vehicles could even collect sensitive data about the health or emotional state of passengers, such as:

- Heart rate
- Stress levels
- Drowsiness

This type of data could be obtained through sensors embedded in the vehicle's seats or steering wheel, or through the analysis of voice patterns and facial expressions.

If this data is not adequately protected, it could be used for purposes beyond those originally intended, such as:

- Targeted advertising: Data on travel patterns and personal preferences could be used to deliver personalized advertisements to passengers.
- Surveillance: Data on vehicle location and passenger activities could be used by law enforcement or other entities to track individuals' movements and behavior.
- Discrimination: Health or emotional data could be used to discriminate against passengers in areas such as insurance or employment.

The potential for misuse of this data necessitates the implementation of robust data protection measures, including:

- Encryption: Protecting data from unauthorized access by encoding it during storage and transmission.
- Data anonymization: Removing personally identifiable information from data to reduce the risk of individual identification.
- Access controls: Restricting access to data to only authorized individuals or entities.
- Data minimization: Collecting only the data that is strictly necessary for the intended purpose.
- Purpose limitation: Using data only for the specific purposes for which it was collected.
- Transparency: Informing users about what data is being collected and how it will be used.
- User consent: Obtaining explicit consent from users before collecting and processing their data.

The Role of Legislation and Regulations

To address the growing data privacy concerns in robotics, several countries and regions have enacted legislation and regulations aimed at protecting individuals' privacy.

The European Union's General Data Protection Regulation (GDPR) is one of the most comprehensive and influential privacy laws in the world. The GDPR establishes a set of principles and requirements for the collection, processing, and storage of personal data, including:

- Consent: Organizations must obtain explicit consent from individuals before collecting their personal data.
- Data minimization: Organizations should only collect the data that is necessary for the intended purpose.
- Purpose limitation: Data should only be used for the specific purposes for which it was collected.
- Right to access: Individuals have the right to access their personal data and obtain information about how it is being used.
- Right to rectification: Individuals have the right to correct inaccurate or incomplete data.
- Right to erasure ("right to be forgotten"): Individuals have the right to request the deletion of their personal data.

- Data security: Organizations must implement appropriate technical and organizational measures to protect data from unauthorized access, use, or disclosure.

In the context of robotics, regulations like the GDPR are essential for ensuring that robots respect individuals' privacy and that data is handled ethically and responsibly. As robots become more prevalent in everyday life, it is crucial that data protection laws evolve to keep pace with technological advancements and address the unique privacy challenges posed by these intelligent machines.

50 multiple choice questions (MCQs) with correct answers based on **Ethical and Social Implications** in AI-based robotics:

Section 15.1: Job Displacement and Economic Impact

1. **Which sector has seen significant job displacement due to industrial robots?**
   a) Education
   b) Manufacturing
   c) Hospitality
   d) Legal
   Answer: b) Manufacturing
2. **What is a major cause of concern with AI-based automation?**
   a) Slower productivity
   b) Increased hardware costs
   c) Job displacement
   d) Poor internet access
   Answer: c) Job displacement
3. **Which of the following jobs is most at risk due to robotic automation?**
   a) Software developer
   b) Truck driver
   c) Nurse
   d) Lawyer
   Answer: b) Truck driver
4. **What does "job displacement" refer to in the context of robotics?**
   a) Moving jobs to different cities
   b) Elimination of jobs due to automation
   c) Offering better roles to employees
   d) Outsourcing to other countries
   Answer: b) Elimination of jobs due to automation
5. **How can governments help mitigate job losses from robotics?**
   a) Increase import duties
   b) Ban robotics
   c) Promote upskilling programs
   d) Cut taxes for companies
   Answer: c) Promote upskilling programs

6. **Which of these is a long-term benefit of robotics despite initial job losses?**
   a) Reduction in education
   b) Elimination of skilled work
   c) Increased economic efficiency
   d) Decreased innovation
   Answer: c) Increased economic efficiency

7. **AI in agriculture might reduce demand for which kind of labor?**
   a) Data scientists
   b) Manual farm workers
   c) AI engineers
   d) Supply chain managers
   Answer: b) Manual farm workers

8. **Which concept supports transitioning workers into new jobs after automation?**
   a) Reskilling
   b) Layoff planning
   c) Corporate taxation
   d) Product redesign
   Answer: a) Reskilling

9. **Which industry is least affected by job displacement due to robotics so far?**
   a) Call centers
   b) Fast food
   c) Construction
   d) Creative arts
   Answer: d) Creative arts

10. **Job displacement is most severe in which type of task?**
    a) Repetitive and predictable tasks
    b) Tasks requiring high creativity
    c) Strategic management
    d) Legal interpretation
    Answer: a) Repetitive and predictable tasks

Section 15.2: Robot Rights and Human Control

11. **Robot rights refer to:**
    a) Freedom of movement
    b) Legal status of AI entities
    c) Software licenses
    d) Ownership laws
    Answer: b) Legal status of AI entities

12. **Which area raises the greatest concern for autonomous decision-making?**
    a) Housekeeping
    b) Military operations
    c) Online shopping
    d) Email filtering
    Answer: b) Military operations

13. **Which term describes human control over robot actions?**
    a) Autonomy
    b) Human-in-the-loop
    c) Data privacy
    d) Remote assistance
    Answer: b) Human-in-the-loop

14. **One major concern of increasing robot autonomy is:**
    a) Decrease in electricity use
    b) Increase in sensor prices
    c) Loss of human oversight
    d) Lack of creativity
    Answer: c) Loss of human oversight

15. **Should robots have rights? This is a question of:**
    a) Legal regulation
    b) Software design
    c) Ethical consideration
    d) User interface design
    Answer: c) Ethical consideration

16. **Who is liable if a robot causes harm autonomously?**
    a) The user
    b) The manufacturer
    c) The AI programmer
    d) It's legally unclear
    Answer: d) It's legally unclear

17. **What principle insists humans must always maintain control over AI systems?**
    a) Open-source principle
    b) Asimov's Law
    c) Human-centric AI
    d) Binary law
    Answer: c) Human-centric AI

18. **Which scenario questions the need for ethical robot behavior?**
    a) Smart home assistants
    b) Autonomous surgery bots
    c) Cleaning bots
    d) Sorting machines
    Answer: b) Autonomous surgery bots

19. **Which of these supports robot rights discussions?**
    a) Robotic empathy simulation
    b) Human-machine interface
    c) AI sentience
    d) High-resolution imaging
    Answer: c) AI sentience

20. **The ethical issue of 'robot rights' is primarily based on:**
    a) Computing power
    b) Legal jurisdiction
    c) Robot consciousness
    d) Cloud compatibility
    Answer: c) Robot consciousness

Section 15.3: Data Privacy in Robotics

21. **Robots often collect user data via:**
    a) Satellites
    b) Sensors and cameras
    c) Optical disks
    d) Microphones only
    Answer: b) Sensors and cameras

22. **What is a primary concern in data privacy in robotics?**
    a) Robot overheating
    b) Unauthorized data access
    c) Power supply issues
    d) Mechanical errors
    Answer: b) Unauthorized data access

23. **Robots in healthcare may collect which type of sensitive data?**
    a) Favorite food
    b) Heart rate
    c) Internet speed
    d) Book preferences
    Answer: b) Heart rate

24. **What regulation protects user data in the EU?**
    a) GDPR
    b) DMCA
    c) IEEE
    d) ISO9001
    Answer: a) GDPR

25. **One method to ensure privacy in robots is:**
    a) Disabling all sensors
    b) Offline storage only
    c) Data encryption
    d) Using only mechanical systems
    Answer: c) Data encryption

26. **Which robot would likely raise more privacy concerns?**
    a) Manufacturing robot
    b) Autonomous vacuum cleaner
    c) Companion robot with facial recognition
    d) Sorting robot in warehouses
    Answer: c) Companion robot with facial recognition

27. **Data collected by robots should be:**
    a) Shared freely
    b) Stored permanently
    c) Minimized and anonymized
    d) Displayed publicly
    Answer: c) Minimized and anonymized

28. **What is one risk of cloud-connected robots?**
    a) Faster movement
    b) Dependency on local hardware
    c) Higher electricity bills
    d) Remote hacking threats
    Answer: d) Remote hacking threats
29. **Which of these is an example of a privacy invasion by a robot?**
    a) Monitoring factory output
    b) Sending medical data without consent
    c) Updating software
    d) Navigating indoors
    Answer: b) Sending medical data without consent
30. **Facial recognition in service robots is controversial due to:**
    a) Performance limitations
    b) Appearance design
    c) Ethical and privacy concerns
    d) High battery usage
    Answer: c) Ethical and privacy concerns

Mixed and Advanced Application-Based Questions

31. **The rise of AI-based robotics requires changes in:**
    a) Construction codes
    b) Environmental law
    c) Legal and ethical frameworks
    d) Electrical wiring
    Answer: c) Legal and ethical frameworks
32. **What can result from lack of robot accountability?**
    a) Slower manufacturing
    b) Unfair legal judgments
    c) Reduced AI capabilities
    d) Data storage failures
    Answer: b) Unfair legal judgments
33. **Data privacy violations by robots can lead to:**
    a) Higher product ratings
    b) Legal action and fines
    c) Better performance
    d) Longer battery life
    Answer: b) Legal action and fines
34. **Ethics in robotics ensures:**
    a) Better app interfaces
    b) Compliance with circuit design
    c) Responsible use of AI systems
    d) Lower development costs
    Answer: c) Responsible use of AI systems

35. **Unemployment from robotics is most likely in jobs that are:**
    a) Analytical
    b) Non-repetitive
    c) Predictable
    d) Strategy-based
    Answer: c) Predictable

36. **Robot rights may include:**
    a) Voting rights
    b) Protection from abuse
    c) Tax exemptions
    d) Citizenship
    Answer: b) Protection from abuse

37. **Data collected by AI systems must adhere to:**
    a) Fictional standards
    b) Ethical use policies
    c) Unwritten protocols
    d) Random models
    Answer: b) Ethical use policies

38. **Human-in-the-loop control is necessary for:**
    a) Maximizing memory usage
    b) Ethical decision-making
    c) Enhancing CPU power
    d) GPU optimization
    Answer: b) Ethical decision-making

39. **Job reskilling programs aim to:**
    a) Automate tasks
    b) Train robots
    c) Prepare humans for new roles
    d) Reduce taxes
    Answer: c) Prepare humans for new roles

40. **Which type of robot would likely need the highest ethical scrutiny?**
    a) Vacuum cleaner robot
    b) Factory welding robot
    c) Military drone
    d) Barcode scanner robot
    Answer: c) Military drone

41. **Robot consciousness is still:**
    a) Widely available
    b) Fully achieved
    c) A debated concept
    d) A programming error
    Answer: c) A debated concept

42. **Who benefits most from ethical AI implementation?**
    a) Robots
    b) Consumers and society
    c) Only researchers
    d) Batteries
    Answer: b) Consumers and society

43. **Autonomy in AI robots must be balanced with:**
   a) High cost
   b) Human oversight
   c) Hardware control
   d) Frequent maintenance
   Answer: b) Human oversight

44. **Robot abuse laws are being explored due to:**
   a) Software issues
   b) Manufacturing errors
   c) Increasing human-robot interaction
   d) Decreasing robot usage
   Answer: c) Increasing human-robot interaction

45. **Unauthorized robot data access can lead to:**
   a) High-speed computing
   b) Enhanced intelligence
   c) Identity theft
   d) Longer battery life
   Answer: c) Identity theft

46. **Privacy-first design in robotics ensures:**
   a) Cost reduction
   b) Legal compliance and trust
   c) Better sensors
   d) Voice recognition
   Answer: b) Legal compliance and trust

47. **Which term describes robots making decisions without human input?**
   a) Human-in-the-loop
   b) Machine error
   c) Autonomy
   d) Overclocking
   Answer: c) Autonomy

48. **Why is ethical robotics important for society?**
   a) To promote AI games
   b) To lower hardware prices
   c) To prevent harm and bias
   d) To increase exports
   Answer: c) To prevent harm and bias

49. **Which sector might face legal scrutiny due to AI-based job losses?**
   a) Tourism
   b) Healthcare
   c) Automation and tech
   d) Music industry
   Answer: c) Automation and tech

50. **Future laws in robotics will likely focus on:**
   a) App development
   b) Sensor design
   c) Ethics, privacy, and control
   d) Graphics resolution
   Answer: c) Ethics, privacy, and control

Chapter 16: Future Trends in AI and Robotics

The fields of artificial intelligence (AI) and robotics are rapidly evolving, with ongoing research and development pushing the boundaries of what these technologies can achieve. Several key trends are poised to shape the future of AI and robotics, transforming the way humans interact with machines and impacting various aspects of society. This chapter will explore three prominent trends: collaborative robots (cobots), swarm intelligence, and human-robot symbiosis.

16.1 Collaborative Robots (Cobots)

Collaborative robots, often referred to as cobots, represent a transformative shift in the field of robotics, moving away from the traditional paradigm of isolated, high-speed industrial robots towards a model of human-robot collaboration. While conventional industrial robots are typically designed to operate autonomously within structured and often fenced-off environments, performing repetitive and often hazardous tasks in isolation from human workers, cobots are specifically engineered to work in close proximity to, and in direct cooperation with, humans within a shared workspace. This close interaction enables humans and robots to combine their respective strengths – the precision, speed, and endurance of robots with the cognitive abilities, adaptability, and problem-solving skills of humans – leading to significant improvements in productivity, enhanced safety in the workplace, and greater flexibility in a wide range of industrial and non-industrial applications.

A Departure from Traditional Industrial Robotics

Traditional industrial robots, while highly effective in automating large-scale manufacturing processes, are often characterized by:

- **High speed and power:** Designed for maximum throughput, these robots typically operate at high speeds and with significant force, posing a safety risk to humans in close proximity.
- **Limited flexibility:** These robots are typically programmed for specific, repetitive tasks and are difficult to reprogram or redeploy for different applications.
- **Isolation:** To ensure safety, traditional industrial robots are often physically separated from human workers by safety barriers, fences, or light curtains, limiting human-robot interaction.
- **High cost and complexity:** The installation, programming, and maintenance of traditional industrial robots can be complex and expensive, requiring specialized expertise.

Cobots, in contrast, are designed to overcome these limitations and facilitate a more harmonious and productive relationship between humans and robots.

Key Characteristics of Cobots

Cobots possess several distinguishing characteristics that differentiate them from traditional industrial robots and enable them to work safely and effectively alongside humans:

- **Enhanced Safety:** Safety is a paramount consideration in the design of cobots. These robots are equipped with a variety of advanced safety features, including:
    - **Force and torque sensors:** These highly sensitive sensors are integrated into the robot's joints and end-effector (the "hand" of the robot) to detect even the slightest contact or collision with a human or object.
    - **Collision detection and avoidance:** When a collision is detected, the cobot can automatically stop its motion or move away from the point of contact, preventing injuries.
    - **Speed and separation monitoring:** Some cobots use vision systems and other sensors to monitor the distance and speed between the robot and human workers. If the distance becomes too small or the speed too high, the robot's motion can be slowed down or stopped.
    - **Safety-rated control systems:** Cobots are designed with safety-rated control systems that ensure reliable and predictable behavior, even in the event of a malfunction.
    - **Lightweight design:** Cobots are often made from lightweight materials, reducing the inertia and impact force in the event of a collision.
- **Ease of Programming and Use:** Cobots are designed to be user-friendly and intuitive, making them accessible to a wider range of users, including those without extensive programming expertise. This is achieved through features such as:
    - **Hand guiding:** Workers can physically guide the robot arm through the desired motions, and the robot can record and repeat the sequence.
    - **Tablet-based interfaces:** Many cobots are programmed using intuitive tablet interfaces with graphical programming tools, eliminating the need for complex coding.
    - **Offline programming:** Simulation software allows users to program the robot's movements offline, without interrupting production.
    - **Simplified setup:** Cobots are often designed for easy installation and setup, with minimal integration effort required.
- **Inherent Flexibility and Adaptability:** Cobots are designed to be more flexible and adaptable than traditional robots, enabling them to be easily redeployed for different tasks and in different work environments. This flexibility is achieved through:
    - **Lightweight and mobile design:** Cobots are typically lightweight and compact, making them easy to move and reposition.
    - **Modular design:** Some cobots have a modular design, allowing components to be easily added or removed to customize the robot for specific tasks.
    - **Quick change tooling:** Cobots can be equipped with quick-change end-effectors, allowing them to switch between different tools (e.g., grippers, screwdrivers, welding torches) quickly.
- **Integration with AI and Machine Learning:** The capabilities of cobots are further enhanced by their integration with artificial intelligence (AI) and machine learning (ML) technologies. This allows cobots to:
    - **Perceive their environment:** Cobots can use sensors such as cameras, force sensors, and proximity sensors to perceive their surroundings and understand the context of their work.

- **Learn from experience:** Cobots can learn from their interactions with humans and their environment, improving their performance over time.
- **Adapt to changing conditions:** Cobots can adapt to changes in the work environment, such as variations in the position of parts or the presence of obstacles.
- **Perform more complex tasks:** AI and ML enable cobots to perform more complex tasks that require decision-making, problem-solving, and adaptability.

Applications of Cobots Across Industries

Cobots are finding increasing adoption across a wide range of industries, transforming the way work is performed and creating new opportunities for human-robot collaboration. Some key application areas include:

- **Manufacturing:** Cobots are revolutionizing manufacturing processes by automating tasks such as:
  - **Assembly:** Cobots can work alongside human assembly line workers, performing repetitive or physically demanding tasks such as screwing, bolting, or fitting parts, while humans handle more complex or delicate operations.
  - **Material handling:** Cobots can transport parts and materials between workstations, reducing the physical strain on workers and improving efficiency.
  - **Quality control:** Cobots equipped with vision systems can perform precise inspections, identifying defects and ensuring product quality.
  - **Welding and painting:** Cobots can perform these hazardous tasks with precision.
- **Logistics and Warehousing:** Cobots are used in warehouses and distribution centers to automate tasks such as:
  - **Picking and packing:** Cobots can assist workers in selecting and packaging orders, reducing the time and effort required.
  - **Sorting:** Cobots can sort items based on size, shape, or destination, improving the efficiency of order fulfillment.
  - **Palletizing:** Cobots can stack boxes or other items on pallets, reducing the physical strain on workers.
- **Healthcare and Medical:** Cobots are being developed and deployed in healthcare settings for applications such as:
  - **Patient handling:** Cobots can assist nurses and caregivers in lifting and transferring patients, reducing the risk of injury.
  - **Rehabilitation:** Cobots can be used to guide patients through exercises and provide feedback on their progress.
  - **Surgery:** Cobots can assist surgeons in performing minimally invasive procedures with greater precision and dexterity.
  - **Drug dispensing:** Cobots can accurately and efficiently dispense medication.
- **Agriculture and Farming:** Cobots are being used in agriculture to automate tasks such as:
  - **Harvesting:** Cobots can harvest fruits, vegetables, and other crops with precision and speed.

- **Weeding:** Cobots can identify and remove weeds, reducing the need for manual labor and herbicides.
    - **Crop monitoring:** Cobots equipped with sensors can monitor crop health and growth, providing valuable data to farmers.
    - **Planting and seeding:** Cobots can precisely plant seeds.
- **Food and Beverage Industry:** Cobots are being used for:
    - Packaging and palletizing
    - Food processing
    - Quality control
- **Construction:** Cobots can be used for:
    - Bricklaying
    - Material handling
    - Inspection
- **Retail:** Cobots can be used for:
    - Inventory management
    - Customer service
    - Delivery

Benefits of Cobots: Transforming the Workplace

The adoption of cobots offers a multitude of potential benefits for businesses, workers, and the overall economy:

- **Significant Increase in Productivity:** By combining the strengths of humans and robots, cobots can dramatically increase productivity in various tasks and industries. Robots can perform repetitive, physically demanding, or time-consuming tasks with greater speed, accuracy, and consistency, freeing up human workers to focus on more complex, creative, and strategic activities that require human cognitive abilities.
- **Enhanced Workplace Safety:** Cobots are designed to work safely alongside humans, minimizing the risk of workplace accidents and injuries. Their advanced safety features, such as force and torque sensors, collision detection, and speed and separation monitoring, enable them to operate in close proximity to humans without posing a significant hazard. This can lead to a reduction in workplace injuries, worker compensation claims, and lost work time.
- **Greater Operational Flexibility:** Cobots offer a high degree of flexibility in production and other operations. They can be easily reprogrammed and redeployed for different tasks, allowing businesses to adapt quickly to changing market demands, product variations, or production schedules. This flexibility can improve responsiveness, reduce downtime, and enable the production of smaller batch sizes.
- **Reduction in Operational Costs:** In many cases, cobots can help businesses reduce operational costs. By automating tasks, cobots can reduce labor costs, increase efficiency, and minimize waste. They can also operate continuously without the need for breaks or shift changes, further improving productivity and reducing overhead costs.
- **Augmentation of Human Capabilities:** Cobots can augment and enhance human capabilities, allowing workers to focus on more complex, creative, and strategic aspects of their work. By offloading mundane or physically demanding tasks to robots, humans

can devote their time and energy to activities that require their unique cognitive skills, such as:

- o Problem-solving
- o Decision-making
- o Innovation
- o Critical thinking
- o Communication
- o Collaboration

This can lead to increased job satisfaction, improved worker morale, and a more fulfilling and engaging work experience.

Diagram of a Collaborative Robot Working with a Human

```
graph LR
    A[Human Worker] -- "Collaboration" --> B(Collaborative Robot);
    B -- "Task Assistance" --> C[Workpiece/Product];
    B -- "Safety Sensors" --> A;
    A -- "Guidance & Oversight" --> B;
style A fill:#90EE90,stroke:#333,stroke-width:2px
style B fill:#87CEFA,stroke:#333,stroke-width:2px
style C fill:#FFFFE0,stroke:#333,stroke-width:2px
```

Diagram Description:

- **Human Worker:** Represents the human operator working in collaboration with the cobot.
- **Collaborative Robot:** Represents the cobot, equipped with sensors and safety features.
- **Workpiece/Product:** Represents the object or product that is being worked on.
- **Collaboration:** Indicates the collaborative interaction between the human worker and the cobot.
- **Task Assistance:** Shows the cobot assisting the human worker in performing a specific task.
- **Safety Sensors**: Shows the cobot using sensors to ensure safety.
- **Guidance & Oversight:** Shows the human worker providing guidance and oversight to the cobot.

In this diagram, the human worker and the cobot are working together on a workpiece or product. The cobot assists the human worker by performing tasks that are repetitive, physically demanding, or require precision, while the human worker provides guidance, oversight, and uses their cognitive abilities to handle more complex aspects of the task. The cobot's safety sensors ensure that it can work safely in close proximity to the human worker.

16.2 Swarm Intelligence

Swarm intelligence (SI) is an innovative and rapidly growing field of study that draws its primary inspiration from the collective, decentralized, and self-organized behaviors observed in various natural systems. These systems, despite the relative simplicity of their individual components or members, are capable of exhibiting remarkably complex and seemingly intelligent behaviors at the group level. Examples of such systems include:

- **Ant colonies:** Ants, individually possessing limited cognitive abilities, can collectively establish highly efficient foraging trails to locate and retrieve food sources, often over considerable distances.
- **Bee swarms:** Bees can coordinate their activities to perform intricate tasks such as building complex hives, regulating temperature, and foraging for nectar, exhibiting collective decision-making processes.
- **Flocks of birds:** Birds flying in flocks can maintain cohesive formations, navigate complex environments, and evade predators through coordinated movements, without any centralized control.
- **Schools of fish:** Fish swimming in schools can exhibit synchronized movements, avoid obstacles, and defend themselves against predators through collective behavior.

These natural systems demonstrate that complex global patterns and solutions can emerge from a multitude of simple local interactions among individual agents. Swarm intelligence algorithms and principles are increasingly being applied to the control of multi-robot systems, enabling them to perform complex tasks in a distributed, robust, and coordinated manner.

Core Principles of Swarm Intelligence

Swarm intelligence is characterized by several fundamental principles that govern the behavior of the system:

- **Decentralization:** In a swarm intelligent system, control is not vested in a single, central entity or controller. Instead, control is distributed among the individual agents or robots that comprise the system. Each agent operates autonomously, making decisions based on its own local perception of the environment and its interactions with neighboring agents. This decentralized approach eliminates the single point of failure that can plague centralized systems, making swarm systems more robust and resilient.
- **Self-Organization:** The global behavior of a swarm intelligent system arises from the local interactions among the agents, without any explicit, centralized coordination or global plan. Agents follow simple rules and communicate with each other directly, and the overall system behavior emerges spontaneously from these local interactions. This self-organizing principle allows swarm systems to adapt dynamically to changing conditions and to exhibit emergent properties that are not explicitly programmed into the individual agents.
- **Locality of Interactions:** Agents in a swarm intelligent system interact with each other and their immediate environment based on local information. Each agent has a limited perception range and is only aware of the state of its nearby neighbors and the immediate surroundings. Agents do not have a global view of the entire system or the overall task. Instead, they rely on local communication and sensing to coordinate their actions and make decisions. This locality of interactions makes swarm systems scalable and efficient, as agents do not need to process or transmit large amounts of global information.

- **Emergence:** One of the most striking characteristics of swarm intelligence is the emergence of complex and seemingly intelligent behaviors at the group level, resulting from the simple interactions among the individual agents. These emergent behaviors are not explicitly programmed into the agents but rather arise spontaneously from their collective interactions. Examples of emergent behaviors include:
    - **Path formation:** Ants create efficient paths to food sources through the deposition and following of pheromone trails.
    - **Collective decision-making:** Bees choose a new hive location through a distributed voting process.
    - **Synchronized motion:** Birds in a flock or fish in a school exhibit coordinated movements without a leader.
    - **Task allocation:** Agents in a swarm can specialize in different tasks and distribute workload efficiently.

Swarm Intelligence Algorithms

Several well-established algorithms have been inspired by the principles of swarm intelligence. These algorithms provide computational frameworks for solving optimization, control, and other complex problems:

- **Ant Colony Optimization (ACO):** Inspired by the foraging behavior of ant colonies, ACO algorithms are used to find optimal paths in graphs and solve combinatorial optimization problems. In ACO, artificial "ants" iteratively construct solutions by traversing the graph, leaving behind a "pheromone" trail that indicates the quality of the path. Subsequent ants are more likely to follow paths with higher pheromone concentrations, leading to the discovery of optimal or near-optimal solutions. ACO has been applied to a wide range of problems, including:
    - **Traveling salesman problem (TSP):** Finding the shortest route that visits a set of cities.
    - **Vehicle routing problem (VRP):** Optimizing the routes of vehicles to deliver goods to multiple locations.
    - **Graph coloring:** Assigning colors to the vertices of a graph such that no two adjacent vertices have the same color.
    - **Network routing**
- **Particle Swarm Optimization (PSO):** Inspired by the social behavior of bird flocks and fish schools, PSO algorithms are used to find optimal solutions in continuous search spaces. In PSO, a population of candidate solutions, called "particles," move through the search space, adjusting their positions and velocities based on their own best-found solution (cognitive component) and the best-found solution of their neighbors (social component). Through this iterative process, the particles converge towards the optimal or near-optimal solution. PSO has been applied to problems such as:
    - **Function optimization:** Finding the minimum or maximum of a mathematical function.
    - **Neural network training:** Optimizing the weights of a neural network.
    - **Control system design:** Tuning the parameters of a controller.
    - **Robotics path planning**

Swarm Robotics: Applying Swarm Intelligence to Robot Systems

Swarm robotics is a subfield of robotics that applies the principles of swarm intelligence to the control and coordination of large groups of relatively simple robots. Instead of relying on a single, complex, and centralized controller, swarm robotics aims to achieve complex collective behaviors by programming simple rules of interaction into each individual robot.

Swarm robotics systems typically consist of:

- **A large number of robots:** The robots are often small, inexpensive, and relatively simple in design.
- **Limited individual capabilities:** Each robot has limited sensing, communication, and computational capabilities.
- **Local communication:** Robots communicate with each other directly, within a limited communication range.
- **Distributed control:** There is no central controller; each robot makes decisions based on its local perception and communication.

Potential Applications of Swarm Robotics

Swarm robotics holds immense potential for a wide range of applications, offering solutions to problems that are difficult or impossible to address with traditional single-robot systems. Some key application areas include:

- **Search and Rescue:** Swarms of small robots can be deployed to search for survivors in disaster-stricken areas, such as collapsed buildings, earthquake zones, or flooded regions. The robots can navigate through rubble and confined spaces, locate victims using sensors, and provide information to human rescuers, significantly increasing the chances of finding survivors.
- **Environmental Monitoring:** Swarms of robots can be used to monitor environmental conditions over large and complex areas. For example, robots can be deployed to:
    - Measure air and water quality in polluted areas
    - Monitor forest fires
    - Track wildlife populations
    - Collect data on climate change
- **Infrastructure Inspection and Maintenance:** Swarms of robots can be used to inspect and maintain critical infrastructure, such as bridges, pipelines, power lines, and offshore platforms. The robots can detect damage, corrosion, or other problems, reducing the need for human inspectors to enter hazardous or inaccessible locations.
- **Precision Agriculture:** Swarms of robots can be used in agriculture to perform tasks such as:
    - Planting seeds with precision
    - Applying fertilizers and pesticides selectively
    - Harvesting crops
    - Monitoring crop health and growth

- **Construction and Manufacturing:** Swarms of robots can be used to automate construction and manufacturing processes, such as:
  - Assembling structures
  - Transporting materials
  - Performing welding or painting tasks
  - 3D printing large-scale objects
- **Cleaning and Maintenance:** Swarms of robots can be deployed for cleaning tasks in large or complex environments, such as:
  - Cleaning up oil spills
  - Cleaning large buildings
  - Maintaining solar panel farms
- **Exploration:** Swarms of robots can be used for space exploration, such as:
  - Exploring planets
  - Mining resources
  - Building habitats

Advantages of Swarm Robotics Compared to Single-Robot Systems

Swarm robotics offers several compelling advantages over traditional single-robot systems, making them well-suited for a variety of challenging applications:

- **Robustness and Fault Tolerance:** Swarm systems are inherently more robust to failures than single-robot systems. If one or a few robots in a swarm malfunction or are lost, the remaining robots can continue to operate and complete the task. The system's functionality is not critically dependent on the performance of any single robot.
- **Scalability and Adaptability:** Swarm systems can be easily scaled up or down by adding or removing robots, making them suitable for a wide range of tasks and environments. The system's performance can be adjusted by changing the number of robots, without requiring significant changes to the control algorithm. Swarm systems can also adapt to changing conditions, such as variations in the environment or the task requirements, by dynamically adjusting the robots' behavior.
- **Flexibility and Versatility:** Swarm systems are highly flexible and versatile, capable of performing a variety of tasks in different environments. The robots can coordinate their actions to achieve different goals, and the system can be reprogrammed or reconfigured to perform new tasks.
- **Increased Efficiency and Parallelism:** In some cases, swarm systems can perform tasks more efficiently than single-robot systems by dividing the workload among multiple robots. The robots can work in parallel, exploring different areas or performing different aspects of the task simultaneously, reducing the overall completion time.

Diagram of a Swarm Robotics System

```
graph LR
    A[Robot 1] -- "Local Communication" --> B[Robot 2];
    A -- "Local Communication" --> C[Robot 3];
    B -- "Local Communication" --> C;
    B -- "Local Communication" --> D[Robot 4];
```

```
    C -- "Local Communication" --> D;
    A -- "Environment" --> Z[Task];
    B -- "Environment" --> Z;
    C -- "Environment" --> Z;
    D -- "Environment" --> Z;
style A fill:#87CEFA,stroke:#333,stroke-width:2px
style B fill:#87CEFA,stroke:#333,stroke-width:2px
style C fill:#87CEFA,stroke:#333,stroke-width:2px
style D fill:#87CEFA,stroke:#333,stroke-width:2px
style Z fill:#FFFFE0,stroke:#333,stroke-width:2px
```

Diagram Description:

- **Robot 1, Robot 2, Robot 3, Robot 4:** Represent individual robots in the swarm.
- **Local Communication:** Arrows indicate direct communication between neighboring robots.
- **Environment:** Represents the environment in which the robots are operating.
- **Task:** Represents the overall task that the swarm is trying to accomplish.

In this diagram, the robots are interconnected through local communication links. Each robot interacts with its neighbors and the environment based on local information. The robots coordinate their actions to perform the overall task in a distributed and self-organized manner.

16.3 Human-Robot Symbiosis

Human-robot symbiosis represents a future vision where humans and robots transcend simple collaboration and enter into a close, mutually beneficial relationship. This concept envisions a future where the distinct capabilities of both humans and robots are seamlessly integrated, enabling them to achieve outcomes and perform tasks that neither could accomplish effectively in isolation. This goes beyond the current paradigm of humans using robots as tools; it posits a future where robots become integral partners in various aspects of human life, working in concert with humans to enhance their abilities, improve their well-being, and expand the boundaries of human potential.

Defining Human-Robot Symbiosis

At its core, human-robot symbiosis implies a relationship characterized by:

- **Close interaction:** Humans and robots work in close proximity, often in direct physical contact or with a high degree of coordination.
- **Mutual benefit:** Both humans and robots derive advantages from the relationship, with each contributing unique strengths and compensating for the other's limitations.
- **Integration of capabilities:** The skills, abilities, and knowledge of humans and robots are combined to achieve a shared goal or outcome.
- **Interdependence:** Humans and robots rely on each other to function effectively, with their actions and decisions closely intertwined.

This symbiotic relationship can manifest in various forms, ranging from physical integration to cognitive enhancement and social interaction.

Levels of Human-Robot Symbiosis

Human-robot symbiosis can be conceptualized as occurring at increasing levels of integration and interdependence:

- **Physical Symbiosis:** At this level, robots are physically integrated with the human body, becoming extensions of human capabilities. This integration can take several forms:
    - **Wearable devices:** Robots are worn on the body, providing support, assistance, or enhancement of physical functions.
    - **Exoskeletons:** Wearable robotic structures that augment human strength, endurance, and mobility.
    - **Prosthetics:** Artificial limbs or organs that replace missing or damaged body parts, restoring or enhancing function.
    - **Implantable devices**: Robots that are surgically placed inside the human body for therapeutic purposes
- **Cognitive Symbiosis:** At this level, robots enhance human cognitive abilities, extending the reach of the human mind and improving information processing, decision-making, and learning. This can involve:
    - **Brain-computer interfaces (BCIs):** Devices that establish a direct communication pathway between the human brain and a computer or robot, enabling the control of external devices with neural signals.
    - **AI-powered personal assistants:** Intelligent software agents that assist humans with tasks such as managing information, scheduling, communication, and decision support.
    - **Augmented reality (AR) and virtual reality (VR):** Technologies that overlay digital information onto the real world or create immersive virtual environments, enhancing human perception and understanding.
- **Social Symbiosis:** At this level, robots become integrated into human social structures, interacting with humans in a natural, intuitive, and socially appropriate manner. Robots may take on roles such as:
    - **Companions:** Providing social interaction, emotional support, and companionship to individuals, particularly the elderly or those with disabilities.
    - **Caregivers:** Assisting with daily living activities, providing personal care, and monitoring health.
    - **Educators:** Assisting in educational settings, providing personalized instruction, and facilitating learning.
    - **Collaborators:** Working alongside humans in teams, sharing tasks, and coordinating actions.

Examples of Emerging Technologies and Applications

Several emerging technologies and applications illustrate the evolving nature of human-robot symbiosis:

- **Exoskeletons:** These wearable robotic devices are designed to augment human strength and endurance, enabling workers to perform physically demanding tasks with less effort and reducing the risk of injury. Exoskeletons are finding applications in:
  - **Construction:** Assisting workers in lifting heavy materials, operating tools, and performing repetitive tasks.
  - **Manufacturing:** Supporting workers on assembly lines, reducing fatigue, and improving productivity.
  - **Rehabilitation:** Helping patients with mobility impairments to regain movement and strength.
  - **Military:** Enhancing the physical capabilities of soldiers, allowing them to carry heavier loads and perform tasks more effectively.
- **Brain-Computer Interfaces (BCIs):** BCIs establish a direct communication pathway between the human brain and external devices, such as robots or computers. This technology holds immense potential for:
  - **Assistive technology:** Enabling individuals with paralysis or other disabilities to control prosthetic limbs, wheelchairs, or other assistive devices with their thoughts.
  - **Communication:** Providing new forms of communication for people who are unable to speak or use traditional communication methods.
  - **Human enhancement:** Potentially enhancing human cognitive abilities, such as memory, attention, or learning.
- **Personal Assistant Robots:** AI-powered robots are being developed to assist humans with a wide range of tasks, acting as intelligent companions and helpers. These robots can:
  - **Manage schedules:** Keeping track of appointments, reminders, and tasks.
  - **Provide information:** Answering questions, accessing online resources, and delivering personalized information.
  - **Control smart home devices:** Adjusting lighting, temperature, and security systems.
  - **Provide companionship:** Engaging in conversation, playing games, and offering emotional support.
- **Companion Robots:** These robots are specifically designed to provide companionship, social interaction, and emotional support, particularly for individuals who may experience loneliness or isolation, such as:
  - **Elderly individuals:** Providing companionship, reminding them to take medication, and monitoring their health.
  - **People with disabilities:** Assisting with daily living activities, providing social interaction, and enhancing their independence.
  - **Children:** Acting as educational aids, playmates, and social interaction partners.

Benefits and Challenges of Human-Robot Symbiosis

Human-robot symbiosis offers a compelling vision of the future, promising numerous potential benefits for individuals and society as a whole:

- **Enhanced Human Capabilities:** Robots can augment human physical and cognitive abilities, enabling people to perform tasks that would otherwise be impossible or extremely difficult. This can lead to:
  - Increased strength and endurance: Exoskeletons and other wearable robots can allow humans to lift heavier objects, perform physically demanding tasks for longer periods, and reduce the risk of injury.
  - Improved sensory perception: Robots equipped with advanced sensors can extend human sensory capabilities, allowing us to perceive information beyond the range of our natural senses.
  - Enhanced cognitive functions: BCIs and AI-powered assistants can improve our memory, attention, learning, and decision-making abilities.
- **Improved Quality of Life:** Robots can assist with daily living activities, provide companionship, and enhance social interaction, significantly improving the quality of life for many individuals, particularly those who may be vulnerable or disadvantaged. This can include:
  - Increased independence for people with disabilities: Robots can assist with tasks such as mobility, dressing, eating, and personal care, enabling individuals to live more independently.
  - Reduced burden on caregivers: Robots can assist with caregiving tasks, reducing the physical and emotional strain on family members or professional caregivers.
  - Combating loneliness and social isolation: Companion robots can provide social interaction and emotional support, particularly for elderly individuals or those who lack social connections.
- **Increased Productivity and Economic Growth:** By working closely with robots, humans can become more productive in various tasks and industries, leading to increased efficiency, reduced costs, and economic growth. This can be achieved through:
  - Automation of repetitive or dangerous tasks: Robots can perform tasks that are tedious, dangerous, or physically demanding, freeing up human workers to focus on more complex and creative activities.
  - Enhanced precision and accuracy: Robots can perform tasks with greater precision and accuracy than humans, reducing errors and improving product quality.
  - 24/7 operation: Robots can operate continuously without the need for breaks or rest, increasing production capacity and reducing downtime.
- **New Forms of Human Expression and Creativity:** Robots can enable new forms of artistic expression, communication, and creativity, expanding the boundaries of human imagination. This can involve:
  - Collaborative art creation: Humans and robots working together to create new forms of art, music, or performance.
  - Enhanced communication: Robots facilitating communication between people with different abilities or across language barriers.
  - New forms of entertainment: Robots creating new and engaging forms of entertainment, such as interactive performances or virtual reality experiences.

However, human-robot symbiosis also presents several significant challenges and ethical considerations that must be carefully addressed to ensure that this technology is developed and deployed in a responsible and beneficial manner:

- **Safety:** Ensuring the safety of humans working closely with robots, particularly in applications involving physical interaction, is of paramount importance. This requires:
    - Robust safety mechanisms: Robots must be equipped with sensors, control systems, and safety features that prevent them from causing harm to humans.
    - Rigorous testing and certification: Robots must undergo thorough testing and certification to ensure their safety and reliability.
    - Clear safety guidelines and regulations: Governments and regulatory bodies must establish clear guidelines and regulations for the safe design, deployment, and operation of robots in human-robot symbiotic settings.
- **Privacy:** As robots become more integrated into human lives, collecting and processing increasing amounts of personal data, there are legitimate concerns about the privacy of this information. This necessitates:
    - Privacy-preserving design: Robots should be designed to minimize the collection and storage of sensitive data.
    - Data security measures: Robust security measures must be implemented to protect data from unauthorized access, use, or disclosure.
    - Transparent data policies: Users should be informed about what data is being collected, how it will be used, and who will have access to it.
- **Autonomy and Control:** Determining the appropriate level of autonomy for robots in symbiotic relationships with humans is a complex ethical issue. Questions arise such as:
    - How much control should humans retain over robots?
    - When is it appropriate for robots to make decisions independently?
    - How can we ensure that robots act in accordance with human values and ethical principles?
- **Human Identity and Social Impact:** The close integration of robots with humans may raise profound questions about human identity, what it means to be human, and the potential social and psychological impacts of these technologies. This includes concerns about:
    - The blurring of boundaries between humans and machines: As robots become more integrated into our lives, the line between human and machine may become increasingly blurred.
    - The potential for social isolation: Over-reliance on robots for companionship or assistance could lead to social isolation and a decline in human-to-human interaction.
    - The impact on human relationships: The introduction of robots into social settings could alter human relationships and social dynamics.

Diagram of Human-Robot Symbiosis

```
graph LR
    A[Human] -- "Physical Integration" --> B[Robot];
    A -- "Cognitive Enhancement" --> B;
    A -- "Social Interaction" --> B;
```

```
    B -- "Task Assistance" --> A;
    B -- "Sensory Input" --> A;
style A fill:#90EE90,stroke:#333,stroke-width:2px
style B fill:#87CEFA,stroke:#333,stroke-width:2px
```

Diagram Description:

- **Human:** Represents the human individual involved in the symbiotic relationship.
- **Robot:** Represents the robot involved in the symbiotic relationship.
- **Physical Integration:** An arrow indicating the physical connection or integration between the human and the robot (e.g., wearable devices, implants).
- **Cognitive Enhancement:** An arrow indicating the robot's role in enhancing the human's cognitive abilities (e.g., information processing, decision support).
- **Social Interaction:** An arrow indicating the social interaction and communication between the human and the robot (e.g., companionship, emotional support).
- **Task Assistance:** An arrow indicating the robot's role in assisting the human with various tasks.
- **Sensory Input:** An arrow indicating the robot providing sensory information to the human.

This diagram illustrates the multi-faceted nature of human-robot symbiosis, showing the various ways in which humans and robots can interact and benefit from each other.

50 multiple-choice questions with answers, covering the topics:

- 16.1 Collaborative Robots (Cobots)
- 16.2 Swarm Intelligence
- 16.3 Human-Robot Symbiosis

16.1 Collaborative Robots (Cobots)

1. Which of the following best describes collaborative robots (cobots)?
   a) Robots that operate independently of humans in structured environments.
   b) Robots designed to work alongside humans in shared workspaces.
   c) Robots used exclusively in heavy industrial applications.
   d) Robots that replace humans entirely in the workforce.
   Answer: b
2. What is a primary safety feature of cobots that allows them to work near humans?
   a) High-speed movements
   b) Force and torque sensors
   c) Large physical size
   d) Complete isolation from humans
   Answer: b
3. How are cobots typically programmed?
   a) Complex coding languages
   b) Intuitive interfaces and hand guiding

c) Only by specialized engineers

d) Using punch cards

Answer: b

4. Which of the following is an advantage of cobots in manufacturing?

a) Increased isolation of workers

b) Reduced flexibility

c) Increased productivity and safety

d) Higher initial costs with no long-term benefits

Answer: c

5. In which industry are cobots used for tasks like patient handling and rehabilitation?

a) Automotive

b) Logistics

c) Healthcare

d) Agriculture

Answer: c

6. What is a key benefit of cobots in logistics?

a) Increasing physical strain on workers

b) Assisting with picking, packing, and sorting

c) Replacing all human workers

d) Slowing down the supply chain

Answer: b

7. Which of the following is NOT a characteristic of a cobot?

a) High Speed

b) Safety

c) Ease of Programming

d) Flexibility

Answer: a

8. What type of sensor is crucial for a cobot to detect collisions?

a) Temperature Sensor

b) Force and Torque Sensor

c) Light Sensor

d) Sound Sensor

Answer: b

9. Which of the following is a typical application of cobots in agriculture?

a) High-speed assembly

b) Patient surgery

c) Harvesting and crop monitoring

d) Warehouse management

Answer: c

10. How do cobots enhance human capabilities?

a) By replacing human workers entirely

b) By allowing workers to focus on complex tasks

c) By increasing workplace hazards

d) By limiting job roles

Answer: b

11. Compared to traditional industrial robots, cobots are designed to be:

a) More isolated
b) Less safe
c) More expensive
d) More flexible
Answer: d

12. Which of the following is NOT a benefit of using cobots?
a) Increased productivity
b) Improved safety
c) Reduced flexibility
d) Reduced costs
Answer: c

13. What makes cobots suitable for small and medium-sized enterprises (SMEs)?
a) High complexity
b) Ease of programming and lower costs
c) Large size and weight
d) Requirement for specialized infrastructure
Answer: b

14. How do cobots contribute to reducing workplace accidents?
a) By operating at high speeds
b) By working in isolation
c) By using advanced safety features
d) By increasing human error
Answer: c

15. What is the role of hand guiding in cobot programming?
a) To write complex code
b) To physically move the robot for task recording
c) To operate the robot remotely
d) To calibrate sensors
Answer: b

16. In which application are cobots used to improve precision and reduce strain on workers?
a) High-altitude construction
b) Underwater welding
c) Assembly line production
d) Space exploration
Answer: c

17. Which statement about cobots is true?
a) Cobots are designed to replace humans in all tasks.
b) Cobots are designed to augment human capabilities.
c) Cobots are always stationary and fixed in one place.
d) Cobots are not used in the food industry.
Answer: b

18. What is the impact of cobots on job roles?
a) They eliminate all job roles.
b) They create new job roles and change existing ones.
c) They have no impact on job roles.
d) They only impact low-skill jobs.

Answer: b

19. Which of the following is a challenge associated with cobot implementation?
    a) Decreased productivity
    b) High initial investment
    c) Reduced workplace safety
    d) Limited application areas
    Answer: b

20. What is a key factor driving the increased adoption of cobots?
    a) Increasing labor costs
    b) Demand for greater flexibility and customization
    c) Decreasing technological advancements
    d) Reduced focus on workplace safety
    Answer: b

16.2 Swarm Intelligence

21. What is the primary inspiration for swarm intelligence?
    a) Centralized control systems
    b) Individual animal behavior
    c) Collective behavior of natural systems
    d) Human cognitive processes
    Answer: c

22. Which of the following is an example of a natural system exhibiting swarm intelligence?
    a) A single lion hunting prey
    b) A flock of birds flying in formation
    c) A human brain processing information
    d) A computer operating system
    Answer: b

23. What is a key characteristic of swarm intelligence systems?
    a) Centralized control
    b) Decentralized control
    c) Complex individual agents
    d) Global knowledge
    Answer: b

24. Which algorithm is inspired by the foraging behavior of ants?
    a) Particle swarm optimization (PSO)
    b) Ant colony optimization (ACO)
    c) Genetic algorithm (GA)
    d) Simulated annealing (SA)
    Answer: b

25. What is a potential application of swarm robotics in disaster areas?
    a) Replacing human rescuers entirely
    b) Searching for survivors
    c) Building permanent structures
    d) Controlling weather patterns
    Answer: b

26. What is an advantage of swarm robotics over single-robot systems?
    a) Increased complexity

b) Reduced robustness

c) Improved scalability

d) Higher cost

Answer: c

27. Which of the following is NOT a principle of swarm intelligence?

a) Centralization

b) Self-organization

c) Local interactions

d) Emergent behavior

Answer: a

28. What type of problem is Ant Colony Optimization (ACO) best suited for?

a) Finding optimal paths

b) Optimizing continuous functions

c) Image recognition

d) Natural language processing

Answer: a

29. Which algorithm is inspired by the social behavior of bird flocks and fish schools?

a) Ant colony optimization (ACO)

b) Particle swarm optimization (PSO)

c) Genetic algorithm (GA)

d) Simulated annealing (SA)

Answer: b

30. What is a potential application of swarm robotics in agriculture?

a) Heavy machinery operation

b) Crop monitoring and harvesting

c) Livestock management

d) Soil analysis

Answer: b

31. What is the term for the intelligence that arises from the collective behavior of simple agents?

a) Artificial intelligence

b) Distributed intelligence

c) Swarm intelligence

d) Collective consciousness

Answer: c

32. In swarm intelligence, how do agents typically interact with each other?

a) Through a central control unit

b) Through direct, local communication

c) Through pre-programmed instructions only

d) Through long-range signals

Answer: b

33. Which of the following is a characteristic of emergent behavior in swarm systems?

a) It is explicitly programmed into individual agents.

b) It arises from simple local interactions.

c) It requires a global view of the system.

d) It is predictable and linear.

Answer: b

34. How does swarm intelligence contribute to the robustness of a system?
    a) By relying on a single point of control
    b) By distributing control and functionality
    c) By increasing the complexity of individual agents
    d) By eliminating redundancy
    Answer: b

35. Which application of swarm robotics involves robots working together to assemble structures?
    a) Search and rescue
    b) Environmental monitoring
    c) Construction
    d) Agriculture
    Answer: c

36. What is a key advantage of swarm robotics in exploration missions (e.g., space)?
    a) High individual robot complexity
    b) Ability to cover large areas efficiently
    c) Reliance on a single, powerful robot
    d) Limited adaptability
    Answer: b

37. How does swarm intelligence differ from traditional AI?
    a) It relies on centralized control.
    b) It emphasizes emergent behavior from local interactions.
    c) It requires complex individual agents.
    d) It is not inspired by natural systems.
    Answer: b

38. Which of the following is a challenge in implementing swarm robotics?
    a) Difficulty in scaling up the system
    b) Ensuring reliable communication between robots
    c) Over-reliance on individual robot capabilities
    d) Lack of adaptability to changing conditions
    Answer: b

39. What is the role of pheromone trails in Ant Colony Optimization?
    a) To provide a global map of the environment
    b) To indicate the quality of a path
    c) To control the movement of individual ants
    d) To mark the location of obstacles
    Answer: b

40. How do particles in Particle Swarm Optimization (PSO) adjust their movement?
    a) Based on a pre-defined path
    b) Based on their own best solution and their neighbors' best solutions
    c) Randomly, without any coordination
    d) By following a central leader
    Answer: b

16.3 Human-Robot Symbiosis
41. What does human-robot symbiosis refer to?

a) Robots replacing humans in all tasks
b) A close, mutually beneficial relationship between humans and robots
c) Robots operating in isolation from humans
d) Humans controlling robots from a distance
Answer: b

42. Which of the following is an example of physical symbiosis?
a) AI-powered personal assistants
b) Wearable exoskeletons
c) Social companion robots
d) Autonomous vehicles
Answer: b

43. What is the goal of cognitive symbiosis?
a) To replace human cognitive abilities
b) To enhance human cognitive abilities
c) To isolate humans from technology
d) To control human thoughts
Answer: b

44. Which technology enables humans to control robots directly with their thoughts?
a) Augmented reality (AR)
b) Virtual reality (VR)
c) Brain-computer interfaces (BCIs)
d) Global Positioning System (GPS)
Answer: c

45. What is a potential benefit of human-robot symbiosis in healthcare?
a) Increased workload for healthcare professionals
b) Improved assistance with daily living activities
c) Reduced patient interaction
d) Higher healthcare costs
Answer: b

46. What is a key ethical consideration in human-robot symbiosis?
a) Ensuring robot autonomy
b) Ensuring human safety
c) Limiting robot capabilities
d) Preventing robot interaction with humans
Answer: b

47. Which of the following is an example of a robot integrated into human social structures?
a) Industrial welding robot
b) Autonomous delivery drone
c) Companion robot
d) Surgical robot
Answer: c

48. What is a potential risk associated with human-robot symbiosis?
a) Decreased human productivity
b) Enhanced human creativity
c) Concerns about human identity
d) Reduced technological advancements

Answer: c

49. How do exoskeletons exemplify physical symbiosis?
    a) By providing cognitive enhancement
    b) By being implanted in the brain
    c) By enhancing human strength and endurance
    d) By providing social interaction
    Answer: c

50. What is a primary aim of human-robot symbiosis?
    a) To replace humans with robots
    b) To combine human and robot capabilities
    c) To keep humans and robots separate
    d) To limit robot interaction with the environment
    Answer: b

www.ingramcontent.com/pod-product-compliance
Lightning Source LLC
LaVergne TN
LVHW060121070326
832902LV00019B/3065